Martha Stewart's
NEW PIES & TARTS

Martha Stewart's

NEW PIES & TARTS

150 Recipes for Old-Fashioned and Modern Favorites

From the Editors of
Martha Stewart Living

Photographs by Johnny Miller and others

Clarkson Potter/Publishers
New York

Some photographs and recipes originally appeared in *Martha Stewart Living* publications.

Library of Congress Cataloging-in-Publication Data
Stewart, Martha.
  [New pies and tarts]
  Martha Stewart's new pies and tarts / the editors of Martha Stewart living. — 1st ed.
    p. cm.
  Includes index.
  1. Pies. I. Martha Stewart living. II. Title. III. Title: New pies and tarts.
TX773.S852 2011
641.8'652—dc22
                                    2010017379

ISBN 978-0-307-40509-8

Printed in the United States of America

Photograph credits appear on page 345

Book and cover design by Flavia Schepmans

Cover photographs:
(portrait) Matthew Hranek and (pie and tart) Johnny Miller

10 9 8 7 6 5 4 3

First Edition

Acknowledgments

This book represents the hard work and dedication of many talented individuals, particularly those in the Special Projects Group at Martha Stewart Living Omnimedia: editorial director Ellen Morrissey led the team of editors, including deputy food editor Shira Bocar, managing editor Leigh Ann Boutwell, deputy editor Evelyn Battaglia, and assistant editor Stephanie Fletcher. With design director William van Roden, senior art director Flavia Schepmans created the beautiful design. We are indebted to creative director Eric A. Pike for his guidance, and to photographer Johnny Miller for the majority of the beautiful images (a complete list of photographers appears on page 345). Others who provided ideas and support include:

The tireless team at Martha Stewart Living Omnimedia
Jennifer Aaronson
Elizabeth Adler
Christine Albano
Monita Buchwald
Sarah Carey
Alison Vanek Devine
Erin Fagerland
Bryan Gardner
Catherine Gilbert
Heloise Goodman
Tanya Graff
Aida Ibarra
Anna Kovel
Charlotte March
Sara Parks
Ayesha Patel
Lucinda Scala Quinn
Megan Rice
Emily Kate Roemer
Sarah Smart
Gael Towey
Michelle Wong

Our partners at Clarkson Potter
Rica Allannic
Amy Boorstein
Angelin Borsics
Doris Cooper
Derek Gullino
Maya Mavjee
Mark McCauslin
Marysarah Quinn
Lauren Shakely
Patricia Shaw
Jane Treuhaft
Kate Tyler

TO EVERYONE WHO WANTS MORE GREAT RECIPES FOR
MOUTHWATERING PIES AND TARTS

contents

classic

free-form

sleek

dreamy

rustic

layered

artful

dainty

savory

holiday

introduction

Pies (and tarts) remain among America's favorite desserts, and to bake a delectable example of either is something every home baker should be able to do.

Organized by type of pie or tart, this, our newest book, is wonderfully descriptive, beautifully photographed, vibrantly illustrated, and practically presented. Categories range from classic to rustic, dreamy to artful, and dainty to savory.

I am a pie baker, and I know I will use this book forever: not just the individual recipes, such as the Mile-High Lemon Meringue Pie, or the Sour Cherry Pie, or the Rocky Road Tart, or the Mini Chicken Potpies, which will all find their way into my pie repertoire, but also the Basics chapter at the end of the book, which is so very valuable in the information it bestows, such as the ingredients descriptions, the equipment lists, and most especially the simple-to-follow recipes for inspired pastry doughs, crust styles, and commonly used fillings.

Once mastered, these skills will allow you to create pies and tarts easily. Take a suggestion from me: Make several different pastry doughs and freeze them, well wrapped, in single flat rounds. When the occasion arises for which a pie will please, it is just a matter of rolling out the dough, preparing a filling, and baking off a sweet or savory pie that will most certainly make you a hero!

Martha Stewart

classic

The ten pies and tarts that follow represent the most consistently requested, surefire-hit recipes from among the hundreds published by *Martha Stewart Living* over two decades. Individually, each one ranks among the all-time favorites of the magazine's food editors. Collectively, the assortment includes a nice variety of textures, flavors, and styles, so you're bound to find something to please every taste. Consider this chapter an introduction to the wonderful world of pie- and tart-making for beginners, and for baking enthusiasts, a delicious refresher course.

APPLE PIE, RECIPE PAGE 29

Chocolate Cream Pie

With its foolproof crust and easy custard filling, this pie is a breeze to put together, and a good place to start if you're a novice baker. Instead of rolling out dough, you press a ground-cookie mixture into a pie plate and bake for ten minutes or so. The chocolate filling is a cinch, as are the cream topping and chocolate garnish. The only hard part is waiting for the pie to chill thoroughly, preferably overnight, before savoring the end result. Because of the cornstarch, the filling sets up quite nicely and slices well; nevertheless, if you prefer something with a firmer texture, you can add gelatin (see step 3, below). MAKES ONE 9-INCH PIE

FOR THE CRUST

- 25 chocolate wafers (6 ounces), or 1½ cups wafer-cookie crumbs
- 4 tablespoons unsalted butter, melted
- 2 tablespoons granulated sugar
  Pinch of salt

FOR THE FILLING

- 2½ cups milk
- 4 ounces bittersweet chocolate (preferably 61 percent cacao), chopped
- ½ cup granulated sugar
- ¼ cup cornstarch
- ¼ teaspoon salt
- 1 teaspoon unflavored powdered gelatin (optional)
- 2 tablespoons cold water (optional)
- 4 large egg yolks
- 1 teaspoon pure vanilla extract

FOR THE TOPPING

- 1 cup heavy cream
- ¼ cup confectioners' sugar
  Chocolate curls (see page 343), for garnish

1. Make the crust: Preheat oven to 350°F. In a food processor, pulse wafers until fine crumbs form. Add butter, sugar, and salt, and process until combined. Press mixture firmly into bottom and up sides of a 9-inch pie dish. Refrigerate until firm, about 15 minutes. Bake until crust is fragrant, about 10 minutes. Let cool completely on a wire rack.

2. Make the filling: In a medium saucepan, heat milk and chocolate over medium-high, whisking occasionally, until chocolate is melted. In a small bowl, whisk together granulated sugar, cornstarch, and salt. Add 1 cup of milk mixture and whisk until smooth. Return mixture to saucepan; whisk to combine. Cook over medium heat, stirring constantly, until bubbling and thick, 4 to 5 minutes (about 2 minutes after it comes to a boil).

3. If using gelatin, sprinkle 1 teaspoon over the 2 tablespoons cold water in a small bowl; let stand until softened, about 5 minutes. In a medium bowl, whisk egg yolks. Slowly whisk hot milk mixture into yolks. Return mixture to saucepan, and continue cooking custard over medium heat, stirring constantly, until custard is thick and bubbles appear in center, 1 to 2 minutes. Remove from heat. Add softened gelatin, if using, and whisk until dissolved. Stir in vanilla. Let cool about 10 minutes, whisking 2 or 3 times.

4. Pour custard into baked and cooled crust. Press a piece of plastic wrap directly on surface of custard. Refrigerate until filling is firm, 4 hours or up to 1 day.

5. Make the topping: With an electric mixer on medium-high speed, whisk cream just until soft peaks form. Add confectioners' sugar and whisk until stiff peaks form. Spread whipped cream over custard. Garnish pie with chocolate curls just before serving.

Peach and Berry Tart

Making a pie, or in this case a tart, can be remarkably simple—as easy as baking a batch of cookies, in fact. *Pâte sablée* is essentially a cookie dough. Here it's pressed into a springform pan before baking. In this recipe, cornmeal stands in for some of the flour; its flavor works well with summer fruits, but if you don't have it, you can certainly use all flour. To make the filling, toss fresh fruit with sugar, add it to the partially baked tart shell, then finish baking. Peaches and berries are pictured, but if you have apricots or cherries on hand, feel free to use them instead; this low-key recipe takes kindly to improvisation. MAKES ONE 8-INCH TART

FOR THE CRUST

¾ cup all-purpose flour

½ cup yellow cornmeal, preferably stone-ground

3 tablespoons sugar

¼ teaspoon salt

7 tablespoons unsalted butter, cut into small pieces

1 large egg yolk

½ teaspoon pure vanilla extract

FOR THE FILLING

3 ripe peaches, pitted and sliced into ½-inch wedges

¾ cup assorted fresh berries, such as raspberries, blueberries, and blackberries

¼ cup plus 1 tablespoon sugar

1. Make the crust: Preheat oven to 400°F. In a food processor, pulse flour, cornmeal, sugar, salt, butter, egg yolk, and vanilla until dough just begins to come together. Press dough evenly into the bottom and about 1 inch up the sides of an ungreased 8-inch springform pan or tart pan with a removable bottom; set pan on a rimmed baking sheet. Bake until golden and slightly puffy, about 15 minutes. Using an offset spatula, gently flatten bottom of crust. Reduce heat to 350°F.

2. Meanwhile, make the filling: In a medium bowl, toss together peaches, berries, and sugar.

3. Arrange fruit in crust. Bake until peaches are juicy and tender, 30 to 35 minutes more. Transfer pan to a wire rack to cool slightly. Serve warm or at room temperature.

PRESSING IN THE DOUGH

Pecan Pie

Home cooks in the South take great pride in their pecan pies, but the Thanksgiving classic is well loved in all corners of the United States. Sometimes it's flavored with bourbon (add two tablespoons to the egg mixture in step 2) or chocolate (stir in half a cup of coarsely chopped semisweet chocolate along with the pecans in the same step). Cream cheese gives this crust a slightly tangy flavor. A fluted edge, made by shaping the dough with your knuckles or fingertips, is both decorative and practical—it helps anchor the crust to the pie plate, preventing it from shrinking or sliding as it bakes. MAKES ONE 9-INCH PIE

All-purpose flour, for dusting

Cream Cheese Pie Dough (page 330)

4 cups (13 ounces) pecan halves, toasted (see page 343)

4 large eggs, lightly beaten

1 cup packed dark brown sugar

1 cup light corn syrup

½ cup (1 stick) unsalted butter, melted and cooled

2 tablespoons pure vanilla extract

½ teaspoon salt

1. On a lightly floured surface, roll out dough to a 13-inch round. Fit dough into a 9-inch pie plate. Trim dough, leaving a 1-inch overhang. Turn overhang under, flush with rim. Flute edge. Refrigerate or freeze until firm, about 30 minutes.

2. Preheat oven to 325°F. Set aside 1¼ cups pecan halves; coarsely chop remaining 2¾ cups pecans. Stir together eggs, sugar, corn syrup, butter, vanilla, and salt in a medium bowl until well combined. Stir in chopped pecans, and pour mixture into prepared pie shell, spreading evenly. Arrange reserved pecan halves on top in concentric circles until surface is completely covered.

3. Place pie on a rimmed baking sheet, and bake until filling is just set and crust is golden brown, about 90 minutes. (If nuts are getting too dark, tent pie loosely with foil.) Transfer to a wire rack, and let cool completely before serving. (Pie can be stored at room temperature, loosely covered, up to 1 day.)

Plum Galette

A fresh-baked fruit galette is proof that you don't need specialty equipment—or even a pie plate—to successfully bake a beautiful dessert from scratch. Here, sliced plums are arranged on an irregular round base of *pâte brisée* (ground almonds are sprinkled over the crust first). The dough is then simply folded over the filling to make a rough border. There's no crimping or embellishment required; the unfinished edge is a big part of the appeal. SERVES 8

2 tablespoons all-purpose flour, plus more for dusting

Pâte Brisée (page 322; do not divide into 2 disks)

¼ cup whole raw almonds, toasted (see page 343)

¼ cup plus 1 tablespoon sugar

5 to 6 plums, halved, pitted, and sliced ¼ inch thick (keep sliced halves together)

1 to 2 tablespoons heavy cream, for brushing

1. Preheat oven to 350°F. On a lightly floured piece of parchment, roll out dough into an approximate 16-inch oval, ¼ inch thick. Transfer dough (on parchment) to a large baking sheet.

2. Pulse almonds, 3 tablespoons sugar, and the flour in a food processor until ground to a coarse meal. Sprinkle almond mixture over dough. With a spatula, transfer plum slices to dough, spacing close together and leaving a 2-inch border; press lightly to fan out. Fold edge of dough over fruit. Refrigerate 30 minutes.

3. Brush dough with cream; sprinkle galette evenly with remaining 2 tablespoons sugar. Bake until crust is deep golden, and plums are juicy and bubbling, about 70 minutes. Transfer to a wire rack, and let cool completely.

ARRANGING SLICED PLUMS

Pumpkin Pie

Making a single-crust pie is a natural next step after a free-form galette (page 22). Here, the filling—a custard of pumpkin purée, eggs, and evaporated milk—is quickly mixed by hand in one bowl. The pie's simple construction offers an excellent opportunity to experiment with embellished edges, such as a wreath of autumn leaves (pictured), made with a one-inch leaf cutter, or a wheatlike braid (pictured on page 325; you will need one whole recipe pâte brisée for the shell plus the braid). The key to a great pumpkin pie is to partially bake the crust—called blind baking—before adding the filling. The twice-baked crust stays firm and crisp beneath the creamy custard. MAKES ONE 9-INCH PIE

All-purpose flour, for dusting

½ recipe Pâte Brisée (page 322)

2 large whole eggs, lightly beaten, plus 1 large egg yolk, for egg wash

1 tablespoon water

1 cup packed light brown sugar

1 tablespoon cornstarch

½ teaspoon salt

1 teaspoon ground ginger

1 teaspoon ground cinnamon

⅛ teaspoon ground cloves

1½ cups unsweetened pumpkin purée, canned or fresh (see page 343)

1½ cups evaporated milk

Whipped Cream, for serving (optional; page 340)

1. On a lightly floured surface, roll out 1 disk of dough to a 13-inch round, ⅛ inch thick. Fit into a 9-inch pie plate. Trim excess dough flush with rim (reserve scraps). Pierce bottom of shell all over with a fork. Refrigerate or freeze until firm, about 30 minutes.

2. Meanwhile, on a lightly floured piece of parchment, roll out scraps. Using a 1-inch leaf-shaped cutter, cut out 40 leaves from dough. Transfer cutouts to a parchment-lined rimmed baking sheet. Using a paring knife, etch veins in each leaf. Refrigerate until ready to use.

3. In a small bowl, whisk together egg yolk and the water; lightly brush one side of each leaf with egg wash. Arrange leaves, slightly overlapping, around edge of crust, making sure they do not extend over edge, to prevent them from browning too quickly. Lightly brush bottom of each leaf with egg wash as you work. Refrigerate shell 30 minutes.

4. Preheat oven to 375°F. Line pie shell with parchment; fill with pie weights or dried beans. Bake 20 minutes. Carefully remove weights and parchment, and continue to bake until golden brown, 10 minutes more. Let cool on a wire rack. (Keep oven on.)

5. In a large bowl, whisk together sugar, cornstarch, salt, ginger, cinnamon, cloves, pumpkin, and 2 eggs. Add evaporated milk, and whisk to combine. Pour filling into partially baked crust.

6. Place pie plate on a rimmed baking sheet; bake until edges are set but center is still slightly wobbly, 35 to 40 minutes. Transfer plate to a wire rack to cool completely. Serve with whipped cream, if desired.

Mile-High Lemon Meringue Pie

Lemon meringue pie is a perfectly balanced dessert marked by swirling peaks of sweet, nearly weightless meringue atop a rich mouth-puckering filling. A few tricks are in order, however, to help prevent common mishaps, such as a soggy crust or runny filling. First, the crust must be fully blind-baked so that it gets crisp and firm. A half-butter, half-shortening crust like the one used here has a pleasantly crumbly, tender texture. (Substitute an all-butter crust, if you prefer.) The stove-top custard filling is thickened with egg yolks and cornstarch. It must come to a full boil and then cook for several minutes in order to activate the cornstarch and thicken properly. MAKES ONE 9-INCH PIE

All-purpose flour, for dusting

½ recipe Pâte Brisée, Shortening Variation (page 322)

¼ cup cornstarch

1 cup sugar

1½ teaspoons finely grated lemon zest plus ½ cup fresh lemon juice (from 4 lemons)

¼ teaspoon salt

2 cups water

4 large egg yolks (reserve whites for meringue)

4 tablespoons unsalted butter, room temperature

Mile-High Meringue Topping (page 340)

1. On a lightly floured surface, roll out dough to a 13-inch round. Fit into a 9-inch pie plate. Trim dough, leaving a 1-inch overhang. Tuck overhang under, flush with rim, and crimp edges. Pierce bottom of shell all over with a fork. Refrigerate or freeze until firm, about 30 minutes.

2. Preheat oven to 375°F. Line shell with parchment, and fill with pie weights or dried beans. Bake until edges begin to turn golden, 15 to 18 minutes. Remove weights and parchment. Bake until crust is golden brown, 15 to 18 minutes. Let cool completely on a wire rack.

3. Combine the cornstarch, sugar, zest, and salt in a saucepan. Whisk in the water. Cook over medium heat, stirring, until bubbling and thick, about 7 minutes (about 2 minutes after it comes to a boil).

4. In a medium bowl, whisk egg yolks until combined. Pour in cornstarch mixture in a slow, steady stream, whisking until completely incorporated. Return mixture to saucepan. Cook over medium heat, stirring constantly, until it returns to a boil, 1 to 2 minutes. Remove from heat, and stir in lemon juice. Add butter, 1 tablespoon at a time, whisking until each piece melts before adding the next. Let custard cool in saucepan on a wire rack 10 minutes, whisking occasionally.

5. Pour custard into crust. Press plastic wrap directly on surface of custard. Refrigerate until custard filling is chilled and firm, at least 6 hours or up to overnight.

6. Heap meringue on top of filling, making sure it extends to edge and touches crust (to prevent shrinking). Use a kitchen torch to lightly brown meringue peaks. Alternatively, place pie under the broiler for 1 or 2 minutes; watch carefully to ensure meringue doesn't burn. Serve immediately.

Apple Pie

Apple pie is the best-known example of a fruit pie, and for many, it serves as an introduction to double-crust pie-making. To begin, you'll need a big bowlful of tart, firm apples; use a mix of varieties for the best flavor. The apples are tossed with lemon juice, sugar, spices, and flour, the last of which thickens the juices. Keeping the dough cool as you work is crucial; refrigerate it between steps and before baking to promote a flaky crust and help the pie maintain its shape. A few vents in the top crust will allow steam to escape. For shine and sparkle, brush the top with an egg wash (see page 327) and sprinkle with sanding sugar. Flute or crimp the edges as desired, and feel free to embellish the top crust with cutouts made from scraps of dough. Finally, resist the temptation to cut into the pie before it has completely cooled (about 3 hours); otherwise it will not have time to set properly. MAKES ONE 9-INCH PIE

3 tablespoons all-purpose flour, plus more for dusting

Pâte Brisée (page 322)

1 large egg yolk, for egg wash

1 tablespoon heavy cream, for egg wash

3 pounds assorted apples, such as Macoun, Granny Smith, Cortland, Jonagold, and Empire, peeled, cored, and cut into ¼-inch-thick slices

2 tablespoons fresh lemon juice

¼ cup granulated sugar

1 teaspoon ground cinnamon

¼ teaspoon freshly grated nutmeg

⅛ teaspoon salt

1 tablespoon cold unsalted butter, cut into small pieces

Coarse sanding sugar, for sprinkling

Vanilla ice cream, for serving (optional)

1. On a lightly floured surface, roll out 1 disk of dough to a 13-inch round, ⅛ inch thick. Fit into a 9-inch pie plate (do not trim overhang). Refrigerate or freeze until firm, about 30 minutes.

2. Adjust an oven rack to lowest position. Preheat oven to 425°F. Whisk together egg yolk and cream for egg wash.

3. In a large bowl, toss together apples, flour, lemon juice, granulated sugar, cinnamon, nutmeg, and salt until combined; pour mixture into chilled pie shell, piling in center. Dot mixture with butter.

4. Roll out remaining disk of dough as in step 1. Using a sharp paring knife, cut slits in top of dough. Brush rim of bottom crust with egg wash. Center dough on top of pie plate, and trim with kitchen shears, leaving 1-inch overhang. Tuck dough under bottom piece, and crimp edges as desired. Brush pie with egg wash, and sprinkle generously with sanding sugar. Refrigerate or freeze until firm, about 30 minutes.

5. Transfer pie plate to a parchment-lined rimmed baking sheet. Bake on lowest rack until crust begins to turn light brown, about 25 minutes. Reduce heat to 375°F, and bake until crust is golden brown and juices bubble, 60 to 75 minutes more. (The high initial temperature helps the crust set quickly, keeping it from becoming soggy. Reducing the heat allows the apples to cook through without burning the crust; if top crust or edges are browning too quickly, tent pie with foil.) Transfer pie to a wire rack to cool completely. Serve with vanilla ice cream, if desired.

Lattice-Top Blueberry Pie

A woven lattice makes a striking top for a fruit pie, especially colorful fruit, such as blueberries; the open weave allows a peek at the filling and lets steam escape as the pie bakes. The process of weaving the top is easy to follow—cut the dough into strips, preferably with a fluted pastry wheel, and arrange them on top of the filling. This pie and many others with juicy berry fillings are thickened with cornstarch, which has stronger thickening properties than flour (a more appropriate choice for less juicy apples or pears). You may want to adjust the amount of thickener if the berries are particularly juicy, or if you prefer a firmer or looser pie filling.

MAKES ONE 9-INCH PIE

All-purpose flour, for dusting

Pâte Brisée (page 322)

2 pounds (about 7 cups) fresh blueberries, picked over and rinsed

½ cup granulated sugar

¼ cup cornstarch

¼ teaspoon ground cinnamon

1 tablespoon fresh lemon juice

1 large egg yolk, for egg wash

1 tablespoon heavy cream, for egg wash

Fine sanding sugar, for sprinkling

1. Preheat oven to 400°F. On a lightly floured surface, roll out 1 disk of dough to a 13-inch round, about ⅛ inch thick. Fit dough into a 9-inch pie plate.

2. In a large bowl, toss together berries, granulated sugar, cornstarch, cinnamon, and lemon juice until combined. Pour mixture into pie plate, piling in center.

3. On a lightly floured surface, roll out remaining disk of dough as in step 1. To make lattice, cut dough into ten 1-inch-wide strips using a fluted pastry wheel. Lightly brush edge of dough in pie plate with water. Carefully arrange dough strips on top, weaving to form a lattice (see page 328). Trim dough to a 1-inch overhang. Fold edges under as desired, and crimp with a fork. In a small bowl, whisk together egg yolk and cream for egg wash; brush on top of dough strips and edge of pie shell. Generously sprinkle with sanding sugar. Refrigerate or freeze pie until firm, about 30 minutes.

4. Transfer pie plate to a parchment-lined rimmed baking sheet, and bake until crust begins to brown, about 20 minutes. Reduce heat to 350°F. Continue baking until crust is deep golden brown and juices bubble, 55 minutes more. (If crust browns too quickly, tent pie with foil.) Transfer pie to a wire rack; let cool completely, at least 3 hours, before serving.

Berries and Cream Tartlets

All you need is one formula to produce a nearly infinite variety of French-style fruit tarts. Start with a *pâte sucrée* crust, add pastry cream, and top with fresh fruit. You can scatter the fruit freehand, or arrange it in a pattern to make a *tarte composée* (literally, a "composed tart"). Here, summer berries are mixed and matched, but you can also use stone fruits such as cherries or apricots, or fresh figs or grapes. *Pâte sucrée* is sturdier than *pâte brisée,* making it a good choice for tarts that are unmolded before serving. Because the filling is not baked in the crust, it is necessary to blind-bake the shells completely. Traditionally, French fruit tarts are glazed with jam for a polished sheen, but this step is optional; a light dusting of confectioners' sugar or a few tiny flowering herbs look equally lovely. To make a nine-inch tart, use half a recipe of Pâte Sucrée, and add about five minutes to the baking time.

MAKES TWO DOZEN 3-INCH TARTS

All-purpose flour, for dusting

Pâte Sucrée (page 333)

Vanilla Pastry Cream (page 338)

4 cups mixed fresh berries, such as blackberries, blueberries, raspberries, red currants, or sliced strawberries

½ cup apricot jam (optional)

1. Preheat oven to 375°F. On a lightly floured surface, roll out dough ⅛ inch thick, 1 disk at a time. Cut out twenty-four 4-inch rounds, and fit dough into two dozen 3-inch tart pans. Trim dough flush with rims. Pierce bottoms of shells all over with a fork. Refrigerate or freeze until firm, about 30 minutes.

2. Line tart shells with parchment, and fill with pie weights or dried beans. Bake until edges are golden, about 15 minutes. Remove parchment and weights; continue baking until crusts are golden brown all over, about 10 minutes. Let cool completely on a wire rack.

3. Fill tart shells halfway with pastry cream and top with berries, arranging in concentric circles. If desired, in a small saucepan over low heat, heat apricot jam until loose, then pass through a fine sieve. Gently brush berries with strained jam. Serve immediately or refrigerate up to 2 hours.

ARRANGING AND GLAZING FRUIT

Tarte Tatin

Invented by the Tatin sisters, who owned an inn in the Loire Valley, this dessert is popular all over France, especially in Paris. The tart is baked upside down in a pan in which the apples have been sautéed. When inverted, the finished tart boasts a layer of golden, caramelized fruit atop a base of flaky puff pastry. A copper *Tatin* pan is made specifically for this purpose; its two handles are designed for easy unmolding. However, any oven-safe skillet, such as a cast iron pan, will work. You can also easily substitute pears for the apples. For the ultimate in flavor and texture, make your own puff pastry from scratch; see the recipe on page 334. Otherwise, choose a good-quality, all-butter brand such as Dufour.

MAKES ONE 10-INCH TART

All-purpose flour, for dusting

¼ recipe Puff Pastry (page 334), or 1 box store-bought puff pastry, preferably all-butter, thawed

4 tablespoons unsalted butter, room temperature

½ cup sugar

7 to 9 Golden Delicious apples (3 to 4 pounds), peeled, quartered, and cored

Crème fraîche, for serving (optional)

1. Preheat oven to 425°F. On a lightly floured surface, roll out and trim dough to a 10½-inch square. Brush off excess flour. Using a plate as a guide, cut out a 10-inch round. Transfer to a parchment-lined baking sheet, and refrigerate until firm, about 30 minutes.

2. Meanwhile, generously coat bottom and sides of a 10-inch Tatin pan or ovenproof skillet with the butter. Sprinkle sugar evenly over bottom. Arrange apple quarters closely together in concentric circles in skillet, with rounded sides down. Place over medium-high heat, and cook, without stirring, until juices are deep golden and bubbling, 18 to 20 minutes.

3. Bake 20 minutes (apples will settle slightly). Remove from oven, and place chilled pastry round over apples. Bake until pastry is dark golden brown, 23 to 28 minutes more.

4. Invert tart onto a rimmed platter or large plate. If any apples stick to skillet, gently remove them with a spatula and place on tart. Serve immediately, with crème fraîche, if desired.

ARRANGING FRUIT IN TATIN PAN

free-form

A lack of formal structure, and a playful sense of liberation, unite the pies and tarts in this category. Rather than having pie plates or tart pans define their shapes and outlines, all are formed simply and quickly by hand, on a baking sheet. Many are galettes, marked by their signature foldover edges. Others feature a flaky shell made from puff pastry. By nature, these are among the easiest desserts to prepare from scratch. And their carefree construction is a large part of the appeal. Each example would fit the mood of any unfettered occasion just perfectly.

CHERRY AND ALMOND GALETTE, RECIPE PAGE 48

Thin Pear Tart

Here's a great weeknight dessert option—no rolling pin required. The cream cheese dough comes together quite easily, and is simply patted into a thin round. A single pear is thinly sliced, then tossed in a bowl with pear brandy, sugar, and lemon juice. The mixture is then fanned out over the dough before baking. Whipped cream makes a nice accompaniment, as does a snifter of pear brandy, naturally. SERVES 8

2 ounces cream cheese

4 tablespoons unsalted butter, room temperature

½ cup all-purpose flour, plus more for dusting

½ cup plus 1 tablespoon plus 1½ teaspoons sugar

⅛ teaspoon salt

2 tablespoons fresh lemon juice

2 tablespoons pear brandy (or regular brandy)

1 ripe, firm Bosc or Red Bartlett pear

⅛ teaspoon ground cinnamon

1. Preheat oven to 400°F. Combine cream cheese and butter in a food processor. Add the flour, ¼ cup sugar, and the salt, and process until combined. (Dough will be sticky.) On a parchment-lined rimmed baking sheet, with lightly floured fingers, pat dough into an even 8-inch round.

2. In a medium bowl, combine ¼ cup sugar with the lemon juice and brandy. Halve pear lengthwise, and core (leave skin on). Cut each half lengthwise into ¼-inch-thick slices; transfer to lemon-juice mixture; coat well. Drain slices in strainer. Arrange around outer edge of dough, overlapping slightly, then arrange remaining slices in center. Sprinkle tart with remaining 1 tablespoon plus 1½ teaspoons sugar. Dust pears with the cinnamon. Bake until golden, 25 to 30 minutes. Serve warm or at room temperature.

Mini Rhubarb and Raspberry Galettes

Rhubarb paired with raspberries may not be as common a pie filling as rhubarb and strawberries, but the combination is just as delicious (or even more so, depending on who you ask). Here, the two are simply tossed with cornstarch and sugar, then centered on small rounds of *pâte brisée* to create individual galettes. MAKES 8

Pâte Brisée (page 322; do not divide into 2 disks)

All-purpose flour, for dusting

1½ pounds trimmed rhubarb, cut into ¼-inch pieces (about 5 cups)

8 ounces (about 1½ cups) fresh raspberries

¼ cup cornstarch

2 cups granulated sugar

Coarse sanding sugar, for sprinkling

1. Divide dough evenly into 8 pieces. On a lightly floured surface, roll out each piece to a 7-inch round, ⅛ inch thick. Transfer rounds to 2 large parchment-lined rimmed baking sheets, arranging several inches apart. (If rounds become too soft to handle, refrigerate until firm, about 20 minutes.)

2. In a large bowl, toss to combine rhubarb, raspberries, cornstarch, and granulated sugar.

3. Cover each round of dough with a heaping ½ cup rhubarb mixture, leaving a 1-inch border. Fold edges over rhubarb filling, leaving an opening in center; gently brush water between folds, and press gently so that folds adhere. Refrigerate or freeze until firm, about 30 minutes.

4. Preheat oven to 400°F. Brush edges of dough with water, and sprinkle with sanding sugar. Bake until crusts are golden brown, about 30 minutes. Reduce heat to 375°F, and bake until juices bubble and start to run out from center of each galette, 15 minutes more. Transfer to a wire rack, and let cool completely before serving.

TOSSING FRUIT WITH SUGAR AND CORNSTARCH

Pear and Sour Cherry Flat Pie

A mixture of sweet Bartlett pears and sour cherries fills sheets of flaky puff pastry. Traces of ground black pepper and five-spice powder (a blend of cinnamon, nutmeg, allspice, star anise, and Szechuan pepper used in Chinese cooking) provide exotic notes. SERVES 8 TO 10

All-purpose flour, for dusting

1 box store-bought puff pastry, preferably all butter, thawed, or ¼ recipe Puff Pastry (page 334)

2 medium ripe, firm Bartlett pears (about 1 pound 2 ounces), peeled, halved, cored, and cut into ¼-inch slices

½ cup (about 2 ounces) dried sour cherries

⅓ cup sugar, plus more for sprinkling

1 tablespoon plus 1 teaspoon cornstarch

1 tablespoon fresh lemon juice

⅛ teaspoon salt

⅛ teaspoon freshly ground pepper

⅛ teaspoon five-spice powder

1 large egg, lightly beaten, for egg wash

1. On a lightly floured surface, roll out and trim dough into two 10-by-7½-inch rectangles. Refrigerate or freeze until firm, about 30 minutes.

2. In a bowl, toss to combine pears, cherries, sugar, cornstarch, lemon juice, salt, pepper, and five-spice powder.

3. Transfer 1 rectangle of dough to a parchment-lined rimmed baking sheet. Spoon fruit mixture evenly onto dough, leaving a 1-inch border. Brush border with beaten egg. Lay remaining rectangle of dough over filling; press gently to seal edges. Refrigerate or freeze until firm, about 30 minutes. Meanwhile, preheat oven to 375°F.

4. Trim edges, and brush top with beaten egg. Cut five 5-inch vents in top. Sprinkle top generously with sugar. Bake until crust is golden and juices are bubbling, about 35 minutes. Transfer pie to a wire rack; let cool at least 20 minutes before serving.

Strawberry Galette with Basil Whipped Cream

This springtime stunner is gorgeous to behold—and very enjoyable to eat. Thinly sliced strawberries are laid in a concentric pattern atop a large round of pastry dough. Although the galette needs no embellishment, basil-infused cream lends a sophisticated touch to each slice. SERVES 6 TO 8

¾ cup heavy cream

⅓ cup loosely packed fresh basil leaves, patted dry and chopped

¼ cup plus 3 tablespoons sugar

¾ cup mascarpone cheese

All-purpose flour, for dusting

Pâte Brisée (page 322; do not divide into 2 disks)

1 pound strawberries, hulled (about 3 cups)

2 teaspoons cornstarch

1 tablespoon cold unsalted butter, cut into small pieces

1 large egg yolk, for egg wash

1 tablespoon water, for egg wash

1. Combine cream, basil, and 2 tablespoons sugar in a heatproof bowl. Set bowl over (not in) a pan of simmering water, and stir until sugar dissolves, about 4 minutes. Cover with plastic wrap, and refrigerate at least 1 hour (or up to 2 hours, for more pronounced basil flavor). Strain through a fine sieve into a bowl. Add mascarpone, and whisk until medium peaks form. Cover, and refrigerate until ready to serve, up to 2 hours.

2. On a lightly floured surface, roll out dough ¼ inch thick. Cut out a 10-inch round, and transfer to a parchment-lined rimmed baking sheet. Refrigerate or freeze until firm, about 30 minutes.

3. Preheat oven to 350°F. Meanwhile, cut strawberries lengthwise into ¼-inch-thick slices. Reserve end pieces for another use. Gently toss slices with ¼ cup sugar and the cornstarch, and immediately arrange in concentric circles on dough. Start 1 inch from edge, overlapping slices slightly. Fold edge of dough over berries. Refrigerate 15 minutes. Dot berries with butter.

4. Whisk together egg yolk and the water. Brush dough edge with egg wash, and sprinkle with remaining 1 tablespoon sugar. Bake until crust is golden brown, 40 to 45 minutes. Transfer to a wire rack to cool slightly. Serve galette warm with basil cream.

Peach Tartlets

This late-summer last course offers the opportunity to experience the pleasure of perfect peaches, enhanced only slightly by flaky pastry shells and an easy wine glaze. The peach flavor remains largely unadulterated—just dressed up a bit for dinner. Guests will thank you for your generosity in sharing such a singular taste of the season. MAKES 6

All purpose flour, for dusting

1 box store-bought puff pastry, preferably all butter, thawed, or ¼ recipe Puff Pastry (page 334)

3 ripe, firm peaches, pitted and cut lengthwise into ¼-inch slices

1 large egg yolk, for egg wash

1 tablespoon heavy cream, for egg wash

6 to 12 tablespoons sugar

¼ cup sweet dessert wine, such as Muscat de Beaumes-de-Venise

Whipped Cream, for serving (optional; page 340)

1. Preheat oven to 400°F. On a lightly floured surface, roll out dough ⅛ inch thick. Using a 4-inch round cookie cutter, cut out 6 circles. Transfer to a parchment-lined rimmed baking sheet. Arrange about 8 peach slices in a leaf pattern, overlapping slightly, on each dough round. Refrigerate or freeze until firm, about 30 minutes.

2. In a small bowl, whisk together egg yolk and the heavy cream. Brush edges of tarts with egg wash. Sprinkle each tart evenly with 1 to 2 tablespoons sugar, as desired, depending on tartness. Bake until golden brown, about 25 minutes. Transfer to a wire rack; let cool completely.

3. In a small saucepan, bring dessert wine to a boil; reduce by half, 2 to 3 minutes. Brush glaze over peaches. Serve tartlets with whipped cream, if desired.

Cherry and Almond Galette

Cherries and almonds go hand in hand in many traditional baked goods. To produce this flat tart, lightly sweetened and spiced Bing cherries and ground almonds are heaped onto a rough oval of *pâte sucrée*; the edges of the pastry are then folded over and pleated to form a border, then the whole thing is baked to a gloriously glossy sheen. SERVES 8

All-purpose flour, for dusting

Pâte Sucrée (page 333; do not divide into 2 disks)

¼ cup plus 2 tablespoons sugar

¼ cup whole raw almonds, toasted (see page 343) and cooled

¼ teaspoon freshly grated nutmeg

¼ teaspoon salt

1½ pounds (about 4½ cups) sweet cherries, such as Bing, pitted

2 tablespoons cold unsalted butter, cut into small pieces

1 large egg yolk, for egg wash

1 tablespoon heavy cream, for egg wash

1. On a lightly floured piece of parchment, roll out dough to a 16-inch-long oval, ¼ inch thick. Transfer dough and parchment to a rimmed baking sheet. Refrigerate or freeze until firm, about 30 minutes.

2. In a food processor, pulse ¼ cup sugar, the almonds, nutmeg, and salt until almonds are finely ground. Gently toss mixture with cherries.

3. Preheat oven to 375°F. Spoon cherry mixture over dough, leaving a 2-inch border. Dot with butter. Fold in edges, pressing gently. Refrigerate or freeze until firm, 30 minutes.

4. Whisk egg yolk with cream; brush over edges of tart. Sprinkle entire surface of tart with remaining 2 tablespoons sugar. Bake until golden, 45 to 50 minutes. Transfer to a wire rack; let cool completely.

DOTTING CHERRIES WITH BUTTER

Phyllo Tart with Sugared Pluots

Crisp, flaky sheets of phyllo topped with sugar-coated Pluots celebrate simplicity and summer at once. Pluots, a cross between plums and apricots, are available at farmers' markets and many supermarkets; feel free to substitute any other stone fruit. Have a clean, damp kitchen towel ready to cover the unused sheets of phyllo dough and keep them from drying out while you work. SERVES 8

1½ teaspoons anise seeds

6 sheets store-bought phyllo dough (17 by 12 inches), thawed if frozen

4 tablespoons unsalted butter, melted, for brushing

8 teaspoons sugar

1½ large Pluots, pitted and cut into ¼-inch-thick half-moons (about 25 slices)

1. Preheat oven to 400°F. Toast anise seeds in a skillet over medium heat, shaking occasionally, until fragrant, 3 to 5 minutes. Cool 3 minutes. Crush lightly with a mortar and pestle or the side of a chef's knife.

2. Trim phyllo sheets into 12-by-10-inch rectangles. Lay 1 rectangle on a rimmed baking sheet (keep remaining pieces covered with a damp kitchen towel), and brush lightly with butter, coating entire surface. Sprinkle with 1 teaspoon sugar and ¼ teaspoon anise seeds, and top with another phyllo sheet. Repeat 5 times.

3. Arrange Pluot slices on phyllo in 5 rows of 5 across, spacing each row about ½ inch apart. Sprinkle with remaining 2 teaspoons sugar, and brush Pluot slices with remaining melted butter.

4. Bake until crisp and golden brown, 15 to 17 minutes. Using a spatula, transfer to a wire rack to cool slightly. Cut into squares, and serve warm or at room temperature.

Sun-Dried Strawberry Hand Pies

Scrumptious yet easy to assemble, hand pies are baked in their own containers, so they travel well to picnics, bake sales, and potluck dinners. You don't need a fork to eat one, or even a plate. Each is dainty enough to hold in your hand, and guaranteed to disappear in a few bites. But beyond the appeal of their size and portability lie the delicious components—in this case, a tender crust and tangy filling made from sun-dried strawberries and chunky preserves. You can also use fresh berries, if you prefer: Pair one tablespoon diced small strawberry, and one tablespoon of the jam for each pie; omit step 2. MAKES 20

  All-purpose flour, for dusting

  Hand Pie Dough (recipe follows)

2 cups sun-dried strawberries

1½ cups water

1 vanilla bean, halved lengthwise

2 teaspoons finely grated lemon zest plus 1 teaspoon fresh lemon juice

1 cup chunky strawberry preserves

1 large egg white, for egg wash

¼ cup sugar, for sprinkling

1. On a lightly floured surface, roll out dough ⅛ inch thick. Using a 4½-inch round cookie cutter, cut out 20 rounds, and transfer to parchment-lined rimmed baking sheets. Refrigerate or freeze until firm, about 30 minutes.

2. In a medium saucepan, combine sun-dried strawberries and the water. Scrape in vanilla seeds (reserve pod for another use). Bring mixture to a boil. Reduce heat, and simmer until most of the water has been absorbed, about 20 minutes. Remove from heat, and stir in zest, juice, and preserves. Let cool completely.

3. Let dough stand at room temperature until pliable, 2 to 3 minutes. Spoon 1 tablespoon filling onto center of a dough round, and brush edges with water. Fold round in half; using a fork, press down on edges to seal. Repeat with remaining rounds. Refrigerate or freeze pies 30 minutes.

4. Preheat oven to 375°F. Lightly beat egg white, and brush over dough. Sprinkle pies evenly with the sugar. Bake until golden brown, 20 to 25 minutes. Transfer pies to a wire rack to cool. Serve warm or at room temperature.

·······································

HAND PIE DOUGH
Makes enough for 20 hand pies

3 cups all-purpose flour

¼ teaspoon baking soda

1 teaspoon baking powder

½ teaspoon salt

2 teaspoons finely grated lemon zest

½ cup (1 stick) unsalted butter, room temperature

1 cup sugar

1 large egg

3 ounces cream cheese, room temperature

2 tablespoons low-fat buttermilk

1 teaspoon pure vanilla extract

1. In a medium bowl, whisk together flour, baking soda, baking powder, salt, and zest.

2. With an electric mixer on high speed, beat butter and sugar until pale and fluffy, about 5 minutes. Add egg, and beat until just combined. Add cream cheese, buttermilk, and vanilla; beat until well combined. Add reserved flour mixture, and beat until smooth. Form dough into a ball, and cover with plastic wrap; flatten into a disk, and refrigerate 1 hour or up to overnight, or freeze up to 1 month (thaw in refrigerator before using).

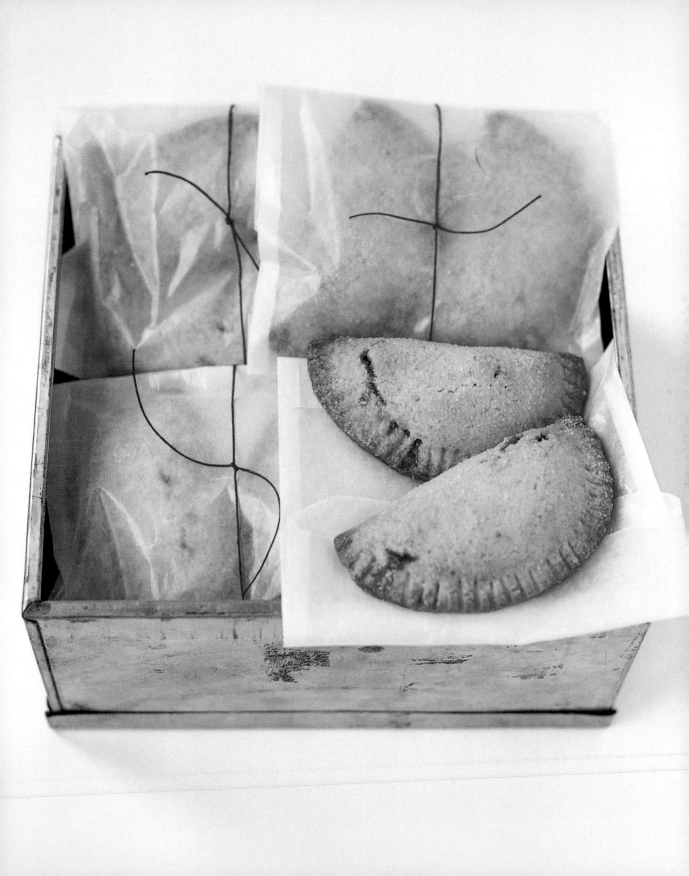

Red Wine–Poached Prune Tart

Prunes, or dried plums (as they are sometimes called), become downright irresistible when drenched in a flavorful concoction of red wine, sugar, cinnamon, and freshly squeezed orange juice. Here, the poached fruit gets baked atop puff pastry for an easy, elegant dessert. SERVES 6

2 cups red wine

Finely grated zest of 1 orange, plus ⅔ cup fresh orange juice (from about 2 oranges)

½ cup plus 2 tablespoons sugar

1 cinnamon stick

1 pound (3 cups) pitted prunes, halved

All-purpose flour, for dusting

1 box store-bought puff pastry, preferably all butter, thawed, or ¼ recipe Puff Pastry (page 334)

1 large egg, for egg wash

1 tablespoon heavy cream, for egg wash

Crème fraîche or Whipped Cream (page 340), for serving

1. In a medium saucepan, bring wine, orange juice, ½ cup sugar, and the cinnamon stick to a boil. Remove from heat; add prunes, and let steep 10 minutes. Use a slotted spoon to transfer prunes to a bowl. Return liquid to a boil; cook until slightly reduced and thickened, 10 to 12 minutes. Remove from heat.

2. Preheat oven to 375°F. On a lightly floured surface, roll out and trim dough to a 12-by-9-inch rectangle. (If necessary, overlap edges of 2 smaller pieces to form a larger rectangle; brush overlap with water to seal, then roll out dough.) Transfer to a parchment-lined rimmed baking sheet. In a small bowl, combine orange zest and remaining 2 tablespoons sugar; sprinkle evenly over pastry. Arrange prunes in rows over pastry, leaving a 1-inch border on all sides. In a small bowl, whisk together egg and cream; brush over edges of pastry.

3. Bake, brushing tart with reserved cooking liquid halfway through, until crust is golden, about 28 minutes. Let cool slightly. Serve warm with crème fraîche or whipped cream.

Apple Crumb Crostata

Consider this a sweet blending of culinary tastes and traditions. As in many Italian desserts, the fruit is minimally sweetened, and seasoned simply with fresh citrus zests. Apples are sautéed until golden, then tumbled onto a round of rich pastry dough to create a *crostata*. The whole thing is finished with a crumb topping with subtle hints of two classic Thanksgiving pie spices, cinnamon and allspice, and served with another all-American favorite, vanilla ice cream. SERVES 10

FOR THE CRUST

- 2½ cups all-purpose flour, plus more for dusting
- ½ cup granulated sugar, plus more for sprinkling
- ½ teaspoon coarse salt
- 1 cup (2 sticks) plus 1 tablespoon cold unsalted butter, cut into small pieces
- 4 large egg yolks, plus 1 large whole egg, lightly beaten, for egg wash
- 3 tablespoons ice water
- Fine sanding sugar, for sprinkling

FOR THE FILLING

- 6 tablespoons unsalted butter
- 3 pounds tart, firm apples, such as Granny Smith, peeled, cored, and cut into ¾-inch cubes
- 1 teaspoon finely grated orange zest
- 1½ teaspoons finely grated lemon zest
- ¼ teaspoon coarse salt
- ½ cup granulated sugar

FOR THE TOPPING

- ¾ cup all-purpose flour
- ¼ cup packed dark brown sugar
- ¼ cup granulated sugar
- ½ teaspoon coarse salt
- ½ teaspoon ground cinnamon
- ¼ teaspoon ground allspice
- ½ cup (1 stick) cold unsalted butter, cut into cubes
- Vanilla ice cream, for serving

1. Make the crust: With an electric mixer on medium speed, beat flour, sugar, salt, and butter until mixture resembles coarse meal. Add egg yolks, and beat slightly. Drizzle ice water over mixture, and beat until just combined. Form dough into a disk; wrap in plastic. Refrigerate until firm, 1 hour or up to 3 days.

2. Make the filling: Melt butter in a large saucepan over medium-high heat. Add apples, zests, and salt, stirring until coated. Sprinkle sugar over mixture, and cook, stirring, until sugar is dissolved, liquid has thickened, and apples are almost golden, about 5 minutes. Transfer to a rimmed baking sheet, and let cool to room temperature.

3. Make the topping: In a food processor, pulse flour, sugars, salt, cinnamon, allspice, and butter just until mixture resembles coarse meal. Refrigerate until ready to use.

4. Preheat oven to 375°F. On a lightly floured piece of parchment, roll out dough to a 14-inch round, ¼ inch thick. Place dough and parchment on a rimmed baking sheet. Pile cooled apple mixture in center, leaving a 3-inch border. Sprinkle crumb mixture evenly over apples. Fold edges of dough over apples, overlapping and leaving an opening in the center.

5. Refrigerate or freeze until dough is firm, about 30 minutes. Lightly brush dough with beaten egg, and sprinkle dough with fine sanding sugar. Bake until pastry is golden brown and apples are tender, 40 to 50 minutes. Serve warm or at room temperature, with vanilla ice cream.

Honeyed Fruit Tartlets

Small puff-pastry squares make great vessels for summer fruits steeped in honey and fresh lime juice. The technique for making the shells is similar to that used to create the French pastries known as *vol-au-vents* (or "flying in the wind," so called for their ethereal texture). *Vol-au-vents* are traditionally filled with savory fillings and served as a first course. Here, plums and strawberries fill the pastries for the last course; feel free to substitute other fresh berries or stone fruits, and to garnish each with a tiny dollop of whipped cream, if you wish. MAKES 12

All-purpose flour, for dusting

1 box store-bought puff pastry, preferably all butter, thawed, or ¼ recipe Puff Pastry (page 334)

1 large egg, for egg wash

1 tablespoon heavy cream, for egg wash

Fine sanding sugar, for sprinkling

8 to 10 small ripe, firm plums, halved, pitted, and cut into ½-inch wedges; or 1¼ pounds (4 cups) whole small or sliced hulled large strawberries

¼ cup honey

Finely grated zest of ½ lime plus 1 to 2 tablespoons fresh lime juice

Pinch of coarse salt

1. Preheat oven to 375°F. On a lightly floured surface, roll out and trim dough to a 12-inch square, then cut dough into twelve 3-by-4-inch rectangles. Transfer to a parchment-lined rimmed baking sheet. Score a ½-inch border inside each rectangle (do not cut all the way through). Refrigerate or freeze until firm, about 30 minutes.

2. Whisk egg and cream in a small dish. Brush onto dough borders, and sprinkle with sanding sugar. Bake until puffed, golden, and cooked through, 25 to 30 minutes. Using an offset spatula, press down on center of each shell (leave borders puffy). Transfer to a wire rack; let cool completely. (Shells can be stored in an airtight container at room temperature up to 2 days.)

3. Stir together fruit, honey, zest, juice, and salt in a medium bowl. Let stand 30 minutes.

4. Just before serving, divide fruit mixture among pastry shells. Drizzle with juice from bowl.

Chocolate-Almond Tart with Fleur de Sel

A homemade dessert does not have to be complicated. This tart involves little more than assembling a few staples from the freezer and the pantry. Think of it as a deconstructed chocolate-almond croissant—one meant for the end of a meal, rather than the start of the day. SERVES 4

1 box store-bought puff pastry, preferably all butter, thawed, or ¼ recipe Puff Pastry (page 334)

1 large egg, lightly beaten, for egg wash

Sanding sugar, for sprinkling

1½ ounces bittersweet chocolate (preferably 61 percent cacao), coarsely chopped

Honey, for drizzling

Sea salt, preferably fleur de sel, for sprinkling

2 tablespoons whole raw almonds, toasted (see page 343) and coarsely chopped

Vanilla ice cream, for serving (optional)

1. Preheat oven to 450°F. Unfold dough on a parchment-lined rimmed baking sheet. Trim edges if needed to form an approximate 10-inch square, and fold in each edge to form a 1-inch border. Pierce center of shell all over with a fork. Brush edges with beaten egg, and sprinkle with sanding sugar. Refrigerate or freeze until firm, about 30 minutes.

2. Bake until pastry is puffed and golden brown, 15 to 20 minutes. Using an offset spatula, press down on middle of shell (leave border puffy). Cover center evenly with chocolate. Drizzle with honey, and sprinkle with salt. Return to oven, and bake just until chocolate melts, about 2 minutes more. Sprinkle with almonds, and cut into 4 squares. Serve with ice cream, if desired, and drizzle with more honey.

Apple Butter Hand Pies

What's more appealing than a batch of fresh-baked, half-moon-shaped pies filled with rich homemade apple butter? Nothing, except maybe a batch of hand pies filled with an assortment of colorful, tasty fruit butters (try peach, plum, apricot, or pear). If you are making your own apple butter, choose eating apples, such as Mutsu, Gala, or Golden Delicious. MAKES 16

All-purpose flour, for dusting
Hand Pie Dough (page 52)

2 cups Apple Butter (recipe follows), or best-quality store-bought fruit butter

¼ cup sugar

¼ teaspoon ground cinnamon

1. On a lightly floured surface, roll out dough ⅛ inch thick. Using a 4½-inch round cookie cutter, cut out 16 rounds. Transfer rounds to parchment-lined rimmed baking sheets, and refrigerate or freeze until firm, about 30 minutes.

2. Spoon about 2 tablespoons apple butter onto half of a round, using the back of the spoon to spread evenly to about ½ inch from edge (make sure the butter is not completely flattened). Quickly brush ice water around circumference of dough, and fold round in half, creating a half-moon shape. Using your fingers, press down on edges to seal and flute edges. Repeat process with remaining dough rounds and apple butter. Place hand pies on a parchment-lined rimmed baking sheet, and refrigerate 30 minutes.

3. Preheat oven to 375°F. Combine sugar and cinnamon in a small mixing bowl. Lightly brush hand pies with water, and sprinkle generously with cinnamon-sugar mixture, dividing evenly. Bake until hand pies are golden brown and crust is just slightly cracked, about 20 minutes. Transfer pies to a wire rack; let cool slightly before serving.

....

APPLE BUTTER
Makes 2 cups

15 apples, such as Mutsu, Gala, or Golden Delicious (about 6½ pounds), peeled, cored, and quartered

1 cup unsweetened apple cider

2 tablespoons Calvados (apple brandy) or regular brandy

1 large cinnamon stick

1 teaspoon ground ginger

½ teaspoon ground cardamom

½ teaspoon freshly grated nutmeg

¼ teaspoon ground mace
    Pinch of ground cloves

1 cup sugar

2 tablespoons fresh lemon juice

1. Combine all ingredients in a large heavy-bottomed saucepan. Cook over medium-high heat, stirring often with a large wooden spoon to prevent scorching, until apples have broken down into a saucelike consistency, about 45 minutes. Mash any large pieces of apple with the back of a spoon, if necessary.

2. Using a heatproof spatula, transfer apple mixture to a small saucepan. Reduce heat to medium-low, and continue cooking, stirring often, until apples are completely broken down and butter is very thick and dark, about 2 hours. Remove from heat, and let cool to room temperature. Refrigerate in an airtight container up to 1 month, or freeze up to 6 months.

Apricot-Pistachio Tart

Few desserts are as vibrantly seasonal and—contrary to its eye-catching appearance—as downright simple as this. Sliced apricots arranged in alternating rows lie on a bed of rich pistachio paste atop puff pastry. Chopped pistachios are scattered on top. **SERVES 8**

1 cup plus 1 tablespoon unsalted raw pistachios, shelled and toasted (see page 343)

½ cup granulated sugar

½ cup (1 stick) cold unsalted butter, cut into ½-inch cubes

1 large whole egg plus 1 large egg yolk, for egg wash

1 teaspoon pure vanilla extract

Pinch of salt

All-purpose flour, for dusting

1 box store-bought puff pastry, preferably all butter, thawed, or ¼ recipe Puff Pastry (page 334)

6 apricots (1¼ pounds), pitted and cut into ¼-inch-thick slices

1 tablespoon heavy cream, for egg wash

2 tablespoons turbinado or other raw sugar

¼ cup apricot jam

1½ tablespoons water

1. In the bowl of a food processor, pulse to combine 1 cup pistachios and the granulated sugar. Add butter; process until paste forms. Add whole egg, the vanilla, and salt; process to combine.

2. On a lightly floured surface, roll out and trim dough to 17-by-9-inch rectangle. (If necessary, overlap edges of 2 smaller pieces to form a rectangle; brush overlap with water to seal, then roll out.) Transfer to a parchment-lined rimmed baking sheet. Using an offset spatula, spread pistachio mixture evenly over dough, leaving a ¾-inch border.

3. Position short end of rectangle nearest you. Arrange apricots in 4 vertical rows atop pistachio mixture, alternating direction in which apricots face. Fold in edges of dough; use your index finger to make a scalloped border. Refrigerate or freeze until firm, about 30 minutes.

4. Preheat oven to 400°F. Whisk together egg yolk and cream; brush over edges of tart shell. Chop remaining 1 tablespoon pistachios; sprinkle pistachios and turbinado sugar over apricots. Bake until crust is deep golden brown and fruit is juicy, about 35 minutes. Let cool on a wire rack.

5. Meanwhile, combine jam with the water in a small saucepan. Cook over low heat, stirring, until loose, 2 minutes. Pass through a fine sieve into a bowl. Brush glaze over apricots. Serve tart warm or at room temperature.

MAKING THE SCALLOPED BORDER

sleek

Minimally constructed, stylishly modern, and marked (for the most part) by a glossy sheen, the pies and tarts in this section are undeniably elegant. When you are entertaining, you may think of any of these examples in the same vein as the "little black dress"—admirably understated and appropriate for endless occasions and celebrations. Yet for all their sophistication, not one of these desserts is complicated in its assembly—consider that the home cook's secret.

MILK CHOCOLATE PISTACHIO TART, RECIPE PAGE 77

Crème Brûlée Tarts

Crème brûlée—a French restaurant favorite whose name means "burned cream"—is delicious all on its own, but even more so when baked in a crisp tart shell. A kitchen torch is used to caramelize the sugar on the surface of the custard, producing spectacular color and crackle. If you don't have a kitchen torch, use the broiler: chill the tarts for half an hour, then broil them for about a minute. For the best results, prepare the tarts no more than one day in advance, and wait to brûlée them until just before serving. This way, the shells will remain firm and crumbly, and the topping will retain its trademark sheen. MAKES 6

FOR THE CRUST

- 2 cups all-purpose flour, plus more for dusting
- ½ cup sugar
- ½ teaspoon salt
- ½ cup (1 stick) cold unsalted butter, cut into small pieces
- 1 large whole egg plus 1 large egg yolk
- 2 tablespoons ice water

FOR THE FILLING

- 1½ cups heavy cream
- 2 large egg yolks
- 5 tablespoons sugar
- Pinch of salt

1. Make the crust: In a food processor, pulse flour, sugar, and salt until combined. Add butter, and pulse until mixture resembles coarse meal. Whisk together whole egg, egg yolk, and the water. Evenly drizzle egg mixture over flour mixture, and pulse just until dough begins to come together. Pat dough into a disk; wrap tightly in plastic, and refrigerate until firm, about 1 hour.

2. Place six 4-inch tart rings on a parchment-lined rimmed baking sheet. On a lightly floured surface, roll out dough ⅛ inch thick. Cut out six 6-inch rounds and fit into rings, leaving overhang. Patch any holes or tears. Pierce bottoms of shells all over with a fork; refrigerate or freeze until firm, about 30 minutes. Meanwhile preheat oven to 350°F. Trim excess dough flush with rings.

3. Bake shells until lightly browned, rotating pan halfway through and pressing dough flat with an offset spatula if it starts to bubble, about 15 minutes. Let cool completely. Reduce heat to 325°F.

4. Make the filling: In a small saucepan, bring cream almost to a boil; remove from heat. In a bowl, whisk together egg yolks, 3 tablespoons sugar, and the salt. Slowly whisk cream into egg-yolk mixture. Strain through a fine-mesh strainer into another bowl.

5. Divide cream mixture evenly among crusts, filling to top. Carefully transfer to oven and bake just until set, rotating pan halfway through, about 20 minutes. Transfer to a wire rack, and let cool to room temperature. Refrigerate until set, 1 hour.

6. Sprinkle tops evenly with the remaining 2 tablespoons sugar (1 teaspoon per tart). Brûlée with a handheld kitchen torch (or under a broiler). Serve immediately.

Chocolate Mousse Tart with Hazelnuts

Ethereal mousse, made by folding chocolate ganache into sweetened whipped cream, is firmly rooted in a humble cookie-crumb-and-nut crust. Candied hazelnuts are sprinkled on top. MAKES ONE 9-INCH TART

FOR THE CRUST

- 6 graham cracker sheets (about 3 ounces)
- ½ cup skinned hazelnuts (see page 343)
- ¼ teaspoon coarse salt
- 2 tablespoons granulated sugar
- 4 tablespoons unsalted butter, melted and cooled

FOR THE TOPPING

- ⅓ cup skinned hazelnuts (see page 343)
- ¼ cup granulated sugar
- ¼ teaspoon coarse salt
- ¼ cup water

FOR THE FILLING

- 1¾ cups heavy cream
- 5 ounces bittersweet chocolate (preferably 61 percent cacao), coarsely chopped
- 2 tablespoons confectioners' sugar

1. Make the crust: Preheat oven to 350°F. In a food processor, combine graham crackers, hazelnuts, salt, and granulated sugar; process until fine crumbs form. With machine running, slowly pour butter through feed tube and process until combined. Press crumbs into bottom and up sides of a 9-inch fluted tart pan with a removable bottom. Bake until crust is golden brown and fragrant, 12 to 14 minutes. Let cool completely in pan on a wire rack.

2. Meanwhile, make the topping: In a small saucepan, combine hazelnuts, granulated sugar, salt, and water. Bring to a boil; cook 1 minute. Drain hazelnuts and spread in a single layer on a parchment-lined rimmed baking sheet. Bake until nuts are toasted and shiny, 15 minutes. Let cool completely.

3. Make the filling: In a medium saucepan, bring ¾ cup cream to a simmer; remove from heat and add chocolate. Let stand 5 minutes; whisk to combine, then let cool to room temperature. In a large chilled bowl, whip remaining 1 cup cream with the confectioners' sugar until stiff peaks form. Gently fold in chocolate mixture until combined. Pour filling into baked, cooled crust and refrigerate until completely set, 2 hours or, wrapped tightly with plastic, up to 2 days. Top tart with candied hazelnuts before serving.

Panna Cotta Tartlets with Strawberries

A crisp *pâte sucrée* shell and fresh strawberry sauce set off an inverted serving of *panna cotta* (Italian for "cooked cream"). Just a bit of balsamic vinegar in the sauce brings out the flavor of the fruit. If the strawberries are very sweet, you won't need as much sugar—use an amount at the lower end of the range in step five. MAKES 6

2½ teaspoons unflavored powdered gelatin

3 tablespoons water

2½ cups heavy cream

¾ cup sugar, plus up to 2 tablespoons for sauce, as needed

½ cup crème fraîche

½ teaspoon pure vanilla extract

All-purpose flour, for dusting

Pâte Sucrée (page 333)

1 pound strawberries, hulled and halved lengthwise or quartered if large (about 3 cups)

1 teaspoon balsamic vinegar

1. In a small bowl, sprinkle gelatin over the water; let soften 10 minutes.

2. Prepare an ice-water bath. Bring cream and ½ cup plus 2 tablespoons sugar to a simmer in a medium saucepan, stirring occasionally. Add gelatin mixture, and cook over medium-low heat, stirring, until gelatin and sugar are dissolved. Remove from heat. Whisk in crème fraîche and vanilla. Pour into a medium bowl set into ice-water bath. Let cool completely, stirring occasionally. Divide mixture evenly among six 5-ounce ramekins or custard cups. Refrigerate until set, 3 hours or up to 1 day.

3. Place six 4-inch tart rings on a parchment-lined rimmed baking sheet. Divide dough into 6 pieces. On a lightly floured surface, roll out each piece of dough to a 6-inch round, ⅛ inch thick. Gently press each round into a tart ring. Trim excess dough flush with rings. Refrigerate or freeze until firm, about 30 minutes.

4. Preheat oven to 375°F. Pierce bottoms of shells all over with fork. Line shells with parchment, and fill with pie weights or dried beans. Bake until edges are golden, about 18 minutes. Remove parchment and weights; continue baking until surfaces are golden, about 10 minutes more. Let cool on a wire rack. Remove from tart rings.

5. Cook berries, remaining 2 to 4 tablespoons sugar (depending on sweetness of berries), and vinegar in a skillet over medium-low heat, stirring, until juicy, about 5 minutes. Let cool slightly.

6. Dip ramekins in warm water; pat dry. Run a small knife around edge of each panna cotta; gently invert onto a baked, cooled tart shell. Top with berries and sauce, and serve immediately.

Egg Custard Tart with Nutmeg

Old-fashioned yet quietly innovative, this custard tart is satisfyingly rich and creamy. It's also unsparing with the dominant spice, nutmeg—and all the better as a result. MAKES ONE 9-INCH TART

FOR THE CRUST

- 2 cups all-purpose flour, plus more for dusting
- 2 tablespoons granulated sugar
- ¾ teaspoon salt
- ¾ cup (1½ sticks) cold unsalted butter, cut into small pieces
- 1 large egg yolk
- 3 tablespoons ice water

FOR THE FILLING

- 1 vanilla bean, halved lengthwise
- 2 cups heavy cream
- 2 cups milk
- 12 large egg yolks, room temperature
- ½ cup granulated sugar
- 2 teaspoons arrowroot
- ¼ teaspoon freshly grated nutmeg, plus more for sprinkling

  Confectioners' sugar, for dusting

1. Make the crust: In a food processor, pulse flour, sugar, and salt to combine. Add butter, and pulse until combined. Whisk together egg yolk and water; drizzle over flour mixture, and pulse until dough just comes together, not more than 30 seconds. Shape dough into a disk, and wrap in plastic. Refrigerate 1 hour or up to 1 day.

2. Preheat oven to 350°F. On a lightly floured surface, roll out dough to an 11-inch round, ⅛ inch thick. Fit into a 9-by-2-inch round fluted tart pan with a removable bottom. Refrigerate or freeze until firm, about 30 minutes. Line with parchment, and fill with pie weights or dried beans. Bake 15 minutes. Remove weights and parchment, and bake until golden brown, about 25 minutes more. Let cool completely in pan on a wire rack. (Keep oven on.)

3. Make the filling: With the tip of a paring knife, scrape seeds from vanilla bean into a saucepan, and add pod. Add cream and milk, and bring to a simmer. Remove pan from heat, and cover. Let stand 10 minutes.

4. In a large bowl, whisk together egg yolks and granulated sugar until pale and thick, about 2 minutes. Still whisking, add warm cream mixture in a slow, steady stream. Add arrowroot and nutmeg. Whisk until smooth. Strain through a fine sieve into baked and cooled crust. Skim foam from surface.

5. Bake until edges of filling are firm but center is still slightly wobbly, about 40 minutes. Let cool completely in pan on a wire rack. Refrigerate 4 hours (or, wrapped tightly in plastic, up to 1 day). Before serving, unmold, sprinkle with lots of nutmeg, and dust lightly with confectioners' sugar.

Milk Chocolate Pistachio Tart

More than other types of chocolate, milk chocolate melts in the mouth like butter, with a luscious taste and texture. It partners well with all varieties of nuts. Here, pistachios are mixed into the cookie crust, ground into a paste and spread over the partially baked crust, and sprinkled on top as a garnish. Slicing the tart reveals a "racing stripe" formed by the paste between the dark crust and filling. MAKES ONE 9-INCH TART

FOR THE CRUST

- ¾ cup all-purpose flour, plus more for dusting
- ¼ cup unsweetened Dutch-process cocoa powder
- ⅓ cup unsalted shelled pistachios, chopped
- ¼ teaspoon salt
- ½ cup (1 stick) unsalted butter, room temperature
- ¼ cup sugar
- ½ teaspoon pure vanilla extract

FOR THE FILLING

- ½ cup heavy cream
- ¼ cup milk
- 5 ounces milk chocolate, finely chopped
- 1 large egg, lightly beaten

  Pistachio Paste (recipe follows)

  Finely chopped pistachios, for garnish

1. In a bowl, whisk together flour, cocoa, chopped pistachios, and salt. With an electric mixer on medium speed, beat butter until fluffy, about 3 minutes. Add sugar and continue to beat until pale, about 2 minutes. Reduce speed to low, add vanilla, then beat in flour mixture just until incorporated and dough begins to come together. Gather dough into a ball. Wrap in plastic, pat into a disk, and refrigerate about 1 hour.

2. On a lightly floured surface, roll out dough to an 11-inch round, ¼ inch thick. Fit into a 9-inch tart pan with a removable bottom, patching any tears and trimming excess dough flush with rim. Refrigerate or freeze until firm, about 30 minutes.

3. Preheat oven to 325°F. Bake crust until firm, about 30 minutes. Let cool completely on a wire rack. Reduce heat to 300°F.

4. Make the filling: In a small saucepan, heat cream and milk. Pour over chocolate in a small bowl. Let stand 2 minutes. Slowly whisk until smooth. Let cool 10 minutes, then stir in egg until combined. Spread pistachio paste evenly in bottom of crust, pressing firmly with an offset spatula until flat and smooth. Place tart shell on a rimmed baking sheet and pour in chocolate filling. Bake until just set, 30 to 35 minutes. Let cool completely on a wire rack. Sprinkle tart with finely chopped pistachios before serving. Tart can be stored in the refrigerator up to 1 day.

PISTACHIO PASTE

- ½ cup unsalted shelled pistachios
- ¼ cup sugar
- ¼ teaspoon salt
- 1 teaspoon safflower oil

In a food processor, purée pistachios, sugar, and salt until mixture begins to clump together. Add oil, and purée until very smooth and pastelike.

Sour Cherry Clafoutis Tarts

Clafoutis, a rich, creamy custard dessert from the French countryside, is made from a quickly blended batter that is usually poured over fruit and baked. Cherries are the traditional choice, but other stone fruits, such as sliced apricots and plums, as well as berries and figs, are good options. Here, clafoutis makes an unexpected—and utterly delectable— filling for individual tarts. MAKES 6

FOR THE CRUST

- ½ cup (1 stick) unsalted butter, room temperature
- ⅔ cup confectioners' sugar
- 1 large egg yolk
- 1 cup all-purpose flour, plus more for dusting
- ½ teaspoon coarse salt

FOR THE FILLING

- 2 large eggs
- ¼ cup granulated sugar
- ⅔ cup crème fraîche or sour cream
- 1 teaspoon pure vanilla extract
  Pinch of salt
- 6 ounces (about 1¼ cups) sour cherries, pitted and halved

1. Make the crust: With an electric mixer on high speed, beat butter and confectioners' sugar until smooth. Add egg yolk and mix until incorporated. Add flour and salt, and mix just until incorporated. Wrap dough in plastic, pat into a disk, and refrigerate 1 hour or up to 3 days.

2. Set six 4-inch tart rings on a parchment-lined rimmed baking sheet. On a lightly floured surface, roll out dough ¼ inch thick. Cut out six 6-inch rounds and fit into bottoms and up sides of tart rings. Trim dough flush with rims. Pierce bottoms of shells with a fork; refrigerate or freeze until firm, about 30 minutes.

3. Preheat oven to 325°F. Bake until lightly brown, pressing down on crust with an offset spatula if it starts bubbling, about 20 minutes. Let crusts cool completely on a wire rack before filling. Raise heat to 375°F.

4. Make the filling: Gently whisk together eggs, sugar, crème fraîche, vanilla, and salt just until combined. Divide mixture among tart shells and scatter cherry halves in each, dividing evenly. Carefully transfer to oven and bake until just set, 17 to 19 minutes. Let tarts cool slightly on a wire rack before serving.

Honey Acorn-Squash Pie

It's fun to tinker with a familiar formula to create an altogether different dessert. In this twist on pumpkin pie, acorn squash is sweetened with honey and spiced with cinnamon and ginger for the filling, while cornmeal lends texture and flavor to the crust. The checkerboard pattern on the piecrust's edge is simple to do—just snip the dough along the rim at even intervals and bend every other section back toward the center. Don't skip the step of chilling the pie shell before baking—it's crucial to helping the edge retain its shape. MAKES ONE 10-INCH PIE

FOR THE CRUST

- 1½ cups all-purpose flour, plus more for dusting
- ½ cup yellow cornmeal, preferably stone-ground
- ½ cup sugar
- 1 teaspoon salt
- ½ cup (1 stick) cold unsalted butter, cut into small pieces
- 2 large egg yolks plus 1 large egg yolk, for egg wash
- 3 to 4 tablespoons ice water
- 1 tablespoon milk, for egg wash

FOR THE FILLING

- 3 small acorn squash (about 3 pounds)
- ¾ cup honey
- ½ teaspoon ground cinnamon
- ¾ teaspoon ground ginger
- 1 teaspoon salt
- 4 large eggs, lightly beaten
- ½ cup milk
  Whipped Cream (page 340), for serving

1. Make the crust: In a food processor, pulse to combine flour, cornmeal, sugar, and salt. Add butter, and pulse until mixture resembles coarse meal. In a small bowl, lightly beat 2 egg yolks with 3 tablespoons ice water; drizzle over flour mixture, and pulse until dough just begins to come together (add up to 1 tablespoon more ice water if mixture is too crumbly). Shape into a disk, and wrap in plastic. Refrigerate 1 hour or up to 1 day.

2. Meanwhile, make the filling: Halve squashes lengthwise; remove seeds and cut flesh into wedges. In a large, lidded pot fitted with a steamer basket (or colander), bring 2 inches of water to a boil. Place squash in basket (in batches if necessary); cover, and steam until tender when pierced with the tip of a knife, 20 to 30 minutes (check water level periodically). Let cool completely. Scrape flesh from cooled squash, and purée in a food processor until smooth. Add honey, cinnamon, ginger, and salt, then add whole eggs and ½ cup milk. Pulse until thoroughly combined.

3. On a lightly floured surface, roll out dough to a 13-inch round, ⅛ inch thick. Fit into a 10-inch pie plate; trim excess dough flush with rim. Cut edge of dough ½ inch deep at ¾-inch intervals; bend every other section back toward center. Whisk together remaining 1 egg yolk and 1 tablespoon milk; lightly brush edge of crust. Refrigerate or freeze until firm, about 30 minutes.

4. Preheat oven to 425°F. Pour filling into pie shell on a rimmed baking sheet. Bake 10 minutes. Reduce heat to 350°F, and continue to bake 30 to 40 minutes more, or until filling is barely set (it will continue to firm as it cools). If crust is browning too quickly, cover with a foil ring (see page 324). Transfer pie to a wire rack to cool completely. (Filling will separate from crust as it cools.) Serve warm, at room temperature, or cold, with whipped cream. Pie can be made up to 2 days ahead and refrigerated, covered.

Chocolate-Nut Candy Bar Tartlets

Think of one of these glistening tarts as an elegant interpretation of a beloved candy bar: One bite into the chocolate crust reveals a center of soft caramel and toasted nuts. Each batch fills six small tartlet pans (or a seven-inch round tart pan). Vary them by topping some with chocolate ganache and others with chocolate shavings. To make shavings, spread leftover chocolate from step 4 on a baking sheet; refrigerate until firm, then scrape with a knife or a dough scraper. MAKES 6

All-purpose flour, for dusting

½ recipe Pâte Sucrée, Chocolate Variation (page 333)

1 cup sugar

2 tablespoons light corn syrup

2 tablespoons water

½ cup heavy cream

4 tablespoons unsalted butter

1 tablespoon crème fraîche

½ teaspoon pure vanilla extract

Pinch of coarse salt

½ cup (about 2¼ ounces) unsalted macadamia nuts, halved and toasted (see page 343)

6½ ounces bittersweet chocolate (preferably 61 percent cacao), finely chopped

1. Preheat oven to 350°F. On a lightly floured surface, roll out dough ⅛ inch thick. Cut dough into 6 rectangles, 5½ by 4 inches each. Fit dough into four 4½-by-2½-inch tart pans with removable bottoms, pressing into bottoms and up sides. Pierce bottoms of shells all over with a fork. Refrigerate or freeze until firm, about 30 minutes.

2. Place shells on a rimmed baking sheet; bake until dry, 15 to 18 minutes. Transfer to a wire rack to cool completely.

3. In a small saucepan, bring sugar, corn syrup, and water to a boil; wash down sides of pan with a pastry brush dipped in water to prevent crystals from forming. Reduce heat to low; cook, swirling pan to color evenly, until caramel is a rich amber color. Remove from heat; carefully add ¼ cup cream (it will spatter), butter, crème fraîche, vanilla, and salt. Stir until smooth. Let cool slightly, 1 to 2 minutes; stir in nuts.

4. Melt 5 ounces chocolate in a heatproof bowl set over (not in) a pan of simmering water (alternatively, you can melt in a microwave oven). Pour 1½ tablespoons melted chocolate into each crust; with an offset spatula, spread to coat evenly. Refrigerate until set, about 10 minutes. Pour caramel mixture into each shell, dividing evenly.

5. Bring ¼ cup cream to a boil in a small saucepan. Pour over remaining 1½ ounces chocolate in a heatproof bowl; whisk until smooth. Cool until slightly thickened, about 10 minutes. Pour about 1 tablespoon over caramel in 3 shells; smooth with an offset spatula. Store tartlets at room temperature, in an airtight container, up to 1 day.

Caramelized Lemon Tart

Lemon tarts are perennially popular, and this brûléed one has garnered most-favored-dessert status among *Martha Stewart Living* readers since it was first published in the magazine back in 1992. With its caramelized top, vibrant filling, and buttery crust, the eye- and palate-pleasing tart is sure to garner more rave reviews for many years to come. You can also make it in an 8-inch round tart pan. MAKES ONE 14-BY-4-INCH TART

All-purpose flour, for dusting

½ recipe Pâte Sucrée (page 333)

6 large egg yolks

Finely grated zest of 2 lemons and ½ cup fresh lemon juice (from about 2 lemons)

1 cup plus 2 to 3 tablespoons sugar

½ cup (1 stick) cold unsalted butter, cut into small pieces

1. Preheat oven to 375°F. On a lightly floured surface, roll out dough ⅛ inch thick. Press into bottom and up sides of a 14-by-4-inch rectangular tart pan with a removable bottom. Pierce bottom of shell all over with a fork. Trim excess dough flush with rim. Refrigerate or freeze until firm, about 30 minutes.

2. Line shell with parchment; fill with pie weights or dried beans. Bake shell until edges just turn golden, about 15 minutes. Remove weights and parchment; bake until golden brown, 10 to 12 minutes more. Let cool completely on a wire rack.

3. Whisk together yolks, zest, juice, and 1 cup sugar in a heavy saucepan. Bring to a simmer, whisking constantly. Cook until mixture is thickened, and bubbles appear around edges, 8 to 10 minutes. Strain through a fine sieve into a bowl. Whisk in butter, one piece at a time, until completely smooth. Pour filling into crust. Refrigerate, uncovered, until set, about 2 hours.

4. Just before serving, sift remaining 2 to 3 tablespoons sugar evenly over top of filling. Carefully caramelize sugar with a handheld kitchen torch (or under a broiler) until deep amber. Tart is best eaten the day it is made, but can be stored in an airtight container at room temperature up to 1 day.

CARAMELIZING THE TOP

Crisp Coconut and Chocolate Pie

Despite its chic appearance, this dessert is really an uncomplicated icebox pie at heart. And it's gluten-free, to boot. The pie requires only four ingredients—butter, chocolate, cream, and shredded coconut. The press-in crust comes together in seconds in a food processor. After it's baked, the shell is filled with velvety ganache, which sets to a lovely, smooth sheen. MAKES ONE 9-INCH PIE

FOR THE CRUST

- 4 tablespoons unsalted butter, softened
- 11 ounces (about 6 cups) sweetened shredded coconut

FOR THE FILLING

- 1¼ cups heavy cream
- 8 ounces bittersweet chocolate (preferably 61 percent cacao), finely chopped

1. Make the crust: Preheat oven to 350°F. In a food processor, process butter and one-third of coconut until mixture forms a ball, 1 to 2 minutes. Transfer to a medium bowl. Sprinkle remaining two-thirds coconut over mixture, and combine with your fingers.

2. Place a 9-inch pie plate on a parchment-lined rimmed baking sheet. Press coconut mixture into bottom and up sides of pan to form crust, leaving top edges loose and fluffy. Place a foil ring (see page 324) over edge to prevent burning. Bake until center begins to brown, 10 to 15 minutes; remove foil, and bake until edges are browned, 4 to 6 minutes more. Transfer crust to a wire rack to cool completely.

3. Make the filling: Bring cream just to a boil in a small saucepan; pour over chocolate in a medium heatproof bowl. Let sit 10 minutes, then stir until chocolate is completely melted and mixture is combined. Pour into coconut crust. Refrigerate until filling is set, 1 hour or up to 1 day.

POURING GANACHE INTO CRUST

Pumpkin Flans in Pastry Shells

A signature holiday pie—pumpkin—is reinterpreted as a dinner-party dessert for any time of year. If you don't have the exact pans called for, just be sure that the pastry shells are slightly larger than the flans. MAKES 8

2¾ cups sugar

1 cup water

2¼ cups milk

1½ cups unsweetened pumpkin purée, canned or fresh (see page 343)

2 teaspoons finely grated peeled fresh ginger (from a 1½-inch piece)

½ teaspoon ground cinnamon

¼ teaspoon freshly grated nutmeg

¾ teaspoon salt

5 large whole eggs plus 2 large egg yolks

2 teaspoons pure vanilla extract

All purpose flour, for dusting

Pâte Brisée (page 322)

Whipped Cream (page 340) or crème fraîche, for serving (optional)

1. Prepare an ice-water bath. Combine 2 cups sugar and the water in a small saucepan over medium-high heat. Cook, stirring, until sugar dissolves. Cover pan; bring to a boil. Leave cover on until condensation washes down sides of pan. Remove cover; boil until syrup turns deep amber. Quickly dunk bottom of pan in ice water, and remove. Rapidly divide caramel among eight 4-inch ramekins or custard cups. Swirl to coat bottoms. Let cool. (This can be done several hours ahead of time, and ramekins left at room temperature.)

2. Preheat oven to 325°F. In a saucepan, bring milk just to a boil. Remove from heat. In a large bowl, whisk to combine pumpkin, remaining ¾ cup sugar, the ginger, cinnamon, nutmeg, salt, whole eggs, and egg yolks until smooth. Mix in vanilla and hot milk; pass through a fine sieve, discarding solids. Pour mixture into caramel-lined ramekins, filling each 1 inch high; transfer ramekins to a large roasting pan.

3. Place roasting pan in oven; carefully pour very hot water into roasting pan to reach halfway up outsides of ramekins. Loosely tent with foil. Bake 60 to 65 minutes, or until centers of flans are nearly set; a thin-bladed knife inserted into center should come out clean. Carefully transfer ramekins to a wire rack to cool completely. Refrigerate overnight, covered with plastic wrap.

4. Preheat oven to 375°F. Place eight 5-inch flan rings or tart pans on a parchment-lined rimmed baking sheet. On a lightly floured surface, roll out each disk of dough ⅛ inch thick. Cut out eight 7-inch rounds. Fit dough into flan rings; trim flush with rims. Pierce bottoms of shells all over with a fork. Refrigerate or freeze until firm, about 30 minutes.

5. Line shells with parchment; fill each with pie weights or dried beans. Bake 20 minutes, and remove weights and parchment; bake 6 to 8 minutes more, or until shells are golden brown. Let shells cool completely on wire rack. Remove from flan rings.

6. To unmold each flan, dip ramekin bottoms in a pan of hot water, and pat them dry with a towel. Carefully run a knife around inside edge to loosen flan. Place a pastry shell on a plate. Gently invert flan into shell so it is centered, with caramel sauce filling edges. Serve with whipped cream or crème fraîche, if desired.

Marbleized Lemon Tart with Sage

Anyone who samples this sunny lemon tart can tell you that appearances don't deceive: The dessert tastes every bit as bright and springlike as it looks. Egg yolks, sugar, and freshly squeezed lemon juice create a velvety curd that is poured into a crunchy cornmeal shell flecked with lemon zest and fresh sage. Before it is chilled to set, crème fraîche is dolloped over the curd filling and teased into a swirling pattern with a wooden skewer. MAKES ONE 9-INCH TART

FOR THE CRUST

- 2¼ cups all-purpose flour, plus more for dusting
- ¾ cup coarse yellow cornmeal, preferably stone-ground
- 3 tablespoons sugar
- 1 tablespoon plus 1 teaspoon finely chopped fresh sage leaves
- 1½ teaspoons salt
- ½ teaspoon finely grated lemon zest
- ¾ cup (1½ sticks) cold unsalted butter, cut into small pieces
- 3 large egg yolks
- ¼ cup plus 1 tablespoon ice water

FOR THE FILLING

- ¼ teaspoon unflavored powdered gelatin
- 1 tablespoon water
- 6 large egg yolks
- 1 cup sugar
- ¼ teaspoon salt
- ½ cup fresh lemon juice
- ½ cup (1 stick) unsalted butter, cut into tablespoons
- 3 tablespoons crème fraîche

1. Make the crust: Pulse flour, cornmeal, sugar, sage, salt, and zest in a food processor until combined. Add butter; pulse just until mixture resembles coarse meal. Whisk together egg yolks and ice water in a small bowl. Drizzle egg mixture evenly over flour mixture, and pulse just until dough holds together. Divide dough in half, and shape each portion into a disk. Wrap in plastic, and refrigerate 1 hour or up to 2 days.

2. On a lightly floured surface, roll out 1 disk of dough to an 11-inch round. Gently press into a 9-inch tart pan with a removable bottom; trim excess dough flush with rim. Refrigerate or freeze until firm, about 30 minutes. Reserve remaining dough for another use (it can be frozen up to 3 months; thaw in refrigerator before using).

3. Preheat oven to 375°F. Pierce bottom of shell all over with a fork. Bake until golden brown, about 25 minutes. Let cool.

4. Make the filling: In a small bowl, sprinkle gelatin over the water, and let stand until softened, about 5 minutes. Prepare an ice-water bath.

5. Whisk together egg yolks, sugar, and salt in a large heatproof bowl. Gradually whisk in lemon juice. Place bowl over (not in) a pan of simmering water, and whisk constantly until mixture has thickened. Whisk in softened gelatin. Remove from heat, and whisk in butter, a few pieces at a time, until smooth. Let cool, stirring occasionally. Place bowl with yolk mixture over ice bath, and stir until slightly thickened, about 2 minutes.

6. Pour curd into crust; smooth top. Dollop small spoonfuls of crème fraîche all over top. Using a wooden skewer or the tip of a knife, swirl crème fraîche into curd to create a marbleized pattern. Refrigerate until set, 2 hours, or, wrapped in plastic, up to 1 day.

dreamy

Cream pies and the like are wildly appealing desserts with lots of loft, thanks to fresh ingredients like eggs and cream, whipped, folded, and heaped into crisp pastry shells. Each of these examples has genuine retro appeal, with few techniques required for assembly: The shells are partly or fully pre-baked; fillings often consist of stove-top custards and puddings; and many of the toppings are as simple as soft swirls of sweetened whipped cream. This is comfort food at its most impressive, deliciously billowy best.

KEY LIME PIE, RECIPE PAGE 103

Butterscotch Praline Cream Pie

Evoke memories of puddings, candies, and other childhood delights with this lush butterscotch beauty. Its grown-up look and taste derive from browned butter and brown sugar in the filling and jewel-like shards of hazelnut praline scattered on top. MAKES ONE 9-INCH PIE

All-purpose flour, for dusting
½ recipe Pâte Brisée (page 322)
6 tablespoons unsalted butter
1 cup packed dark brown sugar
1 cup heavy cream
¼ cup cornstarch
¾ teaspoon salt
2 cups milk
4 large egg yolks
1 teaspoon pure vanilla extract
Crushed Hazelnut Praline (page 341)

Whipped Cream (page 340)

1. On a lightly floured surface, roll out dough to a 13-inch round, ⅛ inch thick. Fit into a 9-inch pie plate. Trim dough, leaving a 1-inch overhang. Tuck overhang under, flush with rim, and crimp edges. Pierce bottom of shell all over with a fork. Refrigerate or freeze until firm, about 30 minutes.

2. Preheat oven to 375°F. Line shell with parchment; fill with pie weights or dried beans. Bake until edges begin to turn gold, 15 to 18 minutes. Remove weights and parchment. Bake until crust is golden brown, 12 to 15 minutes more. Let cool completely on a rack. (Crust can be wrapped in foil and stored up to 1 day at room temperature.)

3. Melt butter in a saucepan over medium heat until browned, 8 to 10 minutes. Stir in sugar and cook until dissolved, about 5 minutes. Slowly pour cream down side of pan, stirring constantly until smooth (caramel will bubble). Remove from heat.

4. Whisk cornstarch, salt, and milk in a small bowl until smooth. Whisk into butter mixture until well combined. Cook over medium-high heat, stirring constantly, until mixture is bubbling and thick, about 7 minutes total (about 2 minutes after it comes to a boil).

5. Whisk egg yolks in a medium bowl until combined. Whisk in milk mixture in a slow, steady stream until completely incorporated. Return mixture to saucepan, and cook over medium heat, stirring constantly, just until it returns to a boil, 1 to 2 minutes. Pour through a fine sieve into a large bowl, and stir in vanilla. Let custard cool, whisking occasionally, 10 minutes.

6. Pour custard into piecrust. Press plastic wrap directly on surface of custard. Refrigerate until filling is completely set, 4 hours (or, wrapped tightly with plastic, up to 1 day).

7. Reserve 2 tablespoons crushed praline, and fold remaining praline into whipped cream. Spread cream over pie, and sprinkle reserved praline on top. Serve immediately.

Coffee Cream Pie

Long a harmonious pair, here coffee and pie are served together as one. Chocolate-covered espresso beans hint at the flavor of the filling below, which is spiked with both instant espresso and coffee liqueur.

MAKES ONE 9-INCH PIE

¾ cup granulated sugar

¼ cup cornstarch

¼ teaspoon salt

2½ cups milk

2 tablespoons plus 1 teaspoon instant espresso powder, such as Medaglia D'Oro

4 large egg yolks

¼ cup coffee liqueur, preferably Kahlúa

1 teaspoon pure vanilla extract

4 tablespoons unsalted butter, cut into tablespoons and softened

Chocolate Wafer Crust (page 331)

⅓ cup dark chocolate-covered espresso beans

1¼ cups cold heavy cream

1 tablespoon confectioners' sugar

1. Whisk together granulated sugar, cornstarch, and salt in a medium saucepan. Whisk in milk and 2 tablespoons espresso powder, and cook over medium-high heat, stirring constantly, until bubbling and thick, about 7 minutes (about 2 minutes after it comes to a boil).

2. Whisk egg yolks in a medium bowl until combined. Whisk in milk mixture in a slow, steady stream until completely incorporated. Return mixture to saucepan, and cook over medium heat, stirring constantly, just until it returns to a boil, 1 to 2 minutes.

3. Strain through a fine sieve into a large bowl, and stir in coffee liqueur and vanilla. Add butter, 1 tablespoon at a time, whisking until each piece melts before adding the next one. Let custard cool, whisking occasionally, about 10 minutes.

4. Pour custard into baked and cooled crust. Press plastic wrap directly on surface of custard. Refrigerate until filling is firm, 4 hours (or, wrapped tightly with plastic, up to 1 day).

5. With a flat side of a chef's knife, crush espresso beans, 1 at a time. Reserve 1 tablespoon larger pieces for garnish.

6. In a chilled bowl, beat cream, confectioners' sugar, and remaining 1 teaspoon espresso powder until stiff peaks form. Fold small espresso-bean pieces into whipped cream mixture, and spread over pie. Sprinkle with reserved espresso-bean pieces, and serve immediately.

Banana Cream Pie

In the heyday of roadside restaurants, this tempting dessert was typically placed in the rotating glass case near the entrance, the better to entice hungry passersby. It was a good strategy: The pie's velvety banana custard and billowy whipped-cream topping were—and remain—impossible to resist. MAKES ONE 9-INCH PIE

All-purpose flour, for dusting

½ recipe Pâte Brisée (page 322)

½ cup granulated sugar

¼ cup cornstarch

¼ teaspoon coarse salt

2 cups milk

4 large egg yolks

2 tablespoons cold unsalted butter, cut into pieces

3 ripe bananas, halved lengthwise, thinly sliced crosswise

1½ cups heavy cream

2 teaspoons confectioners' sugar

½ teaspoon pure vanilla extract

Chocolate curls, for garnish (see page 343)

1. On a lightly floured surface, roll out dough to a 13-inch round, ¼ inch thick. Fit dough into a 9-inch pie plate. Trim dough, leaving a 1-inch overhang. Tuck overhang under, flush with rim, and crimp edges. Pierce bottom of shell all over with a fork. Refrigerate or freeze until firm, about 30 minutes.

2. Preheat oven to 425°F. Line shell with parchment, and fill with pie weights or dried beans. Bake until edges begin to turn gold, 15 to 18 minutes. Reduce heat to 375°F. Remove weights and parchment, and bake until golden brown, about 20 minutes more. Let cool completely on a wire rack.

3. Combine granulated sugar, cornstarch, and salt in a medium saucepan. Whisk in milk, and cook over medium-high heat, stirring constantly, until bubbling and thick, about 7 minutes (about 2 minutes after it comes to a boil).

4. Whisk egg yolks in a medium bowl until combined. Add milk mixture in a slow, steady stream, whisking until completely incorporated. Return mixture to saucepan, and cook over medium heat, stirring constantly, until it returns to a boil, 1 to 2 minutes.

5. Pour milk mixture through a fine sieve into a bowl. Add butter, and stir until melted. Fold in bananas. Pour into crust. Press plastic wrap directly on surface of custard. Refrigerate until filling is set, 4 hours (or, wrapped in plastic, up to 1 day).

6. In a chilled bowl, beat together cream, confectioners' sugar, and vanilla until soft peaks form. Spread whipped cream over filling. Using a rubber spatula or the back of a spoon, shape topping into peaks. Sprinkle chocolate curls on top, and serve immediately.

Pumpkin Icebox Pie

This timesaving alternative to traditional pumpkin pie doesn't rely on a baked custard for its silky texture. Instead, cream cheese, gelatin, and evaporated milk are combined to create an easy no-bake filling. You can make the crust up to two days ahead; wrap well and store at room temperature before filling. MAKES ONE 9-INCH-SQUARE PIE

FOR THE CRUST

16 cinnamon graham cracker sheets (8 ounces), broken into large pieces

1 tablespoon dark brown sugar

½ teaspoon coarse salt

½ cup (1 stick) unsalted butter, melted and cooled

FOR THE FILLING

1 tablespoon unflavored powdered gelatin

¼ cup ice water

4 ounces cream cheese, room temperature

1½ cups packed dark brown sugar

1 teaspoon ground cinnamon

¼ teaspoon freshly grated nutmeg, plus more for garnish

¾ teaspoon coarse salt

1 large can (29 ounces) unsweetened pumpkin purée

1 can (12 ounces) evaporated milk

FOR THE TOPPING

1 cup heavy cream

1 tablespoon confectioners' sugar

Freshly grated nutmeg

1. Make the crust: Preheat oven to 350°F. In a food processor, combine graham crackers, brown sugar, and salt; process until fine crumbs form. Add butter, and process until combined. Press crumbs evenly into bottom and up sides of a 9-inch-square baking pan. Refrigerate until firm, about 15 minutes. Bake until crust is deep golden brown, 15 minutes. Let cool completely on a wire rack.

2. Make the filling: In a small bowl, sprinkle gelatin over the water and let stand 5 minutes. With an electric mixer on medium speed, beat cream cheese, brown sugar, cinnamon, nutmeg, and salt until smooth. Add pumpkin purée; beat until smooth. In a small saucepan, bring evaporated milk to a simmer. Add softened gelatin and stir until completely dissolved. Pour milk mixture into pumpkin mixture and whisk until completely smooth. Pour filling into cooled crust and refrigerate until completely set, 4 hours (or, wrapped tightly with plastic, up to 2 days).

3. Make the topping: In a chilled bowl, beat cream with confectioners' sugar until soft peaks form. To serve, top pie with whipped cream and sprinkle with nutmeg.

PRESSING IN CRUST

Key Lime Pie

Martha loves Key lime pie, especially the one served at Joe's Stone Crab restaurant in Miami. Small, round, and yellow-green, Key limes pack a lot of punch, with a more pronounced flavor than more widely available, greener Persian limes. They are worth seeking out for the authentic flavor of the Florida Keys, but if you can't find them, you may substitute bottled Key-lime or fresh Persian-lime juice instead. Depending on your preference, you can top the pie with meringue (shown opposite) or sweetened whipped cream (page 340). MAKES ONE 9-INCH PIE

1 can (14 ounces) sweetened condensed milk

4 large eggs, separated

¾ cup fresh Key lime juice (from about 20 Key limes)

Graham Cracker Crust (page 331)

½ cup plus 1 tablespoon granulated sugar

Finely grated lime zest, for garnish (optional)

1. Preheat oven to 325°F. In a bowl, whisk to combine condensed milk, egg yolks, and lime juice. Pour mixture into baked and cooled crust. Bake pie until center is just set, 15 to 17 minutes. Let cool completely on a wire rack.

2. Beat granulated sugar and egg whites in the bowl of a standing electric mixer. Place bowl over (not in) a pan of simmering water, and stir until warm to touch and sugar is dissolved. Attach bowl to mixer; beat on medium-high speed until stiff peaks form and meringue is glossy, about 5 minutes.

3. Top pie with meringue, and garnish with lime zest, if desired. Serve immediately.

Apricot Chiffon Tart

Lightweight, airy chiffon pies are potluck favorites for a reason. The no-bake filling is stabilized with gelatin and lightened with egg whites, resulting in a sturdy yet ethereal tart that can be made well ahead of serving time yet still hold its shape. MAKES ONE 9-INCH TART

FOR THE CRUST

- 5 ounces shortbread cookies, such as Walkers, broken
- ⅔ cup whole raw almonds
- ¼ cup sugar
- ½ teaspoon coarse salt
- 4 tablespoons unsalted butter, melted

FOR THE FILLING

- 1¾ pounds fresh apricots (about 10), pitted and quartered
- ¾ cup water plus ⅓ cup cold water
- 1½ cups sugar
- ½ teaspoon coarse salt
- 2 envelopes (4½ scant teaspoons) unflavored powdered gelatin
- 5 large eggs, separated
- Raw almonds, chopped, for garnish

1. Make the crust: Preheat oven to 350°F. Pulse cookies in a food processor until crumbs form. (You should have 1 cup.) Add almonds, sugar, and salt, and process until almonds are finely ground. Add butter, and process just until mixture holds together.

2. Press mixture evenly into bottom and up sides of a 9-inch fluted tart pan with a removable bottom. Refrigerate until firm, about 15 minutes. Bake until golden brown, 17 to 20 minutes. Transfer to a wire rack, and let cool.

3. Make the filling: In a saucepan, bring apricots, ¾ cup water, ¾ cup sugar, and the salt to a boil. Cover, reduce heat, and simmer until apricots are very soft, 10 minutes. Remove from heat; let cool 20 minutes.

4. Purée apricots and liquid in a blender. Strain through a fine sieve into a bowl. (You should have 3 cups purée; reserve ½ cup.)

5. In a small bowl, sprinkle gelatin over remaining ⅓ cup cold water, and let stand until softened, about 5 minutes. Heat 2½ cups apricot purée in a medium saucepan over medium-high. Whisk softened gelatin into purée, and stir until gelatin dissolves.

6. Prepare an ice-water bath. In a medium bowl, whisk together egg yolks and ½ cup sugar. Whisk in one-third of apricot-gelatin mixture, then pour back into pan. Cook over medium-high heat, stirring constantly, until thickened, 2 to 3 minutes. Pour through a sieve into a bowl set in the ice-water bath. Whisk until just beginning to gel, 5 minutes.

7. In a separate bowl, whisk egg whites until soft peaks form. Gradually add remaining ¼ cup sugar, and whisk until stiff peaks form, about 2 minutes. Whisk one-third of whites into apricot-gelatin mixture. Gently fold in remaining whites. Let cool, stirring, until mixture is thick enough to mound, 3 to 5 minutes. Spoon into crust (it will pile high). Refrigerate pie 2 hours or up to 1 day. Before serving, drizzle reserved ½ cup apricot purée on top and sprinkle with chopped nuts.

Note: The eggs in this recipe are not fully cooked; it should not be prepared for pregnant women, babies, young children, the elderly, or anyone whose health is compromised.

FOLDING IN EGG WHITES

Mississippi Mud Pie

A Southern cousin to the chocolate cream pie, this version benefits from the addition of pecans, both in the crust and sprinkled on top. Although recipes vary—some include coffee, for example—a few elements are standard, such as the crumbly chocolate-wafer crust and a layer of rich chocolate custard so dark and dense it calls to mind the muddy banks of the Mississippi River. MAKES ONE 9-INCH PIE

FOR THE CRUST

- 25 chocolate wafer cookies (6 ounces), broken into pieces, or 1½ cups wafer-cookie crumbs
- ½ cup pecan halves
- 4 tablespoons unsalted butter, melted

FOR THE FILLING

- ⅔ cup sugar
- ⅓ cup unsweetened cocoa powder
- ⅓ cup cornstarch
- ¼ teaspoon salt
- 2½ cups milk
- 4 large egg yolks
- ¼ teaspoon pure vanilla extract
- 2 tablespoons cold unsalted butter, cut into small pieces

FOR THE TOPPING

- ½ cup heavy cream
- 1 teaspoon sugar
- ¼ teaspoon pure vanilla extract
- Coarsely chopped pecans, for garnish

1. Make the crust: Preheat oven to 375°F. In a food processor, grind wafers and pecans until fine crumbs form. Add melted butter; process until combined. Press mixture into bottom and up sides of a 9-inch pie plate. Refrigerate until firm, about 15 minutes. Bake 8 to 10 minutes; transfer to a wire rack and let cool completely.

2. Make the filling: Combine sugar, cocoa, cornstarch, and salt in a medium saucepan. Slowly whisk in milk. Cook over medium-high, stirring constantly, until bubbling and thick, about 7 minutes (about 2 minutes after it comes to a boil).

3. Whisk egg yolks in a medium bowl until combined. Whisk in milk mixture in a slow, steady stream until completely incorporated. Return mixture to saucepan, and cook over medium heat, stirring constantly, just until it returns to a boil, 1 to 2 minutes. Pour mixture through a fine sieve into bowl. Stir in vanilla and butter, 1 piece at a time, until completely smooth.

4. Pour filling into crust. Press plastic wrap directly on surface of custard; refrigerate 4 hours or up to 1 day.

5. Make the topping: Just before serving, in a chilled bowl, beat cream, sugar, and vanilla until soft peaks form. Spread whipped cream over pie, and sprinkle with pecans.

Rum-Vanilla Cream Pie

Consider this pie comfort food for grown-ups. Rum adds a spirited kick to both the custard filling and the whipped cream topping. A vanilla bean does double duty, as well: Its seeds dot the filling, and the pod infuses the whipped cream topping with a delicate flavor.

MAKES ONE 9-INCH PIE

All-purpose flour, for dusting

½ recipe Pâte Brisée (page 322)

1 cup granulated sugar

¼ cup cornstarch

¼ teaspoon salt

2½ cups milk

1 vanilla bean, halved lengthwise and scraped, pod reserved

4 large egg yolks

¼ cup plus 1 tablespoon (2½ ounces) golden rum, preferably Appleton

4 tablespoons unsalted butter, cut into tablespoons and softened

1 cup heavy cream

1 tablespoon confectioners' sugar

1. On a lightly floured surface, roll out dough to a 13-inch round, ⅛ inch thick. Fit into a 9-inch pie plate. Trim dough, leaving a 1-inch overhang. Tuck overhang under, flush with rim, and crimp edges. Pierce bottom of shell all over with a fork. Refrigerate or freeze until firm, about 30 minutes.

2. Preheat oven to 375°F. Line shell with parchment; fill with pie weights or dried beans. Bake until edges begin to turn gold, 15 to 18 minutes. Remove weights and parchment. Bake until crust is golden brown, 12 to 15 minutes more. Let cool completely on a wire rack. (Crust can be wrapped in foil and stored overnight at room temperature.)

3. Combine granulated sugar, cornstarch, and salt in a medium saucepan. Whisk in milk and vanilla seeds, and cook over medium-high heat, stirring constantly, until bubbling and thick, about 7 minutes (about 2 minutes after it comes to a boil).

4. Whisk egg yolks in a medium bowl until combined. Add milk mixture in a slow, steady stream, whisking until completely incorporated. Return mixture to saucepan, and cook over medium heat, stirring constantly, until it returns to a boil, 1 to 2 minutes.

5. Pour mixture through a fine sieve into a large bowl, and stir in ¼ cup rum. Add butter, 1 tablespoon at a time, whisking until butter melts before adding next piece. Let cool, whisking occasionally, about 10 minutes.

6. Pour custard into crust. Press plastic wrap directly on surface of custard. Refrigerate until custard filling is firm, 4 hours or up to 1 day.

7. Meanwhile, place cream and vanilla pod in a bowl. Cover, and refrigerate 4 hours or up to 1 day.

8. Just before serving, remove pod from cream, and discard. Whisk cream until soft peaks form. Add confectioners' sugar and remaining 1 tablespoon rum, and whisk until stiff peaks form. Transfer to a pastry bag fitted with a ½-inch star tip (such as Ateco #826 or Wilton #8B), and pipe whipped cream over pie. Serve immediately.

PIPING THE WHIPPED CREAM ON TOP

Frozen Chocolate–Peanut Butter Pie

In this diner-style delight, a chocolate-wafer crust anchors a silky-smooth peanut butter and whipped cream filling. Drizzles of melted chocolate and peanut butter decorate the surface. MAKES ONE 9-INCH PIE

FOR THE CRUST

- 36 chocolate wafer cookies (8 ounces), broken into pieces, or 1¾ cups wafer-cookie crumbs
- 6 tablespoons unsalted butter, melted
- 3 tablespoons dark brown sugar
- Pinch of salt

FOR THE FILLING

- 6 ounces cream cheese, room temperature
- ¾ cup confectioners' sugar
- 1 teaspoon coarse salt
- 1¼ cups smooth peanut butter
- 1 tablespoon pure vanilla extract
- 2 cups heavy cream

FOR THE GARNISH

- 1 ounce semisweet chocolate (preferably 55 percent cacao), finely chopped
- 2 tablespoons smooth peanut butter

1. Make the crust: Preheat oven to 350°F. In a food processor, pulse wafers until finely ground. In a bowl, combine wafer crumbs, butter, brown sugar, and salt. Press mixture firmly into bottom and up sides of a 9-inch pie plate. Refrigerate until firm, about 15 minutes. Bake until set, 8 to 10 minutes. Let cool completely on a wire rack.

2. Make the filling: With an electric mixer on medium speed, beat cream cheese, confectioners' sugar, and salt until fluffy. Beat in peanut butter and vanilla.

3. In a chilled bowl, beat cream until soft peaks form. Whisk one-third of whipped cream into peanut butter mixture, then gently fold in remaining whipped cream. Spoon filling into cooled crust. Freeze, uncovered, 4 hours (or up to 1 day, covered with plastic wrap).

4. Garnish the pie: Melt chocolate in heatproof bowl set over (not in) a pan of simmering water. (Alternatively, you can melt it in the microwave.) Transfer melted chocolate to a resealable plastic bag. Snip tip from one corner of bag to make a very small opening. Holding bag about 5 inches above pie, drizzle melted chocolate over top. In a small saucepan over low heat (or in the microwave), melt peanut butter. Place in a resealable plastic bag; snip corner, and drizzle in same manner as melted chocolate. Let pie stand 10 minutes before slicing.

Coconut Cream Pie

The flavor of coconut is especially intense in this pie: Sweetened shredded coconut flakes are blended into the press-in chocolate-wafer crust and the rich custard filling, and then toasted coconut is sprinkled all over the top to finish. MAKES ONE 9-INCH PIE

FOR THE CRUST

- 30 chocolate wafer cookies (about 7 ounces), broken into pieces
- ¼ teaspoon coarse salt
- 5 tablespoons unsalted butter, melted and cooled
- ⅓ cup sweetened shredded coconut

FOR THE FILLING

- ½ cup granulated sugar
- ⅓ cup cornstarch
- ½ teaspoon coarse salt
- 2¾ cups milk
- 4 large egg yolks
- ¾ teaspoon pure vanilla extract
- 1¼ cups sweetened shredded coconut

FOR THE TOPPING

- ½ cup sweetened shredded coconut
- 1½ cups heavy cream
- ¼ cup confectioners' sugar

1. Make the crust: Preheat oven to 350°F. In a food processor, pulse wafers with salt until fine crumbs form. With machine running, add butter and process until mixture resembles wet sand. Transfer to a bowl and stir in coconut until combined. Press mixture into bottom and up sides of a 9-inch pie plate. Refrigerate until firm, about 15 minutes. Bake until crust is fragrant, about 8 to 10 minutes. Let cool completely on a wire rack.

2. Make the filling: Combine granulated sugar, cornstarch, and salt in a medium saucepan. Whisk in milk, and cook over medium-high heat, stirring constantly, until bubbling and thick, about 7 minutes (about 2 minutes after it comes to a boil).

3. Whisk egg yolks in a medium bowl until combined. Add milk mixture in a slow, steady stream, whisking until completely incorporated. Return mixture to saucepan, and cook over medium heat, stirring constantly, until it returns to a boil, 1 to 2 minutes.

4. Strain mixture through a fine sieve into a large bowl, and stir in vanilla and coconut. Pour filling into baked and cooled crust, and smooth top. Refrigerate until filling is completely set, about 4 hours, or, wrapped tightly in plastic, up to 2 days.

5. Make the topping: Preheat oven to 350°F. Spread coconut in an even layer on a rimmed baking sheet. Bake until golden, 10 to 12 minutes, tossing occasionally (check often to ensure coconut doesn't burn). Transfer sheet to a wire rack; let coconut cool completely. In a chilled bowl, whip cream and confectioners' sugar until soft peaks form. Top pie with whipped cream and toasted coconut. Serve immediately.

Yogurt and Blueberry Pie with Granola Crust

Inspired by a beloved breakfast treat—yogurt parfait—this recipe borrows the main components (granola, yogurt, and fruit) and transforms them into a delicious dessert. The pie is not too sweet, but you can adjust it to your preference by drizzling as much honey as you like.

MAKES ONE 9-INCH PIE

FOR THE CRUST

1½ cups plain granola

¼ cup sugar

½ teaspoon ground cinnamon

4 tablespoons unsalted butter, melted

FOR THE FILLING

1 cup plain yogurt

8 ounces cream cheese, room temperature

3 tablespoons sugar

1 teaspoon pure vanilla extract

FOR THE TOPPING

5 ounces (1 cup) blueberries, picked over

Mild honey, such as acacia

1. Make the crust: Preheat oven to 350°F. In a food processor, pulse 1 cup granola with the sugar and cinnamon until fine crumbs form. Drizzle in butter, and process until combined. Add remaining ½ cup granola, and process until combined but mixture is still crumbly.

2. Transfer to a 9-inch pie plate, and press mixture evenly into bottom and up sides. Refrigerate until firm, about 15 minutes. Bake until crust is golden and fragrant, about 10 minutes. Transfer to a wire rack to cool completely.

3. Make the filling: Place yogurt in a cheesecloth-lined sieve set over a medium bowl; let drain at least 30 minutes. Discard liquid.

4. With an electric mixer on medium-low speed, beat cream cheese until very smooth. Add sugar and vanilla; beat until smooth. Add strained yogurt, and beat on low speed until smooth.

5. Pour filling into prepared crust, and refrigerate until set, 6 hours or up to 1 day. Just before serving, arrange blueberries on top, drizzle with honey, and cut into wedges.

Chocolate-Caramel Cream Pie

Chocolate-covered caramels inspired this rich, silken pie. A generous amount of salt throughout balances the sweetness in an unexpected—yet entirely welcome—way. MAKES ONE 9-INCH PIE

All-purpose flour, for dusting

Rich Chocolate Pie Dough (page 332)

¾ cup sugar

¼ cup cornstarch

¾ teaspoon plus a pinch salt

2½ cups milk

4 ounces bittersweet chocolate (preferably 61 percent cacao), finely chopped

4 large egg yolks

1 teaspoon pure vanilla extract

1 tablespoon water

1¼ cups cold heavy cream

Chocolate shavings, for garnish (see page 343)

1. On a lightly floured surface, roll out dough to a 13-inch round, ⅛ inch thick. Fit into a 9-inch pie dish. Trim dough, leaving a 1-inch overhang; tuck overhang under, flush with rim. With the tip of an inverted spoon, press all along outer edge of dough. Pierce bottom of shell all over with a fork. Refrigerate or freeze until firm, about 30 minutes.

2. Preheat oven to 350°F. Line shell with parchment, and fill with pie weights. Bake until edges begin to look dry, 20 to 22 minutes. Remove weights and parchment. Bake until crust is darker around edges and bottom looks dry, 10 to 12 minutes more. Let cool completely on a wire rack. (Crust can be wrapped and stored overnight at room temperature.)

3. In a bowl, whisk together ½ cup sugar, the cornstarch, and ¾ teaspoon salt. In a saucepan over medium-high, combine milk and chocolate, stirring occasionally, until chocolate melts completely. Whisk 1 cup hot milk mixture into sugar mixture until smooth. Whisk milk-sugar mixture into remaining milk mixture in saucepan. Cook over medium, stirring constantly, until bubbling and thick, 4 to 5 minutes.

4. Whisk egg yolks in a medium bowl until combined. Whisk in milk mixture in a slow, steady stream. Return mixture to saucepan. Cook over medium, stirring constantly, until it just begins to bubble, 1 to 2 minutes. Pour through a fine sieve into a large bowl, and stir in vanilla. Let custard cool, whisking occasionally, about 10 minutes. Pour into crust. Press plastic wrap on surface of custard. Refrigerate until set, 4 hours (or, wrapped in plastic, up to 1 day).

5. Prepare an ice-water bath. In a saucepan over medium-high heat, combine remaining ¼ cup sugar, the water, and remaining pinch of salt, stirring until sugar dissolves. Cook, without stirring, until mixture is amber. Carefully pour ½ cup cream in a slow, steady stream down side of saucepan, whisking constantly, until smooth (caramel will bubble). Place saucepan in ice-water bath, stirring occasionally, until cold, 20 minutes.

6. Beat remaining ¾ cup cream until soft peaks form. Gently fold caramel into whipped cream, and whisk until stiff peaks form. Spread whipped cream over pie. Garnish with chocolate shavings. Serve, or refrigerate up to 2 hours.

rustic

For textbook examples of pie, look no further than the following homespun favorites. By and large, these desserts come to mind when you imagine blue ribbons and county fairs, or roadside mom-and-pop fruit stands and farmers' markets. Each is chock-full of easygoing, Sunday-afternoon charm. Whether pinching, fluting, or crimping pastry edges for a double-crust beauty, or scattering the streusel topping over a crumble pie, there's pure satisfaction to be had in preparing—and, of course, eating—any one of these timeless treats.

RASPBERRY-PLUM CRUMB TART, RECIPE PAGE 137

Pear, Fig, and Walnut Pie

This is no ordinary double-crust fruit pie. Fresh pears, dried figs, and toasted walnuts combine to create a wonderful contrast of tastes and textures. Before tossing them with the other ingredients, the figs are simmered in Madeira wine until softened; star anise adds an unexpected flavor note. Use kitchen shears to stem and quarter the figs.

MAKES ONE 9-INCH PIE

¾ cup Madeira wine

5 ounces soft, dried Black Mission figs (scant ⅔ cup), stemmed and quartered

3 whole star anise

All-purpose flour, for dusting

Pâte Brisée (page 322)

3 pounds ripe, firm Anjou pears

¾ cup walnuts, broken into small pieces, toasted and cooled (see page 343)

Fresh juice of 1 lemon

½ cup granulated sugar

¼ teaspoon salt

3 tablespoons cornstarch

2 tablespoons unsalted butter, cut into small pieces

1 large egg yolk, for egg wash

1 tablespoon heavy cream, for egg wash

Fine sanding sugar, for sprinkling

1. Bring wine, figs, and star anise to a boil in a small saucepan. Reduce heat, and simmer until figs are softened, 10 to 12 minutes. Use a slotted spoon to transfer figs to a large bowl. Cook liquid over medium-high heat until reduced to a syrup, about 3 minutes; discard star anise. Pour syrup over figs.

2. Meanwhile, on a lightly floured surface, roll out 1 disk of dough to a 13-inch round. Fit into a 9-inch glass pie plate. Trim dough, leaving a 1-inch overhang; refrigerate or freeze until firm, about 30 minutes. Roll out second disk to a 13-inch round. Cut out steam vent in center with a cookie cutter; refrigerate or freeze dough round and cutout until firm, about 30 minutes.

3. Peel and core pears; slice into ¼-inch-thick wedges. Add pears, walnuts, lemon juice, granulated sugar, salt, and cornstarch to figs and syrup; stir until well combined. Spoon into pie plate, piling high in center. Dot with butter; lightly brush edge of dough with water. Drape second disk of dough over pin; center over filling. Gently press around filling to fit; trim dough, leaving a ½-inch overhang. Fold edge of top crust under bottom one; crimp to seal. Brush water on bottom of cutout; press onto top crust. Beat egg yolk with cream; brush all over dough. Sprinkle pie generously with sanding sugar; freeze until firm, about 30 minutes. Meanwhile, preheat oven to 400°F, with rack in lower third.

4. Transfer pie plate to a parchment-lined rimmed baking sheet, and bake until just golden, 20 to 25 minutes. Reduce heat to 375°F. Bake until juices are bubbling and crust is deep golden brown, about 1 hour. If edges brown too quickly, cover with a foil ring (see page 324). Let pie cool completely on a wire rack.

Roasted-Apple Tartlets

Usher in fall with a half dozen rustic yet refined tartlets. Over a wonderfully sweet "applesauce" made from the roasted fruit and Calvados, two layers of paper-thin apple slices are brushed with butter and sprinkled with sugar to help them caramelize as they bake. The tartlets are delicious still warm from the oven or at room temperature, especially with a snifter of Calvados served alongside for sipping. MAKES 6

1 teaspoon all-purpose flour, plus more for dusting

½ recipe Pâte Brisée (page 322)

5 tart, firm apples, such as Granny Smith

¼ cup plus 3 tablespoons sugar

2 tablespoons fresh bread crumbs

1 tablespoon fresh lemon juice

1 tablespoon plus 1½ teaspoons Calvados or other apple brandy

Pinch of salt

4 tablespoons unsalted butter, melted

¼ cup apricot jam, heated and strained

1. Place six 4-inch tart rings on a parchment-lined baking sheet. On a lightly floured surface, roll out dough ¼ inch thick. Cut out six 5½-inch rounds, rerolling scraps as needed. Press dough into bottoms and up sides of tart rings. Trim excess dough flush with rims. Refrigerate or freeze until firm, about 30 minutes.

2. Preheat oven to 350°F. Peel, core, and slice 2 apples into 8 wedges each. Toss wedges with the flour, ¼ cup sugar, the bread crumbs, 1 teaspoon lemon juice, the Calvados, and salt. Spread in an even layer on a rimmed baking sheet and bake 20 minutes. Toss apples and continue baking until very soft and caramelized around edges, 15 to 20 minutes more. Transfer to a bowl and roughly mash. Let cool completely.

3. Peel, core, and quarter 1 apple. Core and quarter (do not peel) remaining 2 apples and slice all 3 apples very thin, using a mandoline or a very sharp knife. Toss peeled and unpeeled apple slices separately with remaining 2 teaspoons lemon juice. Spread 2 tablespoons mashed apple mixture into each tart shell. Fan peeled apple slices on top of mash. Evenly brush apples with half the melted butter and sprinkle with half the remaining sugar. Repeat layering with unpeeled apple and remaining butter and sugar. Bake tartlets until apples are dark golden brown on edges, about 65 minutes. Brush tops with strained jam. Transfer to a wire rack and let cool slightly.

Buttermilk Pie

This recipe features a twist on an all-American classic. The *pâte brisée* is rolled out on top of graham cracker crumbs for extra crunch and flavor. Because it requires only a handful of staples, the pie can be made any time of year; here, a summery sauce made from fresh berries and stone fruit is spooned over the top. MAKES ONE 9-INCH PIE

4 graham cracker sheets (2 ounces), finely ground (about ½ cup)

½ recipe Pâte Brisée (page 322; omit sugar, add ¼ teaspoon salt)

2 cups low-fat buttermilk

5 tablespoons unsalted butter, melted and cooled

5 large egg yolks

1½ teaspoons pure vanilla extract

1⅓ cups plus 2 tablespoons sugar

¼ cup plus 1 tablespoon all-purpose flour

¼ teaspoon salt

2 teaspoons finely grated lemon zest

3 ripe yellow peaches, pitted and sliced

4 ounces (1 cup) fresh blackberries

1. Spread graham cracker crumbs evenly on a clean surface. Roll out dough on top of crumbs, turning dough to coat both sides, to a 13-inch round, about ⅛ inch thick. Gently fit dough into a 9-inch pie plate, and crimp edges as desired. Refrigerate or freeze until firm, about 30 minutes.

2. Preheat oven to 400°F. Pierce bottom of shell all over with a fork. Line shell with parchment; fill with pie weights or dried beans. Bake until edges are lightly browned, about 25 minutes. Remove parchment and weights, and bake until crust is lightly browned, about 10 minutes more. Let cool completely on a wire rack. Reduce heat to 350°F.

3. In a medium bowl, whisk together buttermilk, butter, yolks, and vanilla. In a large bowl, combine 1⅓ cups sugar, the flour, and salt. Whisk buttermilk mixture into dry ingredients. Pass through a fine sieve into a clean bowl. Whisk in lemon zest.

4. Pour mixture into pie shell; bake until center is just set, about 70 minutes. Let cool, then refrigerate 4 hours, or up to 1 day.

5. In a medium bowl, toss peach slices and blackberries with remaining 2 tablespoons sugar. Cover with plastic wrap, and let macerate at room temperature until juicy, about 30 minutes.

6. Before serving, drizzle fruit and sauce evenly over pie. Serve cold.

Shaker Citrus Pie

This pie exemplifies the thrift—and practicality—of the Shakers. Besides using the entire citrus fruit, peel and all, the filling calls for just two basic ingredients: sugar and eggs. The best-known Shaker pies are made primarily with lemons, but this one calls for oranges as well. Seek out unsprayed fruit whenever possible; also, those with thin skins will have the best flavor. In this recipe, the citrus slices are tossed with sugar and then allowed to macerate overnight; when the fruit is drained, the fragrant syrup is mixed into the filling along with the cut-up fruit. Whole slices adorn the top. The tart cranberry compote makes a nice accompaniment (especially at Thanksgiving), as do dollops of softly whipped cream. MAKES ONE 10-INCH PIE

2   navel oranges (do not peel), washed well

1   lemon (do not peel), washed well

2   cups sugar

    All-purpose flour, for dusting

½   recipe Pâte Brisée (page 322)

4   large whole eggs, plus 1 large egg yolk, for egg wash

1   tablespoon heavy cream, for egg wash

    Cranberry Compote (optional; page 341)

1. Cut oranges and lemon into paper-thin slices, and remove seeds. Julienne 4 of the orange slices and 4 lemon slices; reserve remaining slices. Place all (including reserved slices) into a glass or other nonreactive container, add sugar, toss gently, and refrigerate overnight.

2. On a lightly floured surface, roll out dough ⅛ inch thick; fit into 10-inch pie plate. Trim excess dough, and crimp edge as desired. Refrigerate or freeze until firm, about 30 minutes.

3. Preheat oven to 400°F. Drain fruit over a bowl, reserving syrup; separate whole slices from julienned.

4. With an electric mixer on medium-high speed, beat whole eggs and citrus syrup until pale yellow and fluffy, about 5 minutes. Remove bowl from mixer; stir in julienned orange and lemon. Pour into chilled pie shell; top with reserved fruit slices.

5. In a small bowl, whisk together egg yolk and cream; gently brush over edges of dough. Place pie plate on a parchment-lined rimmed baking sheet and bake 15 minutes. Reduce heat to 350°F; bake, until filling is set, 35 to 40 minutes more. Let pie cool completely on a wire rack, 2 to 3 hours. Serve pie with compote, if desired.

Quince-Apple Pie

References to quince pie date as far back as the 1400s; the dessert later garnered a mention in Shakespeare's *Romeo and Juliet*. Quinces look and taste like a cross between an apple and a pear; in fact, they are usually paired with one or the other, as in this recipe. Here, peeled, halved quinces are first poached in dessert wine with the reserved peels (for their signature rosy color) and a split vanilla bean (for flavor). Baking the pie in a cast-iron skillet helps the crust turn a deep golden brown and gives the pie a truly home-style appeal. You may substitute four additional Granny Smith apples for the poached quinces; soak the raisins in one-third cup of warm Calvados in place of the poaching liquid. MAKES ONE 8-INCH PIE

4 quinces, peeled and halved, peels reserved

1 bottle (375 ml) sweet dessert wine, such as Muscat

1 vanilla bean, halved lengthwise and scraped, pod and seeds reserved

1 cup sugar, plus more for sprinkling

½ cup raisins

4 tart, firm apples, such as Granny Smith

Fresh juice of 1 lemon

¼ cup all-purpose flour, plus more for dusting

1 teaspoon ground cinnamon

½ recipe Pâte Brisée (page 322)

1 tablespoon unsalted butter, cut into small pieces

1. In a saucepan, combine quinces with reserved peel, wine, vanilla pod and seeds, ¼ cup sugar, and enough water to cover. Place cheesecloth or a round of parchment over fruit to keep it submerged; bring to a boil. Reduce heat, and simmer until quinces are tender when pierced with the tip of a paring knife, 25 to 35 minutes. Remove fruit with a slotted spoon. Continue cooking liquid until syrupy and reduced by two-thirds, about 30 minutes.

2. Preheat oven to 375°F. In a medium bowl, cover raisins with reduced poaching liquid. Let cool.

3. Peel and core apples, and cut into ¾-inch-thick wedges. Transfer to a large bowl with lemon juice, and toss to coat. Add remaining ¾ cup sugar, the flour, and cinnamon; toss to combine. Drain raisins (reserve poaching liquid), and add to apple mixture. Using a melon baller, remove core from poached quinces, cut fruit into ¾-inch-thick wedges, and add to apple mixture.

4. On a lightly floured surface, roll out dough to a 14-inch round, ⅛ inch thick, and fit into an 8-inch cast-iron skillet, leaving overhang. Fill with apple-quince mixture, dot with butter, and fold edges over fruit, overlapping as needed and leaving center open. Brush dough with water, and sprinkle with sugar.

5. Bake until crust is golden brown and juices bubble over, about 1 hour, 25 minutes. If fruit in center appears dry, brush with reserved poaching liquid. (If fruit or crust browns too quickly, tent with foil.) Transfer to a wire rack and let cool completely.

Plum and Port Crostata

The filling for this Italian-style tart begins with a flavorful reduction of port wine and brown sugar; half a fresh Thai chile is added for a subtle—but entirely optional—bit of heat. Start with the best fruit you can find. Small, oval Italian prune plums are firmer and sweeter than other plums; plus, since they are a freestone fruit, their pits are not attached to the flesh and are therefore easily removed. MAKES ONE 8-INCH PIE

All-purpose flour, for dusting

½ recipe Pâte Brisée (page 322)

1½ cups ruby port

1¼ cups packed light brown sugar

½ Thai chile, seeded and minced (optional)

1 teaspoon salt

2 pounds Italian prune plums, halved and pitted

¼ cup cornstarch

¼ teaspoon ground cinnamon

1 teaspoon heavy cream, for brushing

Coarse sanding sugar, for sprinkling

1. On a lightly floured surface, roll out dough to a 12-inch round, ⅛ inch thick. Fit into an 8-inch pie plate, leaving a 1-inch overhang. Refrigerate or freeze until firm, about 30 minutes.

2. Simmer port and ½ cup brown sugar in a saucepan until reduced to ½ cup, about 25 minutes. Transfer to a bowl. Add chile, if desired. Cover, and let cool 10 minutes.

3. Meanwhile, preheat oven to 400°F. Stir together remaining ¾ cup brown sugar and the salt, plums, cornstarch, cinnamon, and port syrup. Pour into pie shell. Fold in overhang to form a border; brush dough with cream, and sprinkle with sanding sugar. Bake 30 minutes; reduce heat to 375°F. Bake until crust is golden and center is bubbling, about 90 minutes more. Let pie cool completely on a wire rack.

Honey and Pine Nut Tart

It's not uncommon to encounter tarts like this one all over Italy, where it is known as *crostata di miele e pignoli*. The filling combines two ingredients typical to Italian baking—honey and pine nuts—with those universal to dessert making (eggs, cream, sugar, and butter). If you can find a creamy, spicy, floral variety such as Tasmanian leatherwood honey, use one-quarter cup in the filling, and balance it with one-third cup of pale, mellow honey, such as acacia. Otherwise, use all acacia, as suggested below. The crust is *pasta frolla,* an Italian short pastry with a crunchy, cookielike texture. Be careful not to overcook the tart; the filling should still jiggle in the center when you remove it from the oven, and it will firm as it cools. MAKES ONE 10-INCH TART

FOR THE CRUST

- ¼ cup heavy cream
- 1 large whole egg plus 1 large egg yolk
- ½ teaspoon pure vanilla extract
- 2⅓ cups all-purpose flour, plus more for dusting
- ½ cup sugar
- 1 teaspoon coarse salt
- ½ teaspoon baking powder
- ½ cup (1 stick) plus 2 tablespoons cold unsalted butter, cut into small pieces

FOR THE FILLING

- ½ cup sugar
- ½ cup plus 1 tablespoon mild honey, such as acacia
- 1 teaspoon coarse salt
- ¾ cup (1½ sticks) unsalted butter, cut into small pieces
- ½ cup heavy cream
- 1 large whole egg plus 1 large egg yolk
- 1½ cups pine nuts (6 ounces)

1. Make the crust: Whisk together cream, whole egg, egg yolk, and vanilla in a medium bowl. Pulse flour, sugar, salt, and baking powder in a food processor. Add butter, and pulse just until mixture resembles coarse meal. Drizzle in cream mixture, and pulse until dough just comes together. Shape dough into 2 disks, and wrap each in plastic. Refrigerate about 1 hour. (Dough can be refrigerated up to 2 days or frozen up to 3 months; thaw in refrigerator before using.)

2. On a lightly floured surface, roll out 1 disk of dough to a 14-inch round, ⅛ inch thick (reserve second disk for another use). If dough is soft and sticky, transfer to a parchment-lined rimmed baking sheet and freeze until firm but still pliable, about 5 minutes. Fit dough into a fluted 10-inch tart pan with a removable bottom. Patch any tears with scraps of dough. Freeze shell while making filling.

3. Make the filling: In a medium saucepan, bring sugar, honey, and salt to a boil, whisking until sugar dissolves. Add butter a few pieces at a time, and whisk until incorporated. Transfer honey mixture to a medium bowl, and let cool 30 minutes. Whisk in cream, whole egg, and egg yolk until incorporated.

4. Preheat oven to 325°F. Place tart pan on a parchment-lined rimmed baking sheet. Scatter pine nuts over bottom. Slowly pour filling over pine nuts, redistributing pine nuts evenly with your fingers. Bake until crust is golden brown and center is set but still slightly wobbly, about 1 hour. Transfer tart to a wire rack, and let cool completely before serving.

Strawberry Icebox Pie

Strawberries are America's favorite summer fruit, hands down. Here, a graham-cracker crust holds a luscious strawberry filling topped with swells of sweetened whipped cream. To make the filling sliceable, some of the berries are briefly cooked with a small amount of cornstarch (and cranberry juice, to enhance the color); the rest are stirred in off heat. The result is a pie with a fresh, true strawberry flavor—and all the crumbly, creamy qualities of the best icebox desserts. MAKES ONE 9-INCH PIE

¾ cup plus 2 tablespoons sugar

½ cup unsweetened cranberry juice

2 quarts fresh strawberries, hulled and thinly sliced (reserve a few whole berries for garnish)

¼ cup cornstarch

¼ teaspoon salt

Graham Cracker Crust (page 331)

½ cup heavy cream

1. In a medium saucepan over medium-high heat, combine ¾ cup sugar, the cranberry juice, 2 cups strawberries, the cornstarch, and salt. Using a potato masher, gently mash strawberries. Bring to a boil; reduce to a simmer and cook, stirring frequently, until very thick, about 1 minute. Remove from heat and let cool slightly. Stir in remaining sliced strawberries. Pour into baked, cooled crust. Refrigerate until set, 4 hours or, covered with plastic, up to 1 day.

2. In a large chilled bowl, beat cream until soft peaks form. Sprinkle remaining 2 tablespoons sugar over cream and continue to beat until soft peaks return (do not overbeat). Spread whipped cream over pie, leaving a 1½-inch border around edge. Garnish with reserved whole berries.

Raspberry-Plum Crumb Tart

The press-in crust for this tart, flavored with ground hazelnuts and cinnamon, doubles as a crumble topping that browns atop the fruit-and-custard filling as it bakes. It's another highly adaptable, versatile recipe that works well with any type of stone fruit or berry. MAKES ONE 9-INCH TART

FOR THE CRUST AND TOPPING

- ¾ cup (1½ sticks) cold unsalted butter, cut into pieces, plus more for pan
- ⅓ cup hazelnuts, toasted and skinned (see page 343)
- 1½ cups all-purpose flour
- ½ cup granulated sugar
- ⅓ cup packed light brown sugar
- ½ teaspoon ground cinnamon
- ½ teaspoon salt

FOR THE FILLING

- 3 ripe, firm plums (about 12 ounces)
- 4 ounces (about ¾ cup) raspberries
- 1 tablespoon all-purpose flour
- ¼ cup plus 2 tablespoons granulated sugar
- 1 large whole egg, lightly beaten, and 1 large egg yolk
- ⅓ cup heavy cream
- ¼ cup milk
- ¼ teaspoon ground cinnamon
- ¼ teaspoon salt

  Pinch of freshly grated nutmeg (optional)

1. Make the crust: Preheat oven to 350°F. Butter a 9-inch springform pan. In a food processor, pulse nuts until ground medium fine, about 30 pulses.

2. With an electric mixer on medium speed, mix ground nuts, flour, sugars, cinnamon, and salt just until combined. Add butter, and mix on low speed just until combined, 2 to 3 minutes. Press 3 cups of crumb mixture into bottom of pan and about 1½ inches up sides to form crust. Reserve remaining crumb mixture. Bake crust until set, 18 to 20 minutes. Let cool completely on a wire rack.

3. Make the filling: Slice plums in half, and remove pits. Slice into eighths. Scatter raspberries and sliced plums onto cooled crust.

4. In a medium bowl, whisk together flour and sugar. Whisk in whole egg, egg yolk, cream, milk, cinnamon, salt, and nutmeg, if desired. Pour custard over fruit; sprinkle with reserved crumb mixture. Bake tart until custard has set and is slightly golden, 45 to 50 minutes. Transfer to a wire rack, and let tart cool at least 25 minutes before slicing. Serve warm or at room temperature.

Cheddar-Crust Apple Pie

For some people, apple pie just isn't the same without a slice of cheddar cheese melted on top or served on the side. This recipe does that custom one better by mixing the cheese right into the crust, so you can enjoy the combination of flavors in every bite. The method for making the crust is a simple variation on the standard *pâte brisée* recipe—shredded cheese is added to the dry ingredients with the butter to form the dough. MAKES ONE 9-INCH PIE

¼ cup all-purpose flour, plus more for dusting

Pâte Brisée, Cheddar Variation (page 322)

2 tablespoons fresh lemon juice

4 pounds tart, firm apples, such as Granny Smith

¾ cup sugar

1 teaspoon ground cinnamon

½ teaspoon salt

1. On a lightly floured surface, roll each disk of dough to a 13-inch round, ⅛ inch thick. Transfer 1 round to a parchment-lined rimmed baking sheet for top crust; refrigerate. Fit second round into a 9-inch pie plate for bottom crust. Trim dough, leaving a 1-inch overhang.

2. Place lemon juice in a large bowl. Peel, quarter, and core apples; thinly slice, tossing into bowl with lemon juice as you work. Add flour, sugar, cinnamon, and salt; toss to combine.

3. Fill bottom crust with apple mixture, piling high in center; lightly brush edge of crust with water. Place top crust over filling; press all around edge to seal with bottom crust. Using kitchen shears, trim to a 1-inch overhang; fold under to form edge, and press to seal. Using thumb and forefinger, crimp dough along rim. With a paring knife, cut 5 small slits in center of pie to let steam escape.

4. Preheat oven to 425°F, with rack in lowest position. Place pie plate on a parchment-lined rimmed baking sheet. Bake 20 minutes; reduce heat to 375°F, and bake until crust is golden brown and juices are bubbling, 60 to 70 minutes more. (If edge browns too quickly, tent pie with foil.) Let pie cool completely on a wire rack, at least 4 hours or up to overnight, before serving.

Peach and Crème Fraîche Pie

This pie has all the makings of a favorite summer dish: ease, seasonal flavor, and laid-back appeal. Peaches and cream are a justly celebrated pair, even more so when the "cream" is crème fraîche: Its slight tartness beautifully complements the sweet fruit. As the pie bakes, the crème fraîche sets like a custard, the peaches become tender, and the crumb topping turns golden and perfectly crisp. MAKES ONE 10-INCH PIE

¼ cup confectioners' sugar

3 tablespoons all-purpose flour, plus more for dusting

¼ teaspoon baking powder

⅛ teaspoon salt

4 tablespoons cold unsalted butter, cut into pieces

½ recipe Pâte Sucrée (page 333)

1½ pounds ripe yellow peaches (4 to 5), pitted and quartered

2 tablespoons granulated sugar

¼ cup plus 1 tablespoon crème fraîche

1. In a medium bowl, sift together confectioners' sugar, flour, baking powder, and a pinch of salt. Using a pastry blender or your fingertips, work in butter until mixture resembles coarse meal. Refrigerate crumb topping until ready to use.

2. On a lightly floured surface, roll out dough ⅛ inch thick. Fit into a 10-inch pie plate. Trim dough, leaving a 1-inch overhang; fold under, and crimp as desired. Pierce bottom of shell all over with a fork. Refrigerate or freeze until firm, about 30 minutes.

3. Preheat oven to 400°F. Line shell with parchment, and fill with pie weights or dried beans. Bake 10 minutes. Remove weights and parchment. Bake until pale golden brown, 5 to 8 minutes more. Transfer to a wire rack to cool slightly. Reduce heat to 375°F.

4. In a medium bowl, sprinkle peaches with granulated sugar and remaining pinch of salt; gently toss to coat. Let stand 15 minutes. Spread 2 tablespoons crème fraîche over bottom of crust; sprinkle with one-third crumb mixture. Arrange peaches on top; spread or dot with remaining 3 tablespoons crème fraîche. Sprinkle with remaining crumb topping.

5. Bake pie until crème fraîche is bubbling and crumb topping is golden brown, about 50 minutes. Cover edge of crust with a foil ring (see page 324) if it browns too quickly. Let pie cool on a wire rack at least 20 minutes. Serve warm or at room temperature.

Blackberry Jam Tart

Cornmeal and blackberries appear together in many baked goods and desserts, as their late-summer flavors complement each other beautifully. This recipe calls for you to prepare your own jam, for which you will be rewarded with a few extra jars. Otherwise, seek out a top-quality store-bought jam to use in its place; spike it with two tablespoons kirsch. **MAKES ONE 10-INCH TART**

All-purpose flour, for dusting

½ recipe Pâte Brisée, Cornmeal Variation (page 322)

½ pint Old Bachelor's Jam (recipe follows), flavors stirred together, or 1 cup best-quality store-bought blackberry jam

12 ounces (about 3 cups) fresh blackberries

¼ cup sliced almonds, toasted (see page 343)

1. Preheat oven to 375°F. On a lightly floured surface, roll out dough to a 12-inch round, ¼ inch thick. Press dough into bottom and up sides of a 10-inch spring-form pan. Trim edges to come 1 inch up sides of pan. Refrigerate or freeze until firm, about 30 minutes.

2. Pierce bottom of shell all over with a fork. Bake until golden brown, about 25 minutes. Immediately spread jam in tart shell. Top with blackberries; sprinkle with almonds. Bake 10 minutes more. Transfer to a wire rack to cool slightly. Serve warm.

OLD BACHELOR'S JAM
Any berry will work in Old Bachelor's Jam; here, it's made with blackberries, raspberries, and kirsch. Some say the liqueur-infused jam was named for its capacity to warm single gentlemen on winter nights. Jam will keep for 1 month, stored in airtight containers in the refrigerator.
Makes 4 half-pint jars

2 pounds (about 7 cups) fresh blackberries

3½ cups sugar

2 lemons, halved

2 pounds (about 7 cups) fresh raspberries

½ cup (4 ounces) kirsch or other cherry-flavored liqueur

1. Bring blackberries, 1¾ cups sugar, and juice of 1 lemon to a simmer in a large pot. Cook until sugar dissolves and berries are soft, 4 to 5 minutes. Press a parchment round directly on surface of jam, and refrigerate overnight. Repeat with raspberries and remaining 1¾ cups sugar and juice of 1 lemon in another large pot.

2. Remove parchment rounds; bring each pot to a boil. Cook over medium-high heat until berries are slightly broken down and mixture is consistency of very loose jelly, about 12 minutes for blackberries and about 17 minutes for raspberries.

3. Divide blackberry jam among 4 half-pint glass jars, filling each halfway; top each with 1 tablespoon kirsch. Divide raspberry jam among jars; top each with 1 tablespoon kirsch.

Sweet Potato Soufflé Pie

In dessert making, sweet potatoes are best known as the filling for a rich, dense, single-crust Southern pie. Yet they become surprisingly light when baked in a soufflé. Here, layers of paper-thin phyllo dough overlap to form a crisp pie shell, which stands tall as the filling cools and sinks (this is one soufflé that's supposed to fall). MAKES ONE 9-INCH PIE

FOR THE FILLING

- 2 sweet potatoes, pierced with a fork
- ¼ teaspoon ground ginger
- ½ teaspoon pure vanilla extract
- ¼ teaspoon salt
- 4 large eggs, separated
- 2 tablespoons light brown sugar
- 1 cup milk
- 1 piece (2 inches) fresh ginger, peeled and thinly sliced
- 4 tablespoons unsalted butter
- ¼ cup all-purpose flour
  Pinch of cream of tartar
- ¼ cup granulated sugar

FOR THE CRUST

- ½ cup (1 stick) unsalted butter, melted, plus more for pan
- ⅓ cup granulated sugar, plus more if needed
- ½ teaspoon ground cinnamon, plus more if needed
- 9 sheets phyllo dough (17 by 12 inches), thawed if frozen

1. Make the filling: Preheat oven to 400°F. On a parchment-lined rimmed baking sheet, bake potatoes until tender, 60 to 75 minutes. Let stand until cool enough to handle. Reduce heat to 375°F.

2. Peel potatoes, and press through a ricer into a large bowl (you should have about 1 cup); let cool completely. Stir in ground ginger, vanilla, salt, egg yolks, and brown sugar.

3. Meanwhile, in a medium saucepan, warm milk and fresh ginger over medium heat until just under a boil. Remove from heat; let stand 30 minutes. Pour through a fine sieve into a bowl and discard solids.

4. In a saucepan over medium-high, melt butter. Whisk in flour; cook, whisking, 1 minute. Whisk in ginger-infused milk. Bring to a boil. Reduce heat to medium; cook 1 minute. Stir into potato mixture.

5. Make the crust: Butter a 9-inch springform pan, and place on a parchment-lined rimmed baking sheet. Stir together ⅓ cup granulated sugar and ½ teaspoon cinnamon in a bowl. Brush 1 phyllo sheet with some melted butter. Sprinkle lightly with cinnamon-sugar mixture. Fold in half crosswise; brush with butter. Sprinkle lightly with cinnamon-sugar mixture, and fit into prepared pan, folded side in, allowing a 2½-inch overhang. Repeat with each sheet, overlapping to cover bottom.

6. With an electric mixer on high, whisk egg whites until foamy. Add cream of tartar; whisk until soft peaks form. With machine running, gradually add ¼ cup granulated sugar; whisk until stiff glossy peaks form. Whisk one-third of egg whites into potato mixture. Using a wide flexible spatula, gently but thoroughly fold in remaining egg whites.

7. Pour filling over phyllo; fold overhang over filling. Sprinkle with cinnamon-sugar mixture (if needed, combine 1 to 2 tablespoons more sugar with a pinch of cinnamon). Bake pie until puffed and just set in center, 45 to 50 minutes. Let pie stand until slightly cooled and center has fallen, about 20 minutes. Serve immediately.

Mrs. Dunlinson's Plate Cake

This recipe comes from Julia Dunlinson, mother of *Martha Stewart Living* design director James Dunlinson, who hails from England. Despite the name, plate cakes are actually pies, baked on dinner plates. You will need an eight- to nine-inch ovenproof plate, such as one made from stoneware or ironstone. This recipe is for a raspberry-and-apple-filled pie, but any summer berries can be used; the amount of sugar will vary with the tartness. Whipped cream is divine with tart fruits like gooseberries or black currants (see variations below). MAKES ONE 8- OR 9-INCH PIE

1 teaspoon unsalted butter, for plate

2 pounds tart, firm apples, such as Granny Smith, peeled, cored, and cut into 1½-inch chunks

   Fresh juice of 1 lemon

1 pound (about 3 cups) raspberries

   All-purpose flour, for dusting

   Pâte Brisée (page 322)

½ cup sugar, plus 1 tablespoon for sprinkling

1 large egg, for egg wash

1 teaspoon water, for egg wash

1. Preheat oven to 375°F. Coat an 8- or 9-inch ovenproof plate with butter. In a medium bowl, toss apples with lemon juice. Gently fold in raspberries.

2. On a lightly floured surface, roll out 1 disk of dough to a 9- or 10-inch round (1 inch larger than plate), about ⅛ inch thick. Transfer to plate. Pile fruit high in center of plate, and sprinkle with ½ cup sugar. Brush edge of dough with water.

3. Roll out remaining dough to a round a few inches larger than plate, and center on top of fruit. Trim excess dough, then turn overhang under to seal. Flute edges with fingers or a fork, and make 2 or 3 slits in top, to let steam escape. In a small bowl, whisk egg with water; brush evenly over dough, and sprinkle pie with remaining 1 tablespoon sugar. Transfer plate to a parchment-lined rimmed baking sheet. Bake 40 to 50 minutes, until crust is golden and fruit is bubbling. Let plate cool completely on a wire rack before serving.

Variations: For gooseberry or currant plate cakes, replace fruit in step 1 with 2 pounds (5 cups) gooseberries (trimmed) or fresh black currants and toss with 1½ cups sugar and the lemon juice. In step 2, sprinkle piled fruit with an additional ½ cup sugar. Proceed with recipe.

FILLING PLATE CAKES

Gooseberry Custard Tartlets

Here, handfuls of glossy gooseberries—which are not berries at all, but relatives of tomatillos—settle into custard tarts that are equally appealing for their ease of preparation. The fruit's flavor can vary—some gooseberries are bracing and tangy; others are sweet, reminiscent of apricots, plums, and grapes. Look for gooseberries in farmers' markets and specialty grocers in late June and early July. Or grow them yourself, as Martha does. MAKES 8

All-purpose flour, for dusting

Pâte Brisée (page 322)

2 large whole eggs plus 1 large egg yolk

⅓ cup plus ¼ cup sugar, plus more for sprinkling

1 cup heavy cream

8 cups fresh green gooseberries (about 4 pints), trimmed

1. Preheat oven to 350°F. On a lightly floured surface, roll out dough about ⅛ inch thick. Cut out eight 6-inch rounds, and fit each round into a 4-inch tart pan with a removable bottom. Fold edges under, and press dough into sides of tart pans. Refrigerate or freeze until firm, about 30 minutes.

2. Pierce bottoms of shells all over with a fork. Transfer pans to a rimmed baking sheet. Line shells with parchment, and fill with pie weights or dried beans. Bake until pale golden brown, 25 to 30 minutes. Remove weights and parchment. Let cool completely on a wire rack.

3. Whisk together whole eggs, egg yolk, and ⅓ cup sugar in a small bowl. Pour in cream, whisking until combined.

4. In a separate bowl, toss gooseberries with remaining ¼ cup sugar. Pile sugar-covered gooseberries into tart shells (a scant 1 cup per tart), and slowly pour in custard (about ¼ cup per tart). Dip a pastry brush into each custard filling, and lightly brush onto edges of shell. Sprinkle tops evenly with sugar.

5. Bake until custard is just set and gooseberries are soft, about 35 minutes. Transfer tartlets to a wire rack to cool 15 minutes. Serve warm.

Chewy Chess Tart

Although countless theories exist to explain the name "chess pie," not one is considered definitive. Whatever its origin, the pantry pie relies primarily on sugar, eggs, and butter for its deceptively complex filling. Here, the traditional dessert is reinterpreted as a more modern-looking tart. An easy crumb crust made from store-bought vanilla wafers replaces the standard rolled-out pie dough, and is baked in a fluted tart ring instead of a pie plate. In testing the recipe, our editors found that Nilla wafers worked better than other brands. The filling is thickened with fine cornmeal; during baking, it forms a thin crust on top, which, when sliced, reveals a creamy golden custard. This version just might become a classic in its own right. MAKES ONE 9-INCH TART

FOR THE CRUST

1¼ cups finely ground vanilla wafer cookies (about 45), such as Nilla wafers

5 tablespoons unsalted butter, melted and cooled slightly

2 tablespoons granulated sugar

¼ teaspoon salt

FOR THE FILLING

1 cup granulated sugar

½ cup packed light brown sugar

1 tablespoon fine cornmeal

¼ teaspoon salt

3 large whole eggs plus 1 large egg yolk

½ teaspoon pure vanilla extract

½ cup (1 stick) unsalted butter, melted and cooled slightly

1. Make the crust: Preheat oven to 350°F. In a bowl, mix wafer crumbs, butter, sugar, and salt until combined. Press mixture into bottom and up sides of a 9-inch fluted tart pan with a removable bottom. Refrigerate or freeze until firm, about 15 minutes.

2. Transfer pan to a rimmed baking sheet, and bake until crust is golden, about 12 minutes. Let cool slightly. Reduce heat to 325°F.

3. Make the filling: Mix together sugars, cornmeal, and salt, breaking up clumps. Whisk in whole eggs, egg yolk, and vanilla. Whisk in butter until completely smooth. Pour filling into tart shell. Bake until top is dark golden brown and edge is set but center is still a bit wobbly, 35 to 40 minutes.

4. Transfer pan to a wire rack, and let cool 15 minutes. Refrigerate until cooled completely, 2 hours or up to 1 day. Unmold, then serve.

Red Currant and Raspberry Pie

Fresh currants are one of summer's overlooked treasures. They are just as adaptable to baking as other more common berries, such as blueberries and raspberries. In fact, naturally tart currants are often paired with those sweeter berries for a perfect balance of flavors. Here, red currants and raspberries are tossed together and baked in a double-crust pie liberally sprinkled with sanding sugar. It's exactly the type of dessert you want to make—and eat—after a visit to a farmers' market or roadside fruit stand in high summer. MAKES ONE 10-INCH PIE

All-purpose flour, for dusting

Pâte Brisée (page 322)

10 ounces (2 cups) fresh red currants, stems removed

10 ounces (about 2 cups) fresh raspberries

¼ cup instant tapioca

Finely grated zest and fresh juice of 1 lemon

1 cup granulated sugar

2 tablespoons unsalted butter, cut into small pieces

1 large egg, for egg wash

1 tablespoon milk, for egg wash

Coarse sanding sugar, for sprinkling

1. On a lightly floured surface, roll out 1 disk of dough to a 14-inch round, ⅛ inch thick. Fit dough into a 10-inch pie plate. Refrigerate or freeze until firm, about 30 minutes.

2. In a medium bowl, gently toss together currants, raspberries, tapioca, lemon zest and juice, and granulated sugar to coat. Pour mixture into pie plate, piling fruit in center. Dot filling with butter.

3. Preheat oven to 425°F. Roll out remaining disk of dough, as in step 1. Whisk together egg and milk. Brush edge of dough with some egg wash; place other round of dough on top, and trim to 1-inch overhang. Crimp edges; refrigerate or freeze pie until firm, about 30 minutes.

4. Transfer to a parchment-lined rimmed baking sheet; cut a few steam vents in top of pie. Brush with egg wash, and sprinkle with sanding sugar. Bake 20 minutes. Reduce heat to 350°F. Continue baking until juices are bubbling and crust is golden brown, about 40 minutes more. Let pie cool completely on a wire rack before serving.

Rhubarb Crumble Pie

Rhubarb shines in this scrumptious dessert. For the filling, the rhubarb is simply tossed with sugar, salt, and a bit of cornstarch. The topping can be used on any single-crust fruit pie, or on a crumble itself, naturally. Make a few extra batches and store them in the freezer for convenience; they'll keep up to six months in airtight containers. This pie is best enjoyed the day after it's baked; try it alone or with a scoop of vanilla (or strawberry) ice cream. MAKES ONE 9-INCH PIE

All-purpose flour, for dusting

½ recipe Pâte Brisée (page 322)

1¾ pounds rhubarb, ends trimmed, cut crosswise into ¾-inch pieces (about 6 cups)

1 cup sugar

2 tablespoons cornstarch

Pinch of salt

Crumble Topping (recipe follows)

1. On a lightly floured piece of parchment, roll out dough to a 13-inch round. Fit dough into a 9-inch pie plate. Trim dough, leaving a 1-inch overhang; fold overhang under, and press gently to seal. Crimp edges, as desired. Refrigerate or freeze until firm, about 30 minutes.

2. Preheat oven to 400°F. In a large bowl, toss rhubarb with sugar, cornstarch, and salt. Pour into pie shell; sprinkle evenly with crumble topping. Place pie plate on a parchment-lined rimmed baking sheet.

3. Reduce heat to 375°F. Bake until topping is browned and crust is lightly browned, about 1½ hours. (If topping or crust brown too quickly, tent pie with foil.) Let pie cool completely on a wire rack before serving.

CRUMBLE TOPPING
Makes 2½ cups

¾ cup all-purpose flour

⅓ cup packed light brown sugar

3 tablespoons granulated sugar

Pinch of salt

6 tablespoons cold unsalted butter, cut into small pieces

In a medium bowl, mix flour, sugars, and salt until combined. With your fingertips, work in butter until large clumps form. Refrigerate, covered, until ready to use (up to 3 days).

ASSEMBLING PIE

Ginger-Pear Hand Pies

Brown butter, vanilla-bean seeds, and freshly grated ginger are used here in good measure to flavor individual pear-custard-filled pies. The pleated pastry shells are formed in a standard muffin tin, allowing for easy removal after baking. MAKES 12

FOR THE CRUST

2½ cups all-purpose flour, plus more for dusting

1 teaspoon granulated sugar

1 teaspoon salt

¾ cup (1½ sticks) cold unsalted butter, cut into small pieces

¼ cup cold vegetable shortening, cut into small pieces

1 tablespoon distilled white vinegar

¼ to ½ cup ice water

FOR THE FILLING

2 large eggs

⅔ cup plus 2 tablespoons granulated sugar

2 teaspoons fresh lemon juice

¼ cup plus 3 tablespoons all-purpose flour

¼ teaspoon salt

2 ripe, firm pears, such as Bosc, peeled and chopped into ¼-inch dice

½ cup (1 stick) unsalted butter

1 vanilla bean, halved lengthwise and scraped

2 tablespoons finely grated peeled fresh ginger

Confectioners' sugar, for dusting

1. Make the crust: In a food processor, pulse flour, sugar, and salt until combined. Add butter and shortening; pulse just until mixture resembles coarse meal, 8 to 10 times. Combine vinegar and ¼ cup ice water, and drizzle evenly over mixture; pulse just until dough comes together. If dough is still crumbly, add up to ¼ cup more ice water, 1 tablespoon at a time.

2. Pat dough into 2 disks, and wrap each in plastic. Refrigerate until firm, 1 hour or up to 1 day.

3. On a lightly floured surface, roll out dough ¼ inch thick. Cut twelve 5-inch rounds from dough. Gently press rounds into cups of a 12-cup standard muffin tin, making pleats around edges and gently pressing to seal. Refrigerate or freeze until firm, about 30 minutes.

4. Preheat oven to 375°F. Make the filling: In a medium bowl, whisk together eggs and granulated sugar until thick and pale yellow. Whisk in lemon juice, then flour and salt. Place diced pears in a medium bowl.

5. In a small saucepan, heat butter, vanilla bean and seeds, and grated ginger over medium-high until butter foams and browns, about 5 minutes. Pour mixture through a fine sieve over pears; discard solids. Stir egg mixture into pear mixture until combined.

6. Divide batter among chilled shells. Bake pies until crusts and filling are golden brown, about 30 minutes. Let cool in tins on a wire rack, 30 to 40 minutes. Unmold; let cool completely on rack. Just before serving, dust with confectioners' sugar.

layered

Slice into any of the pies and tarts that follow, and you can see how their multiple components work together to create a delicious whole. In a single serving, the fork goes from one distinct element straight through to the next, for a pleasing combination of flavors and textures in every bite. Often the crust, filling, and topping can be prepared ahead separately, and the dessert composed just before serving. And since you can usually swap one element for another similar one, layered pies and tarts are especially versatile—just another part of their multifaceted appeal.

CHOCOLATE-ESPRESSO TART, RECIPE PAGE 165

Red, White, and Blueberry Cheesecake Tart

Take all the layers of classic cheesecake—crumbly graham-cracker crust, rich, creamy filling, and fresh fruit topping—and combine them in a modern tart. Sour cream ups the tanginess factor of the filling; almonds round out the cookie crust; and sugar sweetens the plums, which are cooked into a jam. Save some of the cooking syrup for tossing with the blueberries before scattering them over the top. MAKES ONE 9-INCH TART

FOR THE CRUST

- 6 graham cracker sheets (about 3½ ounces)
- ⅓ cup whole raw almonds
- ¼ cup sugar
- 4 tablespoons unsalted butter, melted

FOR THE FILLING

- 1 pound (two 8-ounce bars) cream cheese, room temperature
- ½ cup sour cream
- ½ cup sugar
- 1 large egg
- ½ teaspoon pure vanilla extract
- Pinch of salt

FOR THE TOPPING

- 4 red plums (1 to 1½ pounds total), halved, pitted, and cut into ½-inch pieces
- ½ cup sugar
- 1 tablespoon fresh lemon juice
- 10 ounces (2 cups) fresh blueberries

1. Make the crust: Preheat oven to 350°F. In a food processor, pulse graham crackers, almonds, and sugar until finely ground; add butter, and process until combined. Press mixture firmly into the bottom and up sides of a 9-inch tart pan with a removable bottom. Refrigerate until firm, about 15 minutes.

2. Make the filling: Carefully wipe processor blade and bowl clean. Process cream cheese, sour cream, sugar, egg, vanilla, and salt just until smooth. Place tart pan on a rimmed baking sheet; fill with cream cheese mixture. Bake until filling is just set, 30 to 35 minutes. Transfer pan to a wire rack to cool completely.

3. Make the topping: In a medium saucepan, combine plums, sugar, and lemon juice. Cook at a low simmer, stirring until mixture has thickened to a jamlike consistency, 15 to 25 minutes (time will depend on ripeness of fruit). Reserve 1 tablespoon cooking liquid (no solids); cool remaining plum mixture completely.

4. Leaving a 1-inch border, spread cooled plum mixture over tart filling. Reheat reserved plum liquid (on stove or in microwave) until loose. In a medium bowl, combine with blueberries, and scatter on top of plum mixture. Refrigerate until ready to serve, 2 hours or up to 1 day; unmold before serving.

Rice Pudding Tartlets with Blood Oranges

Move rice pudding out of the bowl and into crisp tartlet shells; top each with juicy, ruby red blood-orange segments. The filling is flavored with vanilla bean and blood-orange juice. The tarts can be served warm, at room temperature, or chilled for an afternoon tea or as a delicious final course after dinner. Arrange the blood-orange sections in a floral pattern, then drizzle the tarts with extra juice. MAKES 6

All-purpose flour, for dusting
Pâte Sucrée (page 333)
4 blood oranges
1 cup Arborio rice
4 cups milk
½ vanilla bean, split lengthwise and scraped
Pinch of salt
½ cup sugar
1 cup heavy cream
2 large egg yolks

1. Preheat oven to 400°F. Place six 4-inch tart rings on a parchment-lined baking sheet.

2. On a lightly floured surface, roll out dough ⅛ inch thick. Cut out six 6-inch rounds, and press dough into tart rings. Trim excess dough flush with rims. Pierce bottoms of shells all over with a fork. Refrigerate or freeze until firm, about 30 minutes.

3. Line rings with parchment, and fill with pie weights or dried beans. Bake until edges begin to brown, about 20 minutes. Remove parchment and weights; continue baking until golden brown all over, about 10 minutes more. Transfer to a wire rack to cool completely.

4. Finely grate zest of 1 blood orange. Cut ends off all 4 oranges, and remove peel and pith with a paring knife, following curve of fruit. Working over a bowl to catch juices, slice between membranes to remove segments, being careful to leave them whole. Transfer to a bowl. Squeeze membranes to extract as much juice as possible; reserve ¼ cup juice.

5. In a medium saucepan, bring rice, milk, zest, vanilla bean and seeds, salt, and sugar to a gentle simmer. Cook, stirring occasionally, until rice is tender and most of the liquid has been absorbed, 30 to 35 minutes. Remove from heat, and discard vanilla bean.

6. In a large bowl, whisk together cream, egg yolks, and reserved ¼ cup orange juice. Gradually whisk in rice mixture, and return to saucepan. Place pan over medium-low heat; cook, stirring constantly, until mixture boils and thickens, about 10 minutes. Remove from heat, and let stand 5 minutes. Pour filling into baked tart shells. Arrange orange segments in a floral pattern over rice pudding, and drizzle with juice from bowl. Serve warm, at room temperature, or chilled.

ARRANGING ORANGE SEGMENTS

Chocolate-Espresso Tart

A cocoa shell forms a crisp foundation for two silky-smooth fillings: an even layer of creamy, tangy mascarpone cheese and gorgeous rosettes of espresso-flavored chocolate ganache. The flavors are strong, yet not particularly sweet; if you prefer, you can mix one to two tablespoons of sugar into the mascarpone filling. To produce perfect ganache every time, make sure the mixture is at room temperature before you start to beat it with an electric mixer. Any warmer or colder, and the mixture may seize or become grainy. MAKES ONE 14-BY-4-INCH TART

FOR THE GANACHE

- 8 ounces bittersweet chocolate (preferably 61 percent cacao), finely chopped
- 1¼ cups heavy cream
- 2 tablespoons best-quality ground espresso beans

FOR THE CRUST

- 1 cup all-purpose flour, plus more for dusting
- ¾ teaspoon salt
- ⅓ cup unsweetened Dutch-process cocoa powder
- ½ cup (1 stick) unsalted butter, softened
- ¼ cup sugar
- 1 large egg
- ¾ teaspoon pure vanilla extract
- 3 tablespoons heavy cream

FOR THE FILLING

- 1½ cups mascarpone cheese (12 ounces)

1. Make the ganache: Put chocolate into a medium heatproof bowl. In a small saucepan, bring cream and espresso just to a boil. Pour through a fine sieve over the chocolate; discard solids. Let stand 2 minutes, then whisk until completely smooth. Let cool to room temperature, stirring occasionally, 30 to 45 minutes.

2. Make the crust: Sift flour, salt, and cocoa into a medium bowl. With an electric mixer on medium speed, beat butter and sugar until pale and fluffy, about 4 minutes. Add egg and vanilla, and mix until combined, scraping down sides of bowl as needed. Reduce speed to low. Gradually add flour mixture in 3 batches, alternating with the cream. Shape dough into a thick rectangle; wrap in plastic. Refrigerate until firm, about 1 hour.

3. Preheat oven to 350°F. Roll out dough between 2 pieces of lightly floured parchment to a 16-by-6-inch rectangle, about ¼ inch thick. Press dough into a 14-by-4-inch rectangular tart pan with a removable bottom. Trim excess flush with rim. Pierce bottom of shell all over with a fork. Refrigerate or freeze until firm, about 30 minutes. Bake until dry, 18 to 20 minutes. Transfer to a wire rack to cool completely; unmold.

4. With an electric mixer on medium-high speed, beat ganache until soft peaks form, 6 to 7 minutes. Transfer to a pastry bag fitted with a ⅝-inch star tip (such as Ateco #828 or Wilton #6B).

5. Spread mascarpone cheese evenly over bottom of tart shell with an offset spatula. Pipe rows of ganache rosettes, one next to another, on top of mascarpone to cover. Tart can be refrigerated, covered, up to 1 day before serving.

Almond Macaroon Galette with Strawberries

This stunning dessert may be a showstopper, but its crust is remarkably simple; it's an easy-to-make oversize almond macaroon. The strawberries are macerated in sugar and liqueur before arranging on the tart; if allowed to rest for a couple of hours, the airy base will begin to soak up some of the deliciously boozy syrup. Since it's flourless, the galette is an excellent choice for Passover. MAKES ONE 9-INCH GALETTE

3 large egg whites

2 teaspoons finely grated lemon zest plus 2 teaspoons fresh lemon juice

1 cup confectioners' sugar

1½ cups sliced blanched almonds, toasted (see page 343) and finely ground

Vegetable-oil cooking spray

1½ pints (about 6 cups) fresh strawberries, hulls on

1 tablespoon granulated sugar

1 tablespoon kirsch

3 tablespoons best-quality strawberry jam

1. Preheat oven to 325°F. With an electric mixer on medium speed, whisk egg whites until soft peaks form. Whisk in lemon zest. Gradually add confectioners' sugar, whisking until whites are glossy and hold a ribbon on surface, 6 to 7 minutes. Fold in almonds.

2. Coat the inside of a 9-inch flan ring with cooking spray, and place on a parchment-lined rimmed baking sheet. Spoon batter into mold, and smooth top. Let stand 10 minutes. Place in oven, and prop door open about ½ inch, using a wooden spoon. Bake 10 minutes. Reduce heat to 300°F, and close door completely. Bake until pale golden and set, about 25 minutes. Unmold, and let cool completely on a wire rack.

3. Halve 8 to 10 strawberries lengthwise. Hull remaining strawberries, and cut each lengthwise into 4 slices. Toss slices with granulated sugar, kirsch, and lemon juice in a bowl; let stand at least 30 minutes or up to 2 hours, stirring occasionally.

4. Heat jam in a small saucepan until loose. Brush top of galette with jam. Arrange reserved strawberry halves around edge, with hulls facing out. Working inward, arrange sliced strawberries in a circular pattern, with bottoms facing out, reserving smallest slices for center. Drizzle liquid from strawberries over top. Serve immediately, or let stand up to 2 hours to allow juices to soak into the crust.

Poached Pear and Almond Tart

Pear and almond tart is one of the best known—and most revered—desserts of classic French pastry; it's also one of Martha's favorites. Almonds are sprinkled over the top and flavor both the press-in crust and the frangipane filling. Halved pears, poached in white wine and vanilla, are nestled in neat rows, leaving just enough room in between for the filling to rise during baking and turn a splendid shade of golden brown. MAKES ONE 11-BY-8-INCH TART

FOR THE CRUST

- ½ cup (1 stick) unsalted butter, room temperature, plus 1 tablespoon unsalted butter, melted and cooled, for pan
- ¾ cup whole blanched almonds
- 3 tablespoons sugar
- 1 cup all-purpose flour
- ¼ teaspoon salt
- ¼ teaspoon pure almond extract

FOR THE FILLING

- 3 tablespoons sliced blanched almonds
- ½ cup plus 1 tablespoon sugar
- ¼ teaspoon salt
- ¼ cup plus 2 tablespoons all-purpose flour
- ¼ cup plus 2 tablespoons almond flour or very finely ground blanched almonds
- ½ teaspoon baking powder
- 2 large whole eggs plus 1 large egg yolk, lightly beaten
- 2 tablespoons unsalted butter, melted
- ¼ cup plus 2 tablespoons milk
  Vanilla Poached Pears (page 342)

1. Make the crust: Brush 1 tablespoon melted butter into bottom and up sides of an 11-by-8-inch tart pan with a removable bottom.

2. Pulse whole almonds and 1 tablespoon sugar in food processor until almonds are finely ground. Add remaining ½ cup butter, and process until combined. Add flour, remaining 2 tablespoons sugar, the salt, and almond extract, and pulse until combined.

3. Press dough evenly into bottom and up sides of pan. Refrigerate or freeze until firm, about 30 minutes. Meanwhile, preheat oven to 350°F. Bake crust until golden, 20 to 25 minutes. Transfer to a wire rack to cool.

4. Make the filling: Spread sliced almonds in an even layer on a rimmed baking sheet, and toast in oven, tossing occasionally until golden, about 10 minutes.

5. In a large bowl, whisk together ½ cup sugar, the salt, flour, almond flour, and baking powder. Whisk in eggs and yolk, butter, and milk until well combined. Pour filling into crust.

6. Blot each pear half lightly with paper towels to remove excess syrup. Arrange halves, cut sides down, over filling, packing fruit closely together (3 rows of 3 pears; reserve remaining half for another use). Sprinkle tops of pears with remaining 1 tablespoon sugar. Sprinkle toasted almonds over tart. Transfer tart to a rimmed baking sheet.

7. Bake until filling is puffed and golden brown, 60 to 70 minutes. Transfer tart to a wire rack to cool completely. Unmold just before serving.

Strawberry and Fresh Fig Tart

Fresh figs and strawberries are favorite summer fruits that make a delicious pairing. Here, they are arranged in a *pâte brisée* shell, then surrounded by a hazelnut batter, which turns golden brown as it bakes. The batter is similar to frangipane, a classic filling for French pastries, notably *pithiviers*, and all manner of tarts; it is traditionally made from almonds, but other nuts are also common. Armagnac is a fine French brandy; Cognac or another top-quality brandy can be substituted.

MAKES ONE 10-INCH TART

All-purpose flour, for dusting

½ recipe Pâte Brisée (page 322)

¾ cup hazelnuts, toasted and skinned (see page 343)

½ cup packed light brown sugar

¼ cup granulated sugar

¼ teaspoon salt

½ teaspoon finely grated lemon zest

½ cup (1 stick) unsalted butter, cut into pieces

2 tablespoons Armagnac (or Cognac or other brandy)

2 large eggs

½ teaspoon pure vanilla extract

8 ounces fresh Black Mission figs (about 7), stemmed and halved lengthwise

8 ounces (1½ cups) fresh strawberries, hulled, halved if large

Whipped cream, for serving (optional; page 340)

1. On a lightly floured surface, roll out dough to a 14-inch round, ⅛ inch thick. Fit into bottom and up sides of a 10-inch round tart pan with a removable bottom. Trim excess dough flush with rim. Refrigerate or freeze until firm, about 30 minutes.

2. Preheat oven to 350°F. Pierce bottom of shell all over with a fork; line shell with parchment, and fill with pie weights or dried beans. Bake 30 minutes; remove weights and parchment, and bake until crust is golden brown, about 5 minutes more. Transfer to a wire rack to cool completely.

3. Pulse hazelnuts in a food processor until finely chopped. Add sugars, salt, and zest, and pulse to combine. Add butter, Armagnac, eggs, and vanilla, and process until almost smooth.

4. Spread hazelnut batter evenly in tart shell and top with figs and strawberries. Bake 30 minutes, then reduce heat to 325°F and bake until set and dark brown, about 1 hour more. Transfer to a wire rack to cool. Serve at room temperature, with whipped cream, if desired.

Fresh-Orange and Yogurt Tart

A citrusy dessert can feel like a burst of sunshine on a wintry day. For this easy tart, a ground-almond crust is quickly pulsed in a food processor, then pressed in the pan and baked until golden brown. The no-bake filling, essentially yogurt thickened with gelatin, takes mere minutes to assemble before it is poured into the shell, chilled, and topped with thinly sliced oranges. **MAKES ONE 8-INCH TART**

FOR THE CRUST

- ½ cup whole raw almonds
- ¼ cup granulated sugar
- ½ teaspoon coarse salt
- 1 cup all-purpose flour
- 6 tablespoons cold unsalted butter, cut into pieces

FOR THE FILLING

- 2 teaspoons unflavored powdered gelatin
- 2 tablespoons ice water
- ½ cup heavy cream
- 1½ cups plain Greek-style yogurt
- ¼ cup packed light brown sugar
  Pinch of coarse salt
- 3 navel oranges

1. Make the crust: In a food processor, pulse almonds with granulated sugar and salt until finely ground. Add flour; pulse to combine. Add butter and pulse until combined. Press crumbs into bottom and up sides of an 8-inch fluted tart pan with a removable bottom. Refrigerate or freeze until firm, about 30 minutes.

2. Preheat oven to 350°F. Place tart pan on a rimmed baking sheet and bake until crust is golden brown and set, 30 to 35 minutes. Let cool completely on a wire rack.

3. Make the filling: In a small bowl, sprinkle gelatin over the water and let stand 5 minutes. In a small saucepan, warm cream over medium heat. When it begins to steam, add softened gelatin and stir until dissolved, about 1 minute. In a medium bowl, whisk together yogurt, brown sugar, and pinch of salt. Stir warm cream mixture into yogurt mixture. Pour filling into cooled tart shell and refrigerate until set, 2 hours or (wrapped in plastic) up to 1 day.

4. With a sharp paring knife, slice off ends of oranges. Following curve of fruit, cut away peel, removing as much white pith as possible. Slice oranges into ¼-inch-thick rounds and remove any seeds. Just before serving, arrange orange slices on top of tart.

Rainbow Puff-Pastry Tarts

A French patisserie classic is made modern. The tarts pictured incorporate sliced kiwi fruit, peaches, and strawberries, along with assorted whole berries, but feel free to improvise with your favorite fresh or poached fruit, and to arrange it in whatever pattern pleases you. That's half the fun of a recipe such as this—the shell serves as a blank canvas for your creativity. MAKES TWO 7-INCH SQUARE TARTS

All-purpose flour, for dusting

1 box store-bought puff pastry, preferably all butter, thawed, or ¼ recipe Puff Pastry (page 334)

1 large egg, lightly beaten, for egg wash

Vanilla Pastry Cream (page 338)

2 cups mixed fresh berries, such as blueberries and raspberries

1 ripe, firm peach, peeled (see page 343), pitted, and sliced into thin wedges

2 kiwi fruits, peeled and sliced into thin rounds

1. On a lightly floured surface, gently roll out and trim dough into two 9-inch squares, ⅛ inch thick, being careful not to press too hard around the edges. Cut out (and reserve) eight 1-inch-wide strips (4 from each square), 1 from each edge. Dough squares should be about 7 by 7 inches. Transfer squares to a parchment-lined baking sheet.

2. Pierce dough squares all over with a fork. Using a pastry brush, moisten dough edges with beaten egg, being careful not to let any drip down over the cut edges.

3. Lay reserved 1-inch strips over edges of each square, positioning them to line up exactly, overlapping at corners. Trim strips to fit, if necessary. Brush egg wash underneath each of the 4 overlapping corners to seal them together. Brush tops of strips, being careful not to let egg wash drip down sides. Refrigerate or freeze until firm, about 30 minutes.

4. Preheat oven to 400°F. Bake until well browned and puffed all over, about 15 minutes. Using an offset spatula, press down on center of crust, leaving borders puffy. Return to oven; bake 12 minutes. Transfer to a wire rack to cool. Press down again, if needed. Let cool completely.

5. Whisk pastry cream to loosen. Using a small offset spatula, spread pastry cream over bottoms of crusts, dividing evenly. Arrange fruit as desired on top of pastry cream.

PRESSING DOWN ON CENTER OF SHELL

Chocolate Pear Tart

Chocolate marries well with many different types of fruit, but pears and chocolate make an extra-special pair. Here, a ring of sliced fruit sits atop a deep, dark chocolate filling, which puffs up as it bakes. Arrange the slices so the curved edges all face the same way, with the narrow ends pointing toward the tart's center. MAKES ONE 9-INCH TART

FOR THE CRUST

- ½ cup (1 stick) unsalted butter, room temperature, plus more for pan
- 1 cup (5 ounces) whole blanched almonds
- ¾ cup sugar
- 3 large eggs
- ⅓ cup unsweetened cocoa powder
- 1 teaspoon pure vanilla extract
- ½ teaspoon salt
- ¼ teaspoon pure almond extract (optional)

FOR THE TOPPING

- 3 ripe, firm Bartlett pears
- ½ lemon
- 2 tablespoons apple jelly

1. Preheat oven to 350°F. Brush softened butter into bottom and up sides of a 9-inch tart pan with a removable bottom.

2. Make the crust: In a food processor, pulse almonds and sugar until nuts are very finely ground. Add butter, eggs, cocoa, vanilla, salt, and almond extract, if using; process until combined. Spread mixture evenly in prepared pan.

3. Make the topping: Peel, halve, and core pears; cut lengthwise into ¼-inch-thick slices, rubbing them with lemon as you work (to prevent discoloration). Arrange slices on chocolate mixture, slightly overlapping, without pressing in.

4. Place pan on a rimmed baking sheet; bake until top is puffed and a tester inserted in center of chocolate mixture comes out with only a few moist crumbs attached, 45 to 50 minutes. Transfer pan to a wire rack to cool completely.

5. Heat jelly in the microwave or on the stove just until loose. Gently brush pears with jelly; let set, at least 20 minutes. Unmold tart and serve.

ARRANGING PEAR SLICES

Hazelnut Frangipane Tart with Apricots

Blanched and peeled apricots are arranged just so on a bed of softly whipped crème fraîche—seven halves in a circle, another half cut into thirds and set in the center. MAKES ONE 9-INCH TART

Pâte Sablée (page 332)

⅓ cup plus 2 tablespoons hazelnuts, toasted, skinned, and coarsely chopped (see page 343)

2 tablespoons all-purpose flour

¼ teaspoon coarse salt

4 tablespoons unsalted butter, room temperature

⅓ cup granulated sugar

1 large egg

4 just-ripe apricots

½ cup heavy cream

¼ cup confectioners' sugar

¼ teaspoon pure vanilla extract

¾ cup crème fraîche

3 tablespoons apricot jam

1 tablespoon fresh lemon juice

1. Press dough into bottom and up sides of a 9-inch round tart pan with removable bottom, about ¼ inch thick. Patch, if necessary. Trim excess dough flush with rim. Refrigerate or freeze until firm, about 30 minutes.

2. Preheat oven to 350°F. Line shell with parchment, and fill with pie weights or dried beans. Bake until edges are golden, about 20 minutes. Rotate shell, and remove parchment and weights. Bake until bottom is crisp and lightly golden, 10 to 15 minutes more. Let cool on a wire rack 10 minutes. Reduce heat to 325°F.

3. Pulse ⅓ cup hazelnuts in a food processor until finely ground. Stir together ground hazelnuts, flour, and salt. With an electric mixer, beat butter and granulated sugar until pale and creamy, 3 to 5 minutes. Beat in egg. Add hazelnut mixture, and beat until just combined. Frangipane can be refrigerated in an airtight container up to 1 week.

4. Spoon frangipane into tart shell, and smooth with an offset spatula. Let stand 10 minutes. Bake until set, about 15 minutes. If edges brown too quickly, cover with a foil ring (see page 324). Transfer to a wire rack and let cool.

5. Peel apricots (see page 343); cut in half, and remove pits. Just before serving, beat cream with confectioners' sugar and vanilla until soft peaks form; whisk in crème fraîche. Spread over frangipane. Arrange 7 apricot halves, cut side down, around edge. Cut remaining apricot half into thirds and arrange in center.

6. Heat jam in a saucepan over medium-low until loose. Stir in lemon juice, and let cool for 5 or 10 minutes. Strain through a sieve; discard solids. Brush strained jam over apricots, and spoon remaining glaze over cream. Sprinkle remaining 2 tablespoons hazelnuts around apricots. Serve immediately.

Nectarine and Raspberry Tart

Thanks to its length and the abundance of glistening fruit, this tart makes a striking finale. The tender cornmeal crust is more crumbly than other types, so do not overmix the dough, and be sure to chill well before rolling. It is also a forgiving dough—you can pinch together any holes or tears when fitting it into the tin. **MAKES ONE 14-BY-4-INCH TART**

FOR THE CRUST

- 6 tablespoons unsalted butter, room temperature
- ½ cup granulated sugar
- 2 large egg yolks
- 1 cup all-purpose flour, plus more for dusting
- ⅓ cup yellow cornmeal, preferably stone-ground
- ½ teaspoon salt
- Vegetable-oil cooking spray

FOR THE FILLING

- 4 ounces cream cheese, softened
- ½ cup crème fraîche
- 1½ tablespoons confectioners' sugar
- 3 ripe nectarines, halved, pits removed, cut into ½-inch slices
- 1 cup raspberries

FOR THE GLAZE

- ¼ cup apricot jam

1. Make the crust: With an electric mixer on medium-high speed, beat butter and granulated sugar until pale and fluffy, about 2 minutes. Add yolks, and mix just to combine. Whisk together flour, cornmeal, and salt, and add to yolk mixture; mix just until dough comes together. Press dough into a disk, wrap in plastic, and refrigerate until firm, 1 hour.

2. Coat a 14-by-4-inch rectangular fluted tart pan with cooking spray. On a lightly floured piece of parchment, roll out dough ⅛ inch thick. Fit dough into pan, and trim excess dough flush with rim. Refrigerate or freeze until firm, about 30 minutes.

3. Preheat oven to 350°F with rack in center. Pierce bottom of shell all over with a fork, and bake until crust begins to color, 15 to 20 minutes. Transfer to a wire rack to cool completely. Unmold crust.

4. Make the filling: With an electric mixer on medium speed, beat cream cheese until smooth. Add crème fraîche and confectioners' sugar, and beat until mixture is smooth and fluffy, about 2 minutes. Refrigerate 30 minutes. Spread filling into cooled crust, and arrange fruit on top, pressing in slightly.

5. Make the glaze: Heat jam in a small saucepan over low until loose. Strain through a sieve, and brush warm glaze over raspberries and nectarines. Refrigerate tart up to a few hours if not serving right away.

Rhubarb Tart with Lemon-Yogurt Mousse

This vibrant tart heralds the arrival of spring. First-of-the-season rhubarb stalks are poached in spiced brandy, then spooned over a silken citrus-and-yogurt mousse. The cornmeal crust is baked in a springform pan for extra height. You can bake the crust one day, fill with mousse the next, then chill overnight before topping and serving. The rhubarb can also be poached a day ahead and chilled separately. MAKES ONE 10-INCH TART

All-purpose flour, for dusting

Pâte Sucrée, Cornmeal-Lemon Variation (page 333)

1 teaspoon unflavored powdered gelatin

1 tablespoon plus ⅓ cup cold water

1 tablespoon plus ¾ cup heavy cream

3 tablespoons light brown sugar

1½ cups plain yogurt

1 tablespoon finely grated lemon zest plus 1 tablespoon fresh lemon juice

⅛ teaspoon coarse salt

2 cups granulated sugar

1 cup brandy

1 cinnamon stick

7 whole black peppercorns

1 teaspoon pure vanilla extract

1½ pounds rhubarb, trimmed, halved lengthwise, and cut into 1½-inch pieces

1. Preheat oven to 375°F. On a lightly floured surface, roll out dough ¼ inch thick. Fit dough into bottom and up sides of a 10-inch springform pan. Refrigerate or freeze until firm, about 30 minutes. Line shell with parchment, and fill with pie weights or dried beans. Bake until edges begin to turn gold, about 25 minutes. Remove weights and parchment. Reduce heat to 350°F, and bake until golden brown, 20 to 25 minutes more. Let crust cool in pan on a wire rack.

2. Sprinkle gelatin over 1 tablespoon water in a small bowl, and let stand until softened, about 5 minutes. Combine 1 tablespoon cream and the brown sugar in a small saucepan over medium heat, stirring until sugar dissolves and mixture is warm. Stir in softened gelatin, and remove from heat. Combine yogurt, zest, and pinch of salt in a medium bowl. Add brown-sugar mixture, and whisk until smooth. Whisk remaining ¾ cup cream in a medium bowl until medium peaks form. Gently fold cream into yogurt mixture.

3. Pour filling into crust. Cover, and refrigerate until firm, 4 hours or up to 1 day.

4. Bring granulated sugar and remaining ⅓ cup water to a boil in a medium saucepan, stirring until sugar dissolves. Cook, undisturbed, until light amber, about 7 minutes. Remove from heat; add ¾ cup brandy, the cinnamon, peppercorns, vanilla, and remaining pinch of salt. Return mixture to a boil for 1 minute, then stir in rhubarb. Remove pan from heat. Stir in lemon juice and remaining ¼ cup brandy, cover, and let stand 25 minutes. Refrigerate until cold, about 4 hours. Strain, reserving liquid, and discard cinnamon and peppercorns. Bring reserved liquid to a boil in a medium saucepan until reduced to 1½ cups, about 4 minutes. Let cool completely.

5. Spoon strained rhubarb over mousse, and serve immediately with reduced cooking liquid on the side.

Banana and Coconut Cashew-Cream Tart

This gluten-free, dairy-free, no-cook tart relies on dates and pecans for a sturdy crust, maple syrup for sweetness, and bananas and coconut for tropical flavors. The cashew "cream" is made by grinding cashews with water and vanilla-bean seeds. Soaking the nuts overnight in water ensures a puddinglike texture once they are ground. All in all, it makes an enticing dessert, even for those without food allergies or sensitivities.

MAKES ONE 9-INCH TART

FOR THE CRUST

- 1½   cups whole raw pecans
-       Pinch of coarse salt
- 1½   cups pitted dates
- 2   teaspoons pure maple syrup

FOR THE FILLING

- 1   cup raw cashews, soaked overnight and thoroughly drained
- ½   cup water
- 2   tablespoons plus 2 teaspoons pure maple syrup, plus more to taste
- 1   vanilla bean, halved lengthwise and seeds scraped (reserve pod for another use)
- ¾   cup unsweetened shredded coconut
- 3   or 4 ripe, firm bananas

1. Make the crust: In a food processor, pulse pecans and salt until nuts are coarsely chopped. Add dates; pulse until thoroughly combined, 15 to 20 seconds. Add syrup; pulse just until combined and mixture sticks together. Press nut mixture firmly and evenly into a 9-inch pie plate, wetting your fingers as needed.

2. Make the filling: Grind drained cashews to a coarse paste in a blender. Add the water, syrup, and vanilla seeds; blend until smooth, about 5 minutes, scraping sides as needed. Mixture should reach the consistency of thick pancake batter. Set aside 2 tablespoons coconut; add remainder to blender, and process to combine. Pour into shell, spreading evenly.

3. Thinly slice bananas on the diagonal; beginning at outer edge, arrange slices in slightly overlapping rows, working toward the center. Sprinkle evenly with reserved coconut; serve immediately.

dainty

Play around with scale to re-create full-size pies and tarts in miniature. Such diminutive treats are traditionally considered tea-party fare, welcome at ladies' luncheons, garden parties, bridal showers, and such. Novel shapes and flavor combinations, however, make the following desserts feel right at home in any modern setting. A display of pint-size pies, for example, can serve as a whimsical and entirely fitting last course at a wedding. Look for other such opportunities to present a dozen or so of these endearing desserts.

POPPY-SEED TARTLETS WITH LEMON CURD, RECIPE PAGE 194

Cranberry Meringue Mini Pies

Here, a dozen petite pies are baked in *pâte sucrée*-lined muffin cups. A small amount of blood-orange juice sweetens the tart cranberries, but not overly so. You can assemble and bake the pies a day ahead, but for the best presentation, wait to top each with meringue until just before serving. If you can't find blood oranges, use a regular variety. MAKES 1 DOZEN

All-purpose flour, for dusting

½ recipe Pâte Sucrée, Citrus Variation (page 333)

12 ounces (3¼ cups) fresh cranberries

1½ cups sugar

1½ cups plus ¼ cup water

1½ teaspoons finely grated lemon zest

1 teaspoon finely grated blood orange zest plus ¼ cup fresh blood orange juice

¼ teaspoon salt

⅛ teaspoon ground cinnamon

Pinch of ground cloves

3 tablespoons cornstarch

3 large egg whites

Pinch of cream of tartar

1. Preheat oven to 375°F. On a lightly floured surface, roll out dough ⅛ inch thick. Cut out twelve 4-inch fluted rounds, and fit into cups of a standard 12-cup muffin tin (not nonstick). Pierce bottom of shell in each cup with a fork. Refrigerate or freeze until firm, about 30 minutes.

2. Line shells with parchment, and fill with pie weights or dried beans. Bake 15 minutes. Remove weights and parchment. Bake until bottoms are just turning golden, 5 minutes more. Transfer to wire racks; let cool 5 minutes. Remove shells from tin; let cool completely.

3. Bring 2 cups cranberries, 1 cup sugar, and 1½ cups water to a boil in a medium saucepan. Reduce heat, and simmer mixture, stirring occasionally, until cranberries burst, about 5 minutes. Pour through a fine sieve (in batches, if necessary); discard solids. (You should have about 1¾ cups; if you have less, add water.)

4. Bring strained cranberry juice, ¼ cup sugar, the zests, salt, cinnamon, cloves, and remaining 1¼ cups cranberries to a boil in a medium saucepan, stirring occasionally. Reduce heat; simmer, stirring occasionally, until cranberries are soft but have not burst, about 3 minutes.

5. Meanwhile, combine cornstarch, orange juice, and remaining ¼ cup water in a bowl; whisk into cranberry mixture in saucepan. Bring to a boil, stirring constantly. Cook, stirring, until translucent, 1 minute. Divide mixture among shells. Refrigerate until set, 1 hour or up to 1 day.

6. Whisk egg whites and remaining ¼ cup sugar in a heatproof bowl set over (not in) a pan of simmering water, until sugar has dissolved and mixture is hot to the touch. With an electric mixer, beat on medium speed until foamy. Raise speed to high. Add cream of tartar; beat until medium glossy peaks form. Divide meringue evenly among pies.

7. Use a kitchen torch to lightly brown meringue peaks. Alternatively, preheat broiler, and place pies under broiler for 30 seconds or up to a minute; watch carefully to ensure meringue doesn't burn. Serve immediately.

Port Caramel Chocolate Tartlets

Chocolate and caramel are enhanced with port wine, Spanish Marcona almonds, and fleur de sel, a delicate sea salt, for ultra-rich miniature tarts that are wonderfully unctuous, like fine truffles. The large yield of this recipe makes it perfect for parties; just don't expect to have any left over. These tartlets have a tendency to disappear rather quickly. MAKES 40

FOR THE CRUST

- 2½ cups all-purpose flour, plus more for dusting
- ½ cup unsweetened Dutch-process cocoa powder
- ½ cup sugar
- ¾ teaspoon fleur de sel, or other sea salt
- ½ cup (1 stick) cold unsalted butter, cut into small pieces
- 3 large eggs, lightly beaten

FOR THE FILLING

- 1 cup sugar
- ½ cup water
- ½ cup heavy cream
- 3 tablespoons ruby or tawny port
- 2 tablespoons cold unsalted butter, cut into small pieces
- 1 ounce dark chocolate (preferably 70 percent cacao), finely chopped
- 1 cup salted Marcona almonds (or blanched, roasted, salted almonds), finely chopped
- Fleur de sel, or other sea salt, for sprinkling

1. Make the crust: Pulse flour, cocoa, sugar, and fleur de sel in a food processor until combined. Add butter; pulse until mixture resembles coarse meal. Add eggs, and process just until dough comes together. Pat dough into a disk. Wrap in plastic. Refrigerate until firm, about 1 hour.

2. On a lightly floured surface, roll out dough ⅛ inch thick. Using a 3-inch round cookie cutter, cut 10 rounds from dough. Transfer remaining dough to a dusted baking sheet; refrigerate. Fit dough rounds into 10 round tartlet molds (each 2¼ inches in diameter). Trim excess dough flush with rims. (Refrigerate scraps.) Refrigerate or freeze shells until firm, about 30 minutes.

3. Preheat oven to 350°F. Pierce bottoms of shells all over with a fork. Bake until firm, about 12 minutes. Let cool completely in molds on a wire rack; unmold.

4. Working in batches of 10 and using remaining dough (reroll scraps), repeat steps 2 and 3 to make 40 shells total.

5. Make the filling: Combine sugar and the water in a small saucepan over medium-high heat, gently stirring occasionally, until sugar has dissolved. Continue to cook, without stirring, until syrup comes to a boil, occasionally washing down sides of pan with a wet pastry brush to prevent crystals from forming. Let boil, swirling pan occasionally, until syrup is dark amber. Remove from heat.

6. Carefully stir in cream and port (caramel will steam and spatter). Add butter and chocolate; stir until melted and smooth. Let cool until slightly thickened but still pourable, about 20 minutes.

7. Cover bottoms of tart shells with chopped almonds (about 1 teaspoon per shell). Spoon filling into shells, almost to top. Sprinkle with almonds and fleur de sel. Refrigerate until ready to serve, 3 hours or up to 1 day.

Strawberry-Rhubarb Pielets

An all-time favorite fruit pie—strawberry-rhubarb—is utterly charming in miniature. These pielets would be welcome at a family reunion, graduation party, or other summer occasion. Baking the lattice-topped pies in mini muffin tins makes large batches easy to manage. If you'd like to serve the pielets à la mode, use a melon baller to form tiny scoops of ice cream. MAKES 2 DOZEN

FOR THE CRUST

- 3 cups all-purpose flour, plus more for dusting
- 3 tablespoons granulated sugar
- 1 teaspoon salt
- ¼ cup plus 1 tablespoon cold solid vegetable shortening
- ¾ cup (1½ sticks) cold unsalted butter, cut into small pieces
- ¼ cup plus 2 tablespoons ice water
  Vegetable-oil cooking spray
- 2 large eggs, for egg wash
  Fine sanding sugar, for sprinkling

FOR THE FILLING

- 12 ounces (about 2 cups) fresh strawberries, hulled and cut into tiny dice
- 5 stalks rhubarb, trimmed and cut into tiny dice
- 1 tablespoon finely grated orange zest plus ¼ cup fresh orange juice
- ¼ cup plus 1 tablespoon orange-flavored liqueur, such as Grand Marnier
- 1½ cups granulated sugar

1. Make the crust: In a food processor, pulse flour, granulated sugar, salt, vegetable shortening, and butter until mixture resembles coarse meal, 8 to 10 seconds. Add ice water, 1 tablespoon at a time; pulse until dough just comes together. Divide dough in half; flatten into 2 disks. Wrap each in plastic, and refrigerate 1 hour or up to 1 day.

2. Make the filling: In a bowl, toss together strawberries, rhubarb, zest, juice, liqueur, and granulated sugar.

3. Preheat oven to 350°F. Coat 2 mini-muffin tins with cooking spray. On a lightly floured surface, roll out dough ⅛ inch thick. Cut out 24 rounds using a 3½-inch round cutter; press into cups. Reroll scraps, and using a pastry wheel, cut twenty-eight ¼-inch strips for lattice. Refrigerate or freeze shells and lattice strips until firm, about 30 minutes.

4. Strain fruit mixture and discard liquid; place 2 tablespoons in each tartlet shell. Lightly beat eggs and brush edge of each shell with egg wash. For each row of tartlets, arrange 2 dough strips lengthwise across muffin tin. Place 2 more dough strips crosswise, weaving a lattice over tartlets. Brush with egg wash. Use a 2¼-inch round cutter to trim excess dough. Sprinkle with sanding sugar. Refrigerate or freeze until firm, about 30 minutes. Transfer tins to baking sheets. Bake until golden brown, 60 to 70 minutes.

5. Use a wooden skewer to gently loosen edges of pielets and remove from pans while still hot; if you wait until they cool, fruit juices may harden and make pielets stick. Transfer pielets to a wire rack, and let cool completely. Serve at room temperature. Pielets can be stored at room temperature up to 1 day.

Poppy-Seed Tartlets with Lemon Curd

Each of these tiny tea-party treats features a pastry shell flecked with poppy seeds, rich lemon curd, a candied lemon slice, and a whipped-cream rosette sprinkled with more poppy seeds. Admittedly, making a bunch of them takes more time than a larger dessert, but most of the components can be prepared ahead (the shells and candied lemon will keep nearly a week). Then it's only a matter of filling and topping the tarts just before serving, using a pastry bag and a star-shaped tip to quickly pipe the cream. MAKES 2 DOZEN

All-purpose flour, for dusting

Pâte Sucrée, Poppy Seed Variation (page 333)

2 recipes Lemon Curd (page 339)

⅔ cup heavy cream

2 tablespoons confectioners' sugar

½ teaspoon pure vanilla extract

Candied Lemon Slices (page 339)

Poppy seeds, for garnish

1. Preheat oven to 375°F. On a lightly floured surface, roll out dough ⅛ inch thick. Using a 4-inch round cutter, cut out 24 rounds. Fit dough rounds into 3½-inch tartlet pans. Pierce bottoms of shells all over with a fork. Refrigerate or freeze until firm, about 30 minutes. Place a second tartlet pan of the same size on top; press together lightly. Alternatively, line dough with parchment and fill with pie weights or dried beans.

2. Bake shells 8 to 10 minutes; when dough begins to brown around edges, remove top pan, and continue baking until crust is dry and turns golden brown, 4 to 6 minutes more. Transfer to a wire rack to cool completely. Unmold. (Tartlet shells can be stored in an airtight container at room temperature up to 3 days.)

3. Spoon approximately 2 tablespoons curd into center of each crust.

4. As close to serving time as possible, with an electric mixer on medium speed, beat cream, confectioners' sugar, and vanilla until soft peaks form, about 4 minutes. Fit a pastry bag with a ³⁄₁₆-inch star tip (#35), and fill with whipped cream.

5. Drain candied lemon slices from syrup, and remove any seeds. Place 1 lemon slice on top of each tart, and finish with a rosette of whipped cream. Sprinkle with poppy seeds, and serve.

Apricot Hand Pies

Apricot halves are poached with lemon peel, cracked cardamom pods, sliced fresh ginger, and vanilla-bean seeds to make a luscious filling for little crosshatched hand pies. Plums or peaches can be used in place of apricots; you may need to cut out larger pastry rounds depending on the size of the fruit. Be sure to keep the fruit submerged in poaching liquid or it will turn brown. This recipe is a specialty of Joey Gallagher, whose daughter, photographer Dana Gallagher, is a frequent contributor to *Martha Stewart Living.* MAKES 1 DOZEN

2 cups water

¾ cup granulated sugar

2 strips (1½ inches long) fresh lemon peel, pith removed

1 piece (about ½ inch) fresh ginger, peeled

4 cardamom pods, cracked

½ vanilla bean, halved lengthwise, seeds scraped

6 small just-ripe apricots (¾ pound), halved and pitted

All-purpose flour, for dusting

Pâte Brisée (page 322)

2 tablespoons ice water

Fine sanding sugar, for sprinkling

1. Bring the water, granulated sugar, lemon peel, ginger, cardamom, and vanilla-bean seeds to a boil in a saucepan. Cook until sugar dissolves; reduce heat, and simmer, uncovered, until liquid has thickened slightly, about 10 minutes.

2. Add apricots to pan. Rinse a double thickness of cheesecloth under cold water, and drape over apricots so fruit is covered by cloth and submerged in liquid. (Alternatively, cut a round of parchment to fit pan and cover fruit.) Continue simmering until apricots soften slightly, 2 to 4 minutes, depending on ripeness. Remove from heat, and let cool completely. Use immediately, or transfer apricots and poaching liquid to a storage container. Make sure apricots are completely submerged in liquid at all times. Refrigerate until ready to use, up to 4 days.

3. On a lightly floured surface, roll out 1 disk of dough into a large round, about ⅛ inch thick. Cut out twelve 3-inch rounds. Transfer rounds to a parchment-lined rimmed baking sheet; refrigerate or freeze until firm, about 30 minutes. Repeat process with remaining dough, using a 4-inch cookie cutter to make 12 more rounds; do not refrigerate.

4. Using paper towels, blot poached apricots halves to eliminate excess liquid. Place 1 in center of each chilled 3-inch round. Brush ice water around edges of dough; cover each with an unchilled 4-inch round. Gently press edges together to seal. Refrigerate about 30 minutes.

5. Preheat oven to 425°F. Using a paring knife, slash top of each hand pie in a crosshatch fashion. Brush with water, and generously sprinkle with sanding sugar. Bake 15 minutes. Reduce heat to 350°F. Continue baking until pastry is golden brown, 15 to 20 minutes more. Transfer pies to a wire rack to cool slightly before serving. Or let cool completely, and store in an airtight container at room temperature up to 4 days.

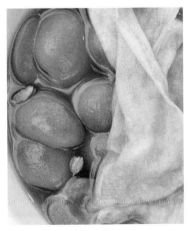

POACHING APRICOTS

Lemon Tartlets with Meringue Caps

Ethereal, light-as-air sweets start with thin tuile cookies that are draped over inverted small brioche molds while still warm. Once cooled, each ruffled cup is filled with velvety curd and topped with a playful baked-meringue peaked cap. You will need a nonstick baking mat for the cups.

MAKES ABOUT 20

4 tablespoons unsalted butter, melted

⅔ cup confectioners' sugar, sifted

5 large egg whites, room temperature

½ cup sifted all-purpose flour

½ teaspoon pure vanilla extract

½ cup granulated sugar

Lemon Curd (page 339)

1. Preheat oven to 325°F. With an electric mixer on medium-high speed, beat butter and confectioners' sugar until pale and fluffy. Mix in 2 egg whites, 1 at a time. Mix in flour and vanilla.

2. Spoon 1 scant teaspoon batter onto a rimmed baking sheet lined with a nonstick baking mat. Using the back of a spoon, spread into a 3-inch circle. Repeat 3 times. Bake until golden, 10 to 12 minutes. Immediately transfer cookies, 1 at a time, to inverted small brioche molds; gently press to shape. Let set, about 30 seconds. Repeat with remaining batter, baking 4 at a time. If cookies become too cool to shape, return them to oven for 20 seconds. Shells can be stored in an airtight container at room temperature up to 3 days. Reduce heat to 200°F.

3. In the bowl of an electric mixer set over (not in) a pan of simmering water, whisk remaining 3 egg whites and the granulated sugar until whites are warm to the touch and sugar has dissolved. Attach bowl to mixer; beat on medium until foamy, then raise speed to high and beat until stiff peaks form and meringue is cool, about 10 minutes. Transfer to a pastry bag fitted with a ⁷⁄₁₆-inch star tip (such as Ateco #825). Pipe twenty 1¼-inch diameter, 2-inch high spirals onto parchment-lined baking sheets, spacing about 1 inch apart. Bake 20 minutes. Reduce heat to 150°F. Bake until dry but not brown, about 2 hours more. Transfer to a wire rack; let cool completely. Meringue caps can be stored in an airtight container at room temperature up to 3 days.

4. To serve, spoon 2 teaspoons lemon curd into each shell. Top each with a meringue cap.

FORMING TUILE CUPS

Wild-Blueberry and Almond Tartlets

Martha originally created this recipe for a boating picnic in Maine. The tartlets are filled with blueberries, both fresh and preserved. Almond flavors the sturdy crust and the cakelike batter for the filling. Use wild blueberries if you can find them; otherwise, cultivated berries will do—the smaller, the better. MAKES 1 DOZEN

FOR THE CRUST

- ⅓ cup blanched almonds
- 1½ cups all-purpose flour, plus more for dusting
- 1 tablespoon sugar
- ½ teaspoon salt
- ½ cup (1 stick) cold unsalted butter, cut into small pieces
- 1 large egg yolk
- 1 to 2 tablespoons ice water

FOR THE FILLING

- 2 large eggs
- ½ cup sugar, plus more for sprinkling
- ¼ cup all-purpose flour
- 3 tablespoons blanched almonds, toasted (see page 343) and finely ground, plus ¼ cup sliced blanched almonds, for topping
- ¼ teaspoon salt
- ¼ cup plus 2 tablespoons blueberry jam
- 3 ounces (½ cup) fresh small blueberries, preferably wild

1. Make the crust: Pulse almonds in a food processor until finely ground. Add flour, sugar, and salt; pulse to combine. Add butter; pulse until mixture resembles coarse meal. Add yolk and 1 tablespoon ice water; pulse until dough just comes together, adding up to 1 tablespoon more ice water, if needed. Shape dough into a disk, and wrap in plastic. Refrigerate until firm, 1 hour or up to 3 days. (Dough can be frozen up to 1 month; thaw in refrigerator before using.)

2. Preheat oven to 375°F. On a lightly floured surface, roll out dough ⅛ inch thick. Cut out twelve 4½-inch rounds. Reroll scraps if necessary. Line twelve 3- or 3¼-inch tartlet pans with dough, pressing into bottoms and up sides; trim excess dough flush with rims. Divide shells between 2 rimmed baking sheets. Pierce bottoms of shells all over with a fork. Refrigerate or freeze until firm, about 30 minutes.

3. Line shells with parchment. Add pie weights or dried beans. Bake until light golden brown, 20 to 22 minutes. Remove weights and parchment. Transfer to wire racks to cool completely.

4. Make the filling: With an electric mixer on medium speed, beat eggs and sugar until pale and thick, about 5 minutes. Using a flexible spatula, fold in flour, ground almonds, and salt.

5. With an offset spatula, spread about 1½ teaspoons jam into each shell. Top with blueberries, dividing evenly. Cover fruit in each tart shell with 2 tablespoons batter. Sprinkle batter evenly with sugar and sliced almonds. Bake until tops rise and are golden, 18 to 20 minutes. Transfer to a wire rack to cool completely. Tartlets can be stored in airtight containers at room temperature up to 1 day.

Coconut Macaroon Tartlets

As delicious—and easy to make—as drop cookies, coconut macaroons make airy shells when pressed and baked in tartlet molds. They will keep for days, and are very versatile. These are filled with vanilla whipped cream and candied ginger, but fresh fruit, citrus curd, and chocolate ganache are other nice options. MAKES 1 DOZEN

FOR THE CRUST

1½ cups shredded unsweetened coconut

2 large egg whites

¼ cup sugar

FOR THE FILLING

1 cup heavy cream

1 vanilla bean, halved lengthwise

2 tablespoons finely chopped crystallized ginger (½ ounce)

1. Make the crust: Preheat oven to 350°F. In a large bowl, combine coconut, egg whites, and sugar until mixture holds together when squeezed.

2. Form 1 heaping tablespoon coconut mixture into a ball. Press ball into a 2-inch brioche or tartlet tin (or mini muffin cup), making a thumbprint in the center and pressing out so mixture forms a ¼-inch-thick crust. Repeat with remaining coconut mixture. Place tins on rimmed baking sheet.

3. Bake crusts until golden brown, about 25 minutes. Set crusts aside until cool enough to handle. Unmold crusts onto a wire rack to cool completely.

4. Make the filling: Pour cream into a chilled mixing bowl. Scrape vanilla seeds into cream; reserve pod for another use. Whisk until soft peaks form. Fill each crust with whipped cream, and garnish with crystallized ginger before serving.

FILLING AND TOPPING TARTLETS

Mini Jam Tarts

Let your imagination be your guide when forming these little tarts; giving each one a singular look enhances its appeal and creates an enticing display, but you can always replicate favorite patterns. Use aspic cutters (available at baking supply stores) or small cookie cutters to make designs, or cut strips of dough to form mini lattice tops. You may also want to vary the flavor—and color—of jam in the fillings. MAKES 16

FOR THE CRUST

- 1¾ cups all-purpose flour, plus more for dusting
- 2 tablespoons sugar
- ¼ teaspoon salt
- ¾ teaspoon ground cinnamon
- ¾ cup (1½ sticks) cold unsalted butter, cut into small pieces
- 2 large egg yolks
- 2 tablespoons ice water
- 1 tablespoon heavy cream, for egg wash

FOR THE FILLING

- 1 cup best-quality jam, in assorted flavors

1. Make the crust: In a food processor, pulse to combine flour, sugar, salt, and cinnamon. Add butter and pulse until mixture resembles coarse meal.

2. Combine 1 egg yolk with the water and drizzle evenly over flour mixture. Pulse just until dough comes together. Press dough into a disk and wrap in plastic. Refrigerate until firm, 1 hour or up to 1 day.

3. Preheat oven to 375°F. On a lightly floured surface, roll out dough just thinner than ¼ inch. Cut out round or square shapes and press into 2- to 3-inch tartlet tins. Trim excess dough flush with rims; fill each shell with 1½ to 2 teaspoons jam, and decorate tops with cutouts or thin strips of dough. (Assembled tarts can be refrigerated for several hours.)

4. Combine remaining egg yolk with the cream; lightly brush over dough. Bake until pastry is golden brown, 20 to 25 minutes. Unmold tarts and let cool completely on a wire rack.

Jumbleberry Mini Tarts

Handy no-fork treats win raves from kids for their lip-smacking taste; busy parents and other home cooks appreciate how easy they are to bake by the dozen. Once the dough is cut into rounds and pressed into mini-muffin cups, it is filled with a toss-together berry filling that becomes wonderfully jamlike during baking. Top each with a tiny dollop of whipped cream. MAKES 2 DOZEN

FOR THE CRUST

- 1 cup plus 2 tablespoons all-purpose flour, plus more for dusting
- ¼ cup confectioners' sugar
- Pinch of salt
- 6 tablespoons cold unsalted butter, cut into small pieces
- 2 to 3 tablespoons ice water

FOR THE FILLING

- ¼ cup granulated sugar
- 1 tablespoon cornstarch
- 1 teaspoon finely grated lemon zest plus 1 tablespoon fresh lemon juice
- Pinch of salt
- 2 cups mixed fresh berries, such as blackberries, blueberries, raspberries, and hulled, sliced strawberries

FOR THE TOPPING

Whipped Cream, for serving (page 340)

1. Make the crust: Pulse flour, confectioners' sugar, and salt in a food processor to combine. Add butter, and pulse until the mixture resembles coarse meal. Add the water, 1 tablespoon at a time, and pulse just until dough forms. Shape dough into a disk. Wrap in plastic; refrigerate until firm, 1 hour or up to 1 day.

2. Cut dough into 24 pieces; on a lightly floured surface, flatten each piece into a 3-inch round. Press a round into bottom and up sides of each cup of two 12-cup nonstick mini muffin tins. Refrigerate or freeze until firm, about 30 minutes.

3. Preheat oven to 400°F. Make the filling: Stir together granulated sugar, cornstarch, zest, juice, and salt in a medium bowl. Add berries; gently toss to coat.

4. Fill shells with berry mixture, dividing evenly. Bake until crusts are golden brown and filling is bubbling, about 25 minutes. Let cool slightly in tins, about 10 minutes. Run a knife around tarts; remove from tins. Let cool completely on a wire rack. Dollop with whipped cream, and serve immediately.

Carrot-Spice Tartlets

Their subtle sweetness and affinity for spices make carrots a natural choice for other baked goods besides the more familiar cakes and muffins. Here, they provide an unexpected flavor for individual tarts with another surprise: pastry crusts coated in crushed gingersnaps. MAKES 8

½ cup finely ground gingersnaps

½ recipe Pâte Brisée (page 322)

6 green cardamom pods

2 tablespoons unsalted butter

½ cup milk

½ cup heavy cream

1 teaspoon finely grated peeled fresh ginger

5 carrots (12 ounces), peeled and cut into ¼-inch slices (2½ to 3 cups)

1 cup sugar

⅛ teaspoon coarse salt

4 large eggs, lightly beaten

   Whipped Cream, for serving (unsweetened; page 340)

   Ground cardamom, for dusting

1. Lightly sprinkle ground gingersnaps on a surface to form a large round, about 18 inches in diameter. Roll out dough on top of crumbs ⅛ inch thick, turning over dough occasionally to coat both sides with cookie crumbs.

2. Cut out eight 5-inch rounds from dough. Press rounds into 4-inch tartlet pans; trim excess dough flush with rims. Pierce bottom of shells all over with a fork. Refrigerate or freeze until firm, about 30 minutes.

3. Preheat oven to 375°F. Line each shell with parchment; fill with pie weights or dried beans. Bake until golden brown, about 30 minutes. Transfer to a wire rack. Remove weights and parchment. Let shells cool completely.

4. Crush cardamom pods with flat side of a large knife to split. Melt 1 tablespoon butter in a small saucepan over medium heat; add crushed cardamom. Cook until fragrant, about 3 minutes. Add milk, cream, and ginger; bring to a simmer, stirring to combine. Cook 15 minutes over medium-low heat, stirring occasionally. Remove from heat; let steep 30 minutes.

5. Melt remaining 1 tablespoon butter in a large sauté pan over medium heat. Add carrots; cook, stirring occasionally, 2 minutes. Stir in sugar and salt. Cover pan; cook until carrots are tender when pierced with the tip of a sharp knife, about 8 minutes. Pour steeped-milk mixture through a fine sieve into pan with carrots; discard solids. Remove from heat; let cool slightly, about 5 minutes. Purée carrot mixture in a food processor until completely smooth; transfer to a bowl.

6. Temper beaten eggs by whisking in up to ¾ cup carrot mixture, ¼ cup at a time, until eggs are warm to the touch. Pour warmed egg mixture into remaining carrot mixture; whisk until thoroughly combined. Let cool.

7. Place shells on a large rimmed baking sheet. Divide filling evenly among shells. Bake until a tester inserted in centers comes out clean, 30 to 35 minutes. Serve tartlets warm with dollops of whipped cream, lightly dusted with ground cardamom.

Persimmon Tartlets with Caramel Cream

The secret to this filling's silkiness and deep caramel flavor is sweetened condensed milk, which is very slowly simmered until thick and golden, then blended with a mixture of cream cheese and crème fraîche. The spicy-sweet graham-cracker crust incorporates ground ginger, cinnamon, and black pepper; persimmon slices adorn the tops. MAKES 1 DOZEN

2 cans (14 ounces each) sweetened condensed milk

1 box (about 1 pound) graham crackers

¼ teaspoon ground ginger

½ teaspoon ground cinnamon

¼ teaspoon salt

¼ teaspoon freshly ground black pepper

1 cup (2 sticks) plus 4 tablespoons unsalted butter, melted

8 ounces cream cheese, room temperature

1½ cups (12 ounces) crème fraîche

1 teaspoon pure vanilla extract

3 ripe Fuyu persimmons, sliced ¼ inch thick

1. Cook condensed milk in a small saucepan over low heat, whisking constantly, until thickened and light golden, about 30 minutes (you should have 1¾ cups). Let cool slightly.

2. Meanwhile, preheat oven to 350°F. Process graham crackers in food processor (working in batches) until finely ground, about 2 minutes; transfer to a medium bowl. Add ginger, cinnamon, salt, and pepper; whisk to combine. Stir in butter. Press 4 or 5 loosely packed tablespoons graham cracker mixture firmly into bottom and up sides of each of twelve 4-inch tart pans with removable bottoms. Place pans on rimmed baking sheets; bake until set, about 10 minutes. Transfer to a wire rack to cool completely. Shells can be stored in airtight containers at room temperature up to 2 days.

3. With an electric mixer on medium-high speed, beat cream cheese until fluffy. Reduce speed to medium. Add crème fraîche, reduced condensed milk, and vanilla. Beat until smooth.

4. Fill cooled crusts with filling and refrigerate until set, 2 hours or up to 1 day. Arrange a persimmon slice on top of each. Unmold tarts before serving.

Blackberry and Cream Tartlets

With scalloped pastry edges and a fruit-streaked, creamy filling, these tarts are almost too pretty to eat, but they're too delicious not to. The filling is similar to a British spoon dessert called fool, which consists of a fruit sauce (in this case, blackberry) folded into whipped cream; more sauce and fruit is spooned on top. Elderflower cordial, another English specialty, flavors the whipped cream; you can omit the liqueur from the recipe if you want. You could also use it to flavor homemade ice cream to serve alongside. MAKES 8

All-purpose flour, for dusting

Pâte Brisée (page 322)

1 pound (about 3 cups) fresh blackberries

¼ cup sugar

1 teaspoon finely grated lemon zest

1 cup heavy cream

2 tablespoons elderflower cordial, such as St. Germain

1. On a lightly floured surface, roll out dough ⅛ inch thick; cut out eight 5-inch rounds, and fit into eight 3½-inch fluted tartlet pans. Trim excess dough flush with rims. Pierce bottoms of shells all over with a fork. Refrigerate or freeze until firm, about 30 minutes.

2. Preheat oven to 375°F. Line shells with parchment; fill with pie weights or dried beans. Bake until golden brown, 15 to 20 minutes. Remove weights and parchment; bake until bottoms of shells are fully browned, about 5 minutes more. Transfer to a wire rack to cool completely.

3. Prepare an ice-water bath. Combine berries, 2 tablespoons sugar, and the zest in a saucepan over medium heat. Cook until berries release their juices, sugar dissolves, and mixture begins to bubble, about 8 minutes. Remove from heat, and set pan in the ice bath to cool.

4. Place cream, remaining 2 tablespoons sugar, and the elderflower cordial in a large chilled bowl; whip until soft peaks form. Gently fold ½ cup berry mixture with juices into whipped cream (leave some streaks). Fill tartlet shells with mixture; top with remaining berries and juice, and serve.

FORMING TART SHELLS

Lime Curd Tartlets in Meringue Shells

In classic French cooking, a large dessert shell made entirely of meringue is called a *vacherin,* so called for its resemblance to a well-known cheese; it is usually layered with whipped cream and fruit. Here, small-scale meringue shells are filled with lime curd, whose bright color is especially striking in contrast with the crisp white shells. MAKES 16

4 large egg yolks plus 2 large whole eggs

¾ cup sugar

Finely grated zest of 2 limes plus ½ cup fresh lime juice (from about 4 limes)

4 tablespoons unsalted butter, cut into small pieces

Swiss Meringue (recipe follows)

1. Whisk together egg yolks and whole eggs. Combine with sugar and lime juice in small saucepan. Cook over medium-low heat, stirring constantly, 8 to 10 minutes, or until mixture is thick enough to coat the back of a spoon.

2. Stir to cool slightly. Strain into a small bowl; add butter, a piece at a time, stirring until smooth. Stir in zest; let cool completely. Cover with plastic wrap; refrigerate until chilled, 30 minutes or up to 2 days.

3. Preheat oven to 200°F. With a pencil, trace sixteen 2-inch circles on parchment; place parchment, penciled side down, on a 12-by-18-inch rimmed baking sheet.

4. Fit pastry bag with a ⁵/₁₆-inch plain tip (#12), and fill with meringue; pipe meringue, starting in center of each circle and spiraling out to circle's edge. Create a ¾-inch-tall wall of meringue peaks by piping along outside of circle using same tip to create smooth peaks, or change tips for a more decorative edge.

5. Bake 20 minutes. Reduce heat to 150°F, and bake until meringue is dry and crisp, but still white, 40 minutes to 1 hour more. Let cool completely on baking sheet. Shells can be kept in an airtight container at room temperature for several weeks, as long as the weather is dry.

6. Fill cooled meringue shells with chilled lime curd; serve immediately.

SWISS MERINGUE

Swiss meringue is best for piping into shapes that will be baked until crisp. It can be kept at room temperature and rewhipped, if necessary. Makes 4 cups

4 large egg whites, room temperature

1 cup sugar

Pinch of cream of tartar

½ teaspoon pure vanilla extract

1. Fill a medium saucepan one-fourth full with water, and bring to a simmer.

2. Combine egg whites, sugar, and cream of tartar in the heat-proof bowl of an electric mixer, and place over (not in) saucepan. Whisk constantly until sugar is dissolved and whites are warm to the touch, 3 to 3½ minutes. (Test by rubbing between your fingers; it should feel smooth, not at all grainy.)

3. With an electric mixer, beat mixture, starting on low speed, gradually increasing to high until stiff, glossy peaks form, about 10 minutes. Add vanilla, and mix until just combined. Use immediately.

Roasted Fig Tartlets

These fanciful tartlets are easy to construct with make-ahead components. The fresh figs can be roasted and then chilled, with the flavorful cooking syrup, for up to a week. The cream filling can be made a day ahead and refrigerated; the fluted pastry shells also can be baked the day before and held overnight at room temperature. MAKES 8

6 ounces cream cheese, room temperature

¾ cup (6 ounces) crème fraîche

3 tablespoons confectioners' sugar

1 cup ruby port

3 star anise

3 cinnamon sticks

1 tablespoon whole black peppercorns

2 strips orange zest (3 inches long and 1 inch wide), plus zest curls for garnish

¼ cup granulated sugar

1 tablespoon honey

2 vanilla beans, halved lengthwise

1½ pounds fresh Black Mission figs (about 24), halved lengthwise

All-purpose flour, for dusting

½ recipe Pâte Sucrée (page 333)

1. With an electric mixer, beat cream cheese until fluffy. Beat in crème fraîche and confectioners' sugar until smooth. (Filling can be refrigerated in an airtight container up to 1 day; bring to room temperature before using.)

2. Preheat oven to 350°F. Combine port, star anise, cinnamon, peppercorns, zest, granulated sugar, and honey in a roasting pan. Use the tip of a paring knife to scrape vanilla seeds into port mixture, then add pods. Add figs, and turn to coat. Roast, basting once, until figs are soft and liquid is syrupy, about 45 minutes. Let cool. (Figs and syrup can be refrigerated in an airtight container up to 1 week.)

3. On a lightly floured surface, roll out dough ⅛ inch thick. Cut out eight 5-inch rounds. Fit dough into 4-inch tartlet pans, and trim excess dough flush with rims. Pierce bottoms of shells all over with a fork. Place shells on a rimmed baking sheet; refrigerate or freeze until firm, about 30 minutes.

4. Bake tartlet shells until golden brown, 12 to 15 minutes. Transfer to a wire rack. Let cool completely.

5. Spoon 2 tablespoons filling into each crust. Top with figs, and drizzle with some syrup. Garnish with orange zest curls. Tartlets can be refrigerated up to 1 hour. Unmold, and serve immediately.

artful

Once you become comfortable working with pastry dough, the possibilities for making decorative top crusts on pies and tarts are nearly limitless. This chapter features strips woven into traditional and unexpected lattices, cutouts that are shingled in an overlapping fashion, and "polka dots" and other patterns formed in lengths of dough. Heeding just a few simple instructions—and a three-part mantra of patience, practice, and proper refrigeration—should encourage success. You can't rush any of these artfully composed pastries, but it's very satisfying to create them. So roll up your sleeves, take a deep breath, and more than anything, remember to chill.

SHINGLED-LEAF BRANDY APPLE PIE, RECIPE PAGE 223

Concord Grape Jam Tart

A cluster of grapes is cut from the top crust of this tart to suggest the fruit inside. Sweet, musky Concord grapes are first made into a jam, then sandwiched between the pastry rounds. You will need a nonreactive pan and a candy thermometer for the jam. MAKES ONE 9-INCH TART

FOR THE CRUST

- 2 cups all-purpose flour, plus more for dusting
- ¼ cup granulated sugar
- ¾ teaspoon coarse salt
- 1 cup (2 sticks) cold unsalted butter, cut into ½-inch pieces
- ¼ cup ice water
- 1 large egg, lightly beaten, for egg wash
- Coarse sanding sugar, for sprinkling

FOR THE FILLING

- 1½ pounds Concord grapes, stems removed
- 3 tablespoons fresh lemon juice
- 1 cup granulated sugar
- Pinch of salt
- Crème fraîche, for serving

1. Make the crust: Pulse flour, granulated sugar, and salt in a food processor. Add butter, and process until mixture resembles coarse meal. Drizzle with the ice water, and pulse until mixture just begins to hold together. Shape dough into 2 disks. Wrap each in plastic, and refrigerate 1 hour or up to 1 day.

2. Make the jam: Combine grapes and lemon juice in a medium nonreactive saucepan over high heat. Cook, stirring frequently, until grapes release their juices, about 7 minutes. Strain through a fine sieve. (You should have 1½ to 2 cups juice.) Return juice to saucepan over high heat, stir in granulated sugar and salt, and bring to a boil. Reduce heat, and simmer until temperature registers 220°F on a candy thermometer, about 8 minutes. Transfer jam to a bowl, and let cool, stirring occasionally. (Jam will keep, covered, up to 2 weeks in refrigerator.)

3. On a lightly floured surface, roll out each disk of dough ⅛ inch thick. Transfer 1 round to a parchment-lined baking sheet, and fit other round into a 9-inch tart pan with a removable bottom. Trim excess dough flush with rim. Refrigerate or freeze shell and round until firm, about 30 minutes.

4. Using the wide bases of 2 metal pastry tips (one ¾ inch in diameter and one 1 inch), cut clusters of holes in dough on baking sheet to resemble a bunch of grapes. Using a paring knife, cut a stem at the top. Freeze dough until firm, about 20 minutes.

5. Preheat oven to 375°F. Spread 1 cup grape jam over tart shell. (Reserve remaining jam for another use.) Brush edge of dough with egg wash. Slide remaining dough round on top, centering design. Press edges to seal, and trim excess dough. Brush top with egg wash, then sprinkle with sanding sugar. Refrigerate tart 30 minutes.

6. Transfer tart to a rimmed baking sheet. Bake 15 minutes, then gently tap pan on counter to release air bubbles. Bake until golden brown and bubbling, 15 to 20 minutes more. Transfer to a wire rack, and let cool completely. Unmold, and transfer to a platter. Serve with crème fraîche.

FORMING PATTERN WITH PASTRY TIPS

Pear-Cranberry Pie with Faux Lattice

Rather than weaving strips of dough under and over one another, the latticelike design for this pie is formed by cutting squares from a round of rolled-out *pâte brisée.* The cutouts are arranged around the edge of the pie plate, in overlapping fashion, for a striking frame. MAKES ONE 9-INCH PIE

All-purpose flour, for dusting

Pâte Brisée (page 322)

4 ripe, firm Bartlett, Bosc, or Anjou pears (about 1¾ pounds)

16 ounces (4⅓ cups) fresh or frozen (thawed) cranberries

⅔ cup packed dark brown sugar

2 tablespoons cornstarch

1 teaspoon coarse salt

2 tablespoons cold unsalted butter, cut into small pieces

1 large egg yolk, for egg wash

1 tablespoon heavy cream, for egg wash

½ cup apricot preserves

1. On a lightly floured surface, roll out 1 disk of dough to a 13-inch round, about ⅛ inch thick. Fit into a 9-inch deep-dish pie plate; trim dough flush with rim. Refrigerate or freeze until firm, about 30 minutes.

2. On lightly floured parchment, roll out remaining disk of dough as in step 1. Top with an inverted 9-inch pie plate, and gently press to make a light indentation. Using a 1-inch square cutter, cut lattice pattern out of round, leaving at least ½ inch between cutouts and edge of indented round. Transfer squares to a parchment-lined rimmed baking sheet. For partial squares where lattice meets edge, make a very light indentation with cutter, then cut out portion inside round with a paring knife.

3. Using a paring knife, cut out the round, leaving an additional ½ inch dough beyond indented circle. Reroll scraps; cut out as many additional squares as possible, and transfer to baking sheet. Transfer parchment with cutout top to another baking sheet. Refrigerate both 30 minutes.

4. Preheat oven to 375°F, with rack in lower position. Peel and core pears. Very thinly slice 2 pears lengthwise; cut remaining 2 pears into 8 wedges each.

5. In a bowl, toss together pears, cranberries, brown sugar, cornstarch, and salt. Pour into pie shell; gently press to make level. Dot with butter. Whisk together egg yolk and cream; lightly brush over edge of pie shell. Gently place another baking sheet on top of chilled lattice (still on parchment); carefully invert. Slide lattice on top of filling, centering; remove parchment. Gently press edges of crust to seal; trim dough, if necessary.

6. Lightly brush lattice with egg wash. Arrange dough squares around edge of pie, overlapping slightly. Lightly brush top of each square with egg wash as you work. Refrigerate 15 minutes. Bake pie on a parchment-lined baking sheet until crust is golden brown and juices are bubbling, about 90 minutes. (Tent with foil if crust browns too quickly.) Let cool on a wire rack 5 minutes.

7. Meanwhile, heat preserves in a saucepan over medium until loose. Pass through a fine sieve into a bowl. Brush warm pie all over with glaze. Let pie cool completely on wire rack.

FORMING PATTERN IN TOP CRUST

Shingled-Leaf Brandy Apple Pie

The layered finish that tops this apple pie is created by shingling the leaves. Pastry cutouts in any shape can be arranged in this manner; here, a flurry of leaves accentuates the pie's autumnal nature. **MAKES ONE 9-INCH PIE**

¼ cup all-purpose flour, plus more for dusting

1½ recipes Pâte Brisée (page 322)

3½ pounds tart, firm apples, such as Granny Smith, Macoun, or Cortland, peeled, cored, and cut into ¼-inch slices

3 tablespoons brandy

2 teaspoons pure vanilla extract

¼ cup granulated sugar

¼ cup packed dark brown sugar

1 teaspoon cinnamon

¼ teaspoon freshly grated nutmeg

⅛ teaspoon allspice

Pinch of salt

1 tablespoon unsalted butter, cut into small pieces

1 large egg yolk, for egg wash

1 tablespoon heavy cream, for egg wash

Fine sanding sugar, for sprinkling

1. On a lightly floured surface, roll out 1 disk of dough to a 13-inch round, ⅛ inch thick. Fit into a 9-inch pie pan. Trim excess dough flush with rim. Refrigerate or freeze until firm, about 30 minutes.

2. Roll out remaining 2 disks of dough about ⅛ inch thick. Place on a parchment-lined baking sheet, and refrigerate or freeze until firm, about 30 minutes. Using a 2¼-inch leaf-shaped cutter, cut out about 65 leaves, and place them in a single layer on the baking sheet. Refrigerate until firm.

3. Preheat oven to 400°F. In a large bowl, toss apples with flour, brandy, vanilla, sugars, cinnamon, nutmeg, allspice, and salt. Fill pie shell with apple mixture. Dot with butter.

4. Score leaves with a paring knife to make veins. Lightly brush edge of pie shell with water. Lightly brush the back of each leaf with water; beginning with the outside edge, arrange leaves in a slightly overlapping ring. Repeat to form another ring slightly overlapping the first. Continue until only a small circle of filling is left uncovered in the center.

5. In a small bowl, whisk together egg yolk and heavy cream. Carefully brush top of leaves and pie edge with egg wash, and sprinkle generously with sanding sugar. Refrigerate or freeze until firm, about 30 minutes.

6. Place pie on a parchment-lined baking sheet, and bake until crust just begins to brown, about 20 minutes. Reduce heat to 350°F, and continue baking until crust is golden brown and juices are bubbling, 85 minutes. Transfer pie to a wire rack to cool completely.

LAYING PASTRY LEAVES OVER FILLING

Pumpkin and Ricotta Crostata

In this pumpkin pie with Italian flavors, loosely arranged scraps of *pasta frolla* are draped over the filling to evoke a lattice design without any weaving. Pine nuts, clustered in groups of three, punctuate the grid.

MAKES ONE 10-INCH CROSTATA

FOR THE CRUST

2¼ cups all-purpose flour, plus more for dusting

½ cup sugar

⅛ teaspoon salt

¾ cup (1½ sticks) plus 2 tablespoons cold unsalted butter, cut into small pieces, plus more for pie plate

1 large whole egg, lightly beaten, plus 1 large egg yolk, lightly beaten

1 teaspoon pure vanilla extract

1 tablespoon finely grated lemon zest

1 large egg white, lightly beaten, for egg wash

FOR THE FILLING

1 cup ricotta cheese, drained 30 minutes in cheesecloth-lined sieve set over bowl

½ cup mascarpone cheese

1 can (15 ounces) unsweetened pumpkin purée

¼ cup plus 1 tablespoon sugar

¼ teaspoon coarse salt

¼ heaping teaspoon freshly grated nutmeg

½ teaspoon pure vanilla extract

2 large egg yolks, lightly beaten

2 tablespoons pine nuts

1. Make the crust: Pulse flour, sugar, and salt in a food processor just until combined. Add butter; pulse until mixture resembles coarse meal.

2. In a bowl, whisk together whole egg, egg yolk, vanilla, and zest. Add egg mixture to bowl of processor; pulse just until dough begins to come together. Divide dough into 2 pieces, and gently press into flat disks. Wrap tightly in plastic. Refrigerate 1 hour or up to 1 day, or freeze up to 1 month (thaw in refrigerator before using).

3. Preheat oven to 350°F. Bring dough to room temperature. On a lightly floured surface, roll out 1 disk dough ¼ inch thick. Transfer to a lightly buttered 10-inch pie plate. Press dough evenly into bottom and up sides of dish. Pierce bottom of shell all over with a fork. Trim excess dough flush with rim; refrigerate scraps in plastic wrap.

4. Bake until pale golden, about 15 minutes. Let cool on a wire rack. Raise heat to 375°F.

5. Make the filling: Process ricotta in a food processor until smooth. Add mascarpone, pumpkin, sugar, salt, nutmeg, and vanilla; process until well combined, about 30 seconds. Add egg yolks; process until combined, about 10 seconds. Pour into shell.

6. On a lightly floured surface, roll out remaining disk of dough, and divide into small pieces. Gently roll pieces with your hands to make ¼-inch-thick ropes. Gently press 1 long rope around top edge of shell (patch 2 ropes together, if necessary). Gently place other pastry ropes on top of filling to create a lattice pattern. Place 3 pine nuts in each square of lattice. Brush pastry pieces with beaten egg white.

7. Bake crostata until crust is golden brown and filling is set, about 40 minutes. Let cool on a wire rack. Crostata can be refrigerated, wrapped in plastic, up to 1 day.

Raisin Pie

This dessert is a specialty of Pennsylvania Dutch country. Chock-full of dark and golden raisins, and flavored with cinnamon, the pie has become a *Martha Stewart Living* reader favorite since the recipe was first published in the magazine. MAKES ONE 9-INCH PIE

All-purpose flour, for dusting

Pâte Brisée (page 322)

2½ heaping cups mixed dark and golden raisins

2 cups ice water

2 tablespoons cornstarch

¾ cup sugar

3 tablespoons cider vinegar

½ teaspoon salt, plus a pinch

1½ teaspoons ground cinnamon

2 tablespoons unsalted butter

1 large egg yolk, for egg wash

1 tablespoon milk, for egg wash

Vanilla ice cream, for serving (optional)

1. On a lightly floured surface, roll out 1 disk of dough to a 12-inch round. Fit dough into a 9-inch pie plate. Refrigerate or freeze until firm, about 30 minutes.

2. In a medium saucepan, combine raisins, ice water, cornstarch, sugar, vinegar, ½ teaspoon salt, the cinnamon, and butter. Bring to a gentle boil. Let boil until very thick, stirring constantly, 2 to 3 minutes. Remove from heat and let cool slightly.

3. Preheat oven to 425°F. Pour raisin mixture into pie shell. On a lightly floured surface, roll remaining disk of dough as in step 1. Using a small round pastry tip, cut out eyelet patterns around edge of dough round. Lay round over raisin mixture. Trim dough, leaving a 1-inch overhang; press lightly to seal, then fold under and press again. Crimp as desired. Refrigerate or freeze until firm, about 30 minutes.

4. In a small bowl, whisk together yolk, milk, and remaining pinch of salt. Brush over crust, and place pie on a parchment-lined rimmed baking sheet. Bake until crust is just golden, 20 minutes. Reduce heat to 375°F. Bake until crust is golden and filling is bubbling, 35 to 40 minutes more. Transfer to a wire rack to cool. Serve with vanilla ice cream, if desired.

Vanilla Bean–Pineapple Tart

For this woven pie-dough pattern, the spacing of the strips is varied to create a seemingly complex geometric design that is actually no more difficult than a basic lattice. Rum-poached pineapple pieces peek out from beneath the open-weave crust. MAKES ONE 11-BY-8-INCH TART

FOR THE CRUST

- 2 cups all-purpose flour, plus more for dusting
- ¼ cup granulated sugar
- ¾ teaspoon coarse salt
- 1 cup (2 sticks) cold unsalted butter, cut into ½-inch pieces
- ¼ cup ice water
- 1 large egg yolk, for egg wash
- 2 tablespoons heavy cream, for egg wash

FOR THE FILLING

- 1 large pineapple (4½ pounds), peeled, quartered, and cored
- ¼ cup packed light brown sugar
- ¼ cup granulated sugar
- 1 vanilla bean, halved lengthwise and scraped
- 2 tablespoons fresh lemon juice
- ½ cup dark rum

WEAVING THE LATTICE ON PARCHMENT

1. Make the crust: Pulse flour, sugar, and salt in a food processor until combined. Add butter, and process just until mixture resembles coarse meal. Drizzle with the ice water, and pulse until mixture just begins to hold together. Shape dough into 2 disks. Wrap each in plastic, and refrigerate 1 hour or up to 3 days.

2. On a lightly floured surface, roll out each disk of dough to a 12-by-9-inch rectangle, ⅛ inch thick. Place 1 rectangle on a parchment-lined rimmed baking sheet, and refrigerate or freeze until firm, 30 minutes. Fit other rectangle into an 11-by-8-inch rectangular tart pan with a removable bottom. Trim dough flush with rim. Refrigerate until ready to use.

3. Make the lattice: Using a clean ruler as a guide, cut chilled rectangle into eighteen ½-inch-wide strips with a sharp knife or pastry wheel. Lay 9 strips of dough on another parchment-lined baking sheet in pairs of parallel lines slightly longer than tart pan. Starting in center, weave 1 new strip under and over strips on baking sheet. Weave a second strip ¼ inch away, this time over, then under. Repeat, weaving pairs of strips across half of tart, spacing pairs 1 inch apart. (If strips become too soft, return to freezer until firm.) Return to center, and repeat with remaining strips to form lattice pattern. Freeze until ready to use.

4. Make the filling: Cut each pineapple quarter crosswise into ⅓-inch-thick slices. Combine sugars, vanilla seeds and pod, and lemon juice in a large sauté pan. Add pineapple, and cook over medium heat, stirring until sugars dissolve and mixture becomes saucy, about 3 minutes. Add rum, and simmer until pineapple has softened and almost all liquid has evaporated, about 20 minutes. Let cool in pan. Discard vanilla pod.

5. Spread pineapple mixture evenly in shell. Combine yolk and cream, and brush along top edges of tart. Carefully slide frozen lattice onto tart, centering it; press edges to seal. Trim excess dough. Brush top of lattice with egg wash. Refrigerate or freeze, uncovered, until firm, about 30 minutes.

6. Preheat oven to 400°F. Transfer tart to a rimmed baking sheet. Bake 15 minutes. Reduce heat to 375°F, and bake until crust is golden and filling is bubbling, 40 to 45 minutes more. (If crust browns too quickly, tent with foil.) Let cool completely in pan on a wire rack.

Sour Cherry Pie

A winning combination of tart and sweet, this county-fair favorite is marked by a tightly woven lattice crust. Sour cherries enjoy a short season—typically a few weeks in late June and early July—so snap them up when you see them, and freeze any extras: Line a baking sheet with parchment and freeze pitted cherries in a single layer. Transfer frozen cherries to a resealable bag; they should keep in the freezer up to one year. MAKES ONE 9-INCH PIE

All-purpose flour, for dusting

Pâte Brisée (page 322)

1 cup granulated sugar

3 tablespoons cornstarch

¼ teaspoon salt

⅛ teaspoon ground cinnamon

2 pounds (about 6 cups) fresh sour cherries, pitted, or 1¾ pounds frozen sour cherries, partially thawed

1 teaspoon pure vanilla extract

2 tablespoons unsalted butter, cut into small pieces

1 large egg, lightly beaten, for egg wash

Coarse sanding sugar, for sprinkling

1. On a lightly floured surface, roll out 1 disk of dough to a 13-inch round, ⅛ inch thick. Fit into a 9-inch pie plate, and trim dough, leaving a ½-inch overhang; refrigerate or freeze until firm, about 30 minutes.

2. On lightly floured parchment, roll out second disk of dough ⅛ inch thick. Using a clean ruler as a guide, cut 14 strips (about ½ inch wide) with a pastry wheel or sharp knife. Place strips (and parchment) on a baking sheet, and refrigerate until firm, 10 minutes.

3. Combine granulated sugar, cornstarch, salt, and cinnamon in a large bowl. Add cherries and vanilla, and toss. Pour cherry mixture into pie plate. Dot with butter. Lightly brush exposed edge of shell with beaten egg.

4. Weave the lattice (see page 328): Lay 7 strips of dough across pie. Fold back every other strip. Lay another strip perpendicular in center of pie. Unfold strips over perpendicular strip. Fold back strips under perpendicular strip. Lay second perpendicular strip next to first. Unfold strips over second perpendicular strip. Repeat, weaving strips across half the pie. Return to center, lay a perpendicular strip on unwoven side of pie, and repeat. Trim strips to 1-inch overhang. Tuck overhang under edge of shell, and crimp to seal. Brush lattice with egg wash, and sprinkle with sanding sugar. Refrigerate or freeze 30 minutes.

5. Preheat oven to 375°F. Transfer pie plate to a parchment-lined rimmed baking sheet. Bake until crust is golden brown and juices are bubbling; if using fresh cherries, begin checking after 1 hour; if using frozen, about 95 minutes. (If top browns too quickly, tent with foil.)

6. Transfer pie to a wire rack; let cool completely. Pie can be kept at room temperature, tented with foil, up to 1 day.

Linzer Tart with Lingonberry Jam

For this Scandinavian-inspired dessert, bittersweet-chocolate-enriched dough is pressed into the pan, and more is rolled into long ropes and pressed to form a herringbone pattern on top. Lingonberry jam is available at specialty stores or Scandinavian markets. **MAKES ONE 9-INCH TART**

FOR THE CRUST

- 3 ounces cold bittersweet chocolate (preferably 61 percent cacao)
- ¾ cup granulated sugar
- 1 cup (5 ounces) whole raw almonds
- 1½ cups all-purpose flour, plus more for dusting
- ½ teaspoon ground cinnamon
- Pinch of salt
- ½ cup (1 stick) plus 1 tablespoon cold unsalted butter, cut into small pieces
- 1 large egg
- 1 tablespoon plus 1½ teaspoons fresh lemon juice
- Confectioners' sugar, for dusting

FOR THE FILLING

- 1 cup lingonberry jam or seedless raspberry jam

1. Preheat oven to 350°F. Make the crust: Break chocolate into pieces. In a food processor, combine chocolate, granulated sugar, and almonds; pulse until finely ground, about 45 seconds.

2. Add flour, cinnamon, and salt, pulsing 3 or 4 times to combine. Add butter, pulsing until mixture resembles coarse meal. Transfer to a bowl.

3. In a small bowl, combine egg and lemon juice. Add to flour mixture, stirring with a fork until mixture comes together.

4. Place a 9-inch springform pan or bottomless tart ring on a parchment-lined rimmed baking sheet. Press about two-thirds of dough into ring, forming a ½-inch-thick shell. Shell should be thicker on the edge, reaching a height of 1 inch on the ring.

5. Using a flexible spatula, spread jam evenly over bottom of shell.

6. Divide remaining dough into quarters. Flour surface and hands well, and roll dough with hands into long thin ropes about ⅓ inch in diameter. Flatten slightly. Arrange decoratively in a herringbone pattern on top of jam, trimming dough as necessary.

7. Bake tart until slightly golden brown around edges, about 50 minutes. Transfer to a wire rack and let cool to room temperature. Refrigerate up to 1 day, wrapped in plastic, and dust lightly with confectioners' sugar before serving.

FORMING HERRINGBONE PATTERN

Strawberry Bandanna Tart

A familiar motif can inspire kitchen artistry: Here, a double-crust strawberry tart is adorned with a stylized bandanna pattern. Aspic cutters, available at baking-supply stores, are used to create the punched grid of tiny ovals and dots. **MAKES ONE 9-INCH SQUARE TART**

8 cups strawberries (about 3 pounds), hulled and sliced ¼ inch thick

1 cup granulated sugar

⅓ cup cornstarch

All-purpose flour, for dusting

Pâte Brisée (page 322)

1 large egg, for egg wash

1 tablespoon water, for egg wash

Fine sanding sugar, for sprinkling

1. Combine strawberries and granulated sugar, and let stand 1 hour. Drain, discarding liquid. Add cornstarch to berries, and stir to combine.

2. Preheat oven to 450°F. On a lightly floured surface, roll out 1 disk of dough to an 11-inch square. Fit into a 9-inch square fluted tart pan with a removable bottom, pressing dough gently into sides. Trim dough flush with rim. Refrigerate or freeze until firm, about 30 minutes. Roll out remaining disk of dough to an 11-inch square. Using aspic cutters, cut out shapes in a bandanna pattern (keeping at least a 2-inch border). Refrigerate or freeze until firm, about 30 minutes.

3. Spread strawberry mixture over shell. Carefully place remaining chilled dough over filling. Trim any overhang.

4. Whisk together egg and water, and brush over top dough. Sprinkle with sanding sugar. Refrigerate or freeze tart until firm, about 30 minutes.

5. Place on a parchment lined rimmed baking sheet, and bake 25 minutes. Reduce heat to 400°F. Bake until filling is bubbling, 30 to 35 minutes more. (If crust browns too quickly, tent with foil.) Transfer tart to a wire rack to cool completely before unmolding. Cut into squares, and serve.

Linzertorte

In Austria, where this handsome dessert originated, linzertorte is enjoyed all year long, but its festive red-and-gold palette makes it especially popular at holiday celebrations. The cookielike crust, rich with ground almonds, is layered with raspberry jam and crisscrossed into a windowpane pattern. MAKES ONE 9-INCH TART

1½ cups all-purpose flour, plus more for dusting

½ cup finely ground toasted almonds

½ teaspoon ground cinnamon

½ teaspoon baking powder

½ teaspoon salt

½ cup (1 stick) unsalted butter

⅔ cup packed light brown sugar

1 large egg

1¼ cups seedless raspberry jam

Confectioners' sugar, for dusting

1. Preheat oven to 350°F. In a medium bowl, whisk together flour, almonds, cinnamon, baking powder, and salt.

2. With an electric mixer, beat butter and brown sugar until smooth. Beat in egg. Gradually add flour mixture, beating on low speed just until mixture comes together.

3. Set aside one-third of dough. On a lightly floured surface, roll out remaining dough ⅛ inch thick. Fit into a 9-inch square or round tart pan, pressing into corners and sides. Trim excess dough flush with rim, and use scraps to patch any holes or tears.

4. Roll out reserved dough into a rectangle at least 13 inches long, ⅛ inch thick. With a pastry wheel, cut lengthwise into ½-inch strips. Transfer strips to a parchment-lined rimmed baking sheet; refrigerate or freeze, along with shell, until firm, about 30 minutes.

5. Heat jam in a small saucepan over medium, stirring occasionally, until loose. Strain through a fine sieve, and let jam cool slightly.

6. Pour jam into shell. Arrange dough strips over jam in a lattice-style pattern (you do not need to weave them over and under). Trim excess dough, and press ends into edge of shell to adhere. Bake until crust is golden brown and jam is bubbling, 30 to 35 minutes. Transfer to a wire rack to cool completely. Just before serving, dust top lightly with confectioners' sugar. Tart can be stored at room temperature, wrapped in plastic, up to 1 day.

Peach-Raspberry Slab Pie

A thin double-crust slab, baked in a rimmed sheet pan, is perfect for pie lovers who prefer a high crust-to-filling ratio. The *pâte brisée* crust is peppered with polka-dot cutouts made with a round pastry tip; you can try this technique on a double-crust pie in any shape, size, or flavor. For easy unmolding, line the baking sheet with parchment paper with a one-inch overhang on long sides before baking the pie.

MAKES ONE 15-BY-10-INCH TART

2¼ pounds peaches (about 9), peeled (see page 343), pitted, and cut into thin wedges

6 ounces (about 1 cup) raspberries

1 cup granulated sugar

¼ cup cornstarch

1 tablespoon fresh lemon juice

⅛ teaspoon salt

All-purpose flour, for dusting

2 recipes Pâte Brisée (page 322; do not divide into disks)

1 large egg yolk, for egg wash

1 tablespoon heavy cream, for egg wash

Fine sanding sugar, for sprinkling

1. Preheat oven to 375°F, with rack in lower third. Gently toss peaches, raspberries, granulated sugar, cornstarch, lemon juice, and salt in a large bowl.

2. On a lightly floured surface, roll out each disk of dough to a 16-by-12-inch rectangle, ⅛ inch thick. Transfer one rectangle to a 15-by-10-inch rimmed baking sheet. Trim excess dough to a ½-inch overhang. Transfer remaining rectangle to a parchment-lined baking sheet. Refrigerate or freeze both until firm, about 30 minutes.

3. Pour fruit mixture into dough-lined baking sheet, and spread into an even layer. Cover with remaining rectangle of dough. Trim edges of top piece of dough to ½-inch overhang. Fold edges of top layer over edges of bottom layer, and pinch to seal.

4. Working in rows, cut about 60 holes from top crust using a 9⁄16-inch plain tip (such as Ateco #807), spacing evenly. Whisk together yolk and cream in a small bowl. Brush crust with egg wash. Sprinkle with sanding sugar.

5. Bake until crust turns golden and filling is bubbling, about 90 minutes. (Tent with foil if crust is browning too quickly.) Let cool completely on a wire rack, about 3 hours, before cutting and serving.

Dried-Fruit Star-Lattice Tart

A lattice crust is easily altered to replicate a number of artisanal basketweave designs, such as this striking six-point star pattern. The filling is also out of the ordinary—a blend of dried, not fresh, fruits is poached in a fragrant spiced syrup. MAKES ONE 11-INCH TART

All-purpose flour, for dusting

Pâte Brisée (page 322; omit sugar)

4 cups water

¾ cup Cognac or other brandy

1 cup sugar

1 vanilla bean, halved lengthwise and scraped

1 cinnamon stick

3 (1-inch) strips orange zest

5 whole cloves

1½ cups dried apricots (11 ounces), preferably California

1 cup pitted prunes

¾ cup dried cranberries

1 large egg yolk, for egg wash

2 tablespoons heavy cream, for egg wash

Créme fraîche, for serving

WEAVING THE LATTICE ON PARCHMENT

1. On a lightly floured surface, roll disks of dough to 14-inch rounds. Place 1 round on a parchment-lined baking sheet; refrigerate or freeze until firm, 30 minutes. Fit other round into an 11-inch fluted tart pan. Trim dough flush with rim. Refrigerate or freeze until firm, 30 minutes.

2. Make the lattice: Using a ruler, cut chilled round into sixteen ½-inch-wide strips with a sharp knife or pastry wheel. Lay 6 strips on another parchment-lined rimmed baking sheet in parallel lines slightly longer than diameter of tart pan. Lay 6 more strips on top, almost perpendicular to first strips. Starting in center, weave 1 new strip diagonally through existing grid, under bottom layer of strips and over top layer. Push diagonal strip into corner of each square (where strips meet) to create a tight fit. Weave a second strip 1 inch away, this time over, then under. Repeat weaving strips across half the tart. (If dough strips become too soft, freeze until firm.) Return to center, and repeat with remaining strips to form a 6-point star pattern. Freeze until ready to use.

3. Bring the water, Cognac, sugar, vanilla seeds and pod, cinnamon, zest, and cloves to a boil in a medium saucepan, stirring until sugar dissolves. Add apricots, prunes, and cranberries; reduce heat, and simmer gently until fruit softens but has not broken down, about 20 minutes. Strain through a sieve into a measuring cup; reserve fruit and liquid separately. Let both cool. Discard vanilla pod, cinnamon stick, orange zest, and cloves. (If you have more than 2 cups liquid, simmer in a small saucepan until reduced; it's fine if you have slightly less than 2 cups.)

4. Spread cooled fruit mixture evenly in tart shell, and brush with ½ cup reserved cooking liquid. Combine egg yolk and cream; brush along top edge of tart. Carefully slide frozen lattice on top of tart, centering over filling, and press edges to seal. Trim excess dough. Brush top of lattice with egg wash. Refrigerate, uncovered, until firm, about 1 hour.

5. Preheat oven to 400°F. Transfer tart to a rimmed baking sheet. Bake 15 minutes. Reduce heat to 375°F, and bake until crust is golden brown and filling is bubbling, 40 minutes more. (If crust browns too quickly, tent with foil.) Brush tart with ½ cup more cooking liquid. Let cool on a wire rack. Unmold; serve with crème fraîche.

holiday

This collection of pies and tarts is designed to honor specific celebrations in high spirit—from New Year's to Christmas and nearly everything in between. Sometimes the occasion announces itself by way of a familiar motif, such as hearts for Valentine's Day or stars and stripes on the Fourth of July. Or perhaps it's the flavor—think pumpkin mousse pie at Thanksgiving. Other times the style of the dessert connotes the holiday, such as the buttermilk cream tart topped with a gorgeous "bouquet" of poached-apple roses, perfect to present at the end of a meal on Mother's Day. All the examples here show that you've gone to a bit of extra effort, and why not? Holidays come but once a year.

CHOCOLATE GANACHE HEART TART, RECIPE PAGE 249

Mini Black and White Chocolate Tartlets

Perfect for a swanky First Night celebration, these stylish treats can be held in one hand while you sip Champagne with the other.

WHITE CHOCOLATE MOUSSE TARTS
Makes 2 dozen

    All-purpose flour, for dusting

    Pâte Sucrée, Chocolate Variation (page 333)

¾ teaspoon unflavored powdered gelatin

2   tablespoons ice water

1¼ cups heavy cream

6   ounces white chocolate, very finely chopped

1. On a lightly floured surface, roll out dough ⅛ inch thick. Line twenty-four 3¾-by-1¾-inch rectangular tart pans, rerolling scraps as needed. Pierce bottoms of shells all over with a fork. Transfer pans to a parchment-lined rimmed baking sheet; refrigerate or freeze until firm, about 30 minutes.

2. Meanwhile, preheat oven to 350°F. Bake shells until dry, 15 to 18 minutes. Let cool completely on a wire rack.

3. In a small bowl, sprinkle gelatin over the ice water. Let soften about 5 minutes. Meanwhile, in a small saucepan, bring ½ cup cream to a boil. Remove from heat. Add softened gelatin, stirring for 30 seconds to dissolve completely.

4. Put the white chocolate in the bowl of a food processor. With machine running, pour in softened gelatin mixture; process until smooth. Transfer to a medium bowl. Cover, and refrigerate until mixture is almost the consistency of pudding, about 15 minutes; stir until smooth.

5. In a medium chilled bowl, whisk remaining ¾ cup cream just until stiff peaks form. Fold into white chocolate mixture until combined.

6. Put mousse in a pastry bag fitted with a ⁵⁄₁₆-inch star tip (#22). Pipe into cooled tart shells.

MARBLEIZED CHOCOLATE TRUFFLE TARTLETS
Makes 2 dozen

    All-purpose flour, for dusting

    Pâte Sucrée, Chocolate Variation (page 333)

15 ounces bittersweet chocolate (preferably 61 percent cacao), finely chopped

1   cup heavy cream

1   tablespoon instant espresso powder

2   ounces white chocolate, coarsely chopped

1. Preheat oven to 350°F. On a lightly floured surface, roll out dough ⅛ inch thick. Fit dough into twenty-four 3-inch fluted tart pans, or the cups of a standard muffin tin. Place pans on a rimmed baking sheet; refrigerate or freeze until firm, about 30 minutes. Bake until dry, 18 to 20 minutes. Let cool completely; unmold shells from pans.

2. Place chopped bittersweet chocolate in a heatproof bowl. In a small saucepan over medium heat, bring cream and espresso powder to a simmer. Pour over chopped chocolate, and let stand 5 minutes. Stir until smooth. Fill baked and cooled tart shells with chocolate mixture.

3. Meanwhile, in a heatproof bowl set over (not in) a pan of simmering water, melt white chocolate, stirring. Transfer to a resealable plastic bag; snip a small opening in the corner. Working quickly, pipe 6 dots of melted white chocolate on filling in each tartlet. Using a wooden skewer or toothpick, swirl dots to marbleize. Gently tap tartlets on work surface to settle filling. Refrigerate until set, 1 hour or up to 1 day.

Pear-Raspberry Heart Pie

The crimson filling is only part of this pie's allure. A gorgeous, sugar-coated crust is also sure to impress any valentine, and you can take your pick of two different styles: Heart-shaped cookie cutters create windows in a double crust, near right, and fashion an overlapping shingled top, far right. Baking times are the same for either variation. MAKES ONE 9-INCH PIE

All-purpose flour, for dusting

Pâte Brisée (page 322)

½ cup granulated sugar

3 tablespoons cornstarch

¼ teaspoon salt

¼ teaspoon ground cinnamon

6 ripe, firm Bartlett pears (about 3 pounds), peeled, cored, and cut into ¼-inch slices

8 ounces (about 1½ cups) fresh raspberries

2 tablespoons fresh lemon juice

2 tablespoons unsalted butter, cut into small pieces

1 large egg yolk, for egg wash

1 tablespoon water, for egg wash

Fine sanding sugar, for sprinkling

1. To make the shingled pie: On a lightly floured surface, roll out 1 disk of dough to a 13-inch round. Fit dough into a 9-inch pie plate, and trim dough, leaving a ¼-inch overhang (reserve scraps). Refrigerate or freeze until firm, about 30 minutes. Roll out second disk ⅛ inch thick. With a 2-inch heart-shaped cookie cutter, cut out 48 hearts, using scraps from bottom crust if necessary. Transfer to a parchment-lined baking sheet; refrigerate or freeze until firm, about 30 minutes.

2. In a large bowl, whisk together granulated sugar, cornstarch, salt, and cinnamon. Add pears, raspberries, and lemon juice, and gently toss to coat. Spoon mixture into pie shell, piling fruit in center. Dot with butter. Tuck overhang under, flush with rim. Brush edge lightly with water. Arrange 22 hearts around edge of pie: Press hearts gently onto edge, alternating direction and overlapping slightly. (To help hearts stick, lightly brush each with water.) Repeat, overlapping 16 hearts for second circle. Repeat, overlapping 10 hearts, points in, for final circle. (Points will create a star-shaped vent about 1½ inches wide.) Combine egg yolk and the water in a small bowl. Brush piecrust with egg wash, then sprinkle with sanding sugar. Refrigerate or freeze pie until firm, 30 minutes.

To make the cutout-heart pie: Following directions in step 1, leave second round of dough whole; cut out hearts in center using heart cutters in varying sizes. Transfer cut-out dough to a parchment-lined baking sheet, and refrigerate or freeze until firm, 30 minutes. Prepare filling as in step 2, but do not tuck overhang under dough. Lightly brush edge of shell with water, then drape top crust over filling, centering design. Trim dough, leaving a ½-inch overhang. Tuck overhang under bottom crust, flush with rim, then crimp edge. Whisk yolk and the water in a small bowl. Lightly brush entire piecrust with egg wash, then sprinkle with sanding sugar. Refrigerate or freeze pie until firm, 30 minutes.

3. Preheat oven to 400°F, with rack in lowest third. Place pie on a parchment-lined baking sheet, and bake until crust is light golden, 20 to 25 minutes. Reduce heat to 375°F. Bake until crust is golden brown and juices are bubbling, about 85 minutes more. Transfer to a wire rack; let cool completely before serving.

Chocolate Ganache Heart Tartlets

Petite chocolate tarts pair the sophistication of truffles with the playfulness of brightly colored Valentine candies—in this case, piped meringue hearts. Each tart is sized for two valentines to share; you can also make one large tart in a ten-and-a-half-inch heart-shaped pan (as pictured on page 242). The baking time will remain the same. MAKES 5

FOR THE CRUST

- 1 cup all-purpose flour, plus more for dusting
- ¼ cup unsweetened Dutch-process cocoa powder
- ⅛ teaspoon salt
- ½ cup (1 stick) unsalted butter, room temperature
- ¼ cup sugar
- ½ teaspoon pure vanilla extract
- Vegetable-oil cooking spray

FOR THE FILLING

- 10 ounces bittersweet chocolate (preferably 61 percent cacao), coarsely chopped
- 1 cup heavy cream
- ½ cup milk
- 1 large egg, lightly beaten
- Meringue Hearts (recipe follows)

1. Make the crust: In a bowl, whisk together flour, cocoa, and salt.

2. With an electric mixer on medium speed, beat butter until fluffy, about 3 minutes. Add sugar, and beat until pale and fluffy, about 2 minutes. Reduce speed to low. Add vanilla and the flour mixture, and mix until dough just begins to hold together, 1 to 2 minutes. Turn out dough onto a piece of plastic wrap, then use wrap to gather dough into a ball. Flatten into a disk, and refrigerate until firm, 1 hour.

3. Coat five 5-inch tart pans with cooking spray. On a lightly floured surface, roll out dough ¼ inch thick. Cut dough into 5-inch rounds, and press into bottom and up sides of tart pans. Trim excess dough flush with rims. Patch any tears. Refrigerate or freeze until firm, about 30 minutes.

4. Preheat oven to 325°F. Place tart pans on a rimmed baking sheet and bake until dry, about 25 minutes. Let cool completely on wire racks.

5. Make the filling: Place chocolate in a bowl. In a small saucepan, bring cream and milk almost to a boil; pour over chocolate. Let stand 2 minutes. Slowly whisk until smooth. Let stand 10 minutes more. Stir in egg. Return crusts to rimmed baking sheet, and pour in filling. Bake until just set, about 25 minutes. Transfer to a wire rack and let cool completely before removing from pans. Garnish with meringue hearts.

MERINGUE HEARTS
Makes about 6 dozen

- 2 large egg whites, room temperature
- ½ cup sugar
- Pinch of cream of tartar
- Gel-paste food coloring, in assorted colors

Preheat oven to 175°F. Place egg whites, sugar, and cream of tartar in a heatproof bowl set over (not in) a pan of simmering water. Whisk until sugar dissolves, about 2 minutes. Transfer to an electric mixer, and beat on medium-high speed until stiff, glossy peaks form, about 7 minutes. Divide meringue into batches, and tint each with food coloring as desired. Transfer to pastry bags fitted with ¼-inch star tips (#18). Pipe hearts (½ to 1 inch each) onto parchment-lined baking sheets. Bake 2 hours. Turn oven off, and let meringues stand in oven 8 hours (or overnight). Meringues can be stored in an airtight container in a cool, dry place up to 2 weeks.

Grasshopper Pie

A refreshing chocolate-and-mint cocktail was the inspiration for grasshopper pie, a favorite of Southern hostesses in the 1950s and '60s. It's just as appealing today, and its green palette makes it a fun and festive choice for a St. Patrick's Day celebration. To make the pie, a crème de menthe concoction is whipped into a cloud of nearly weightless filling and chilled in a chocolate wafer shell. Each slice is topped with whipped cream and chocolate shavings. This recipe has been updated from the original one, with fresh mint in the filling and shredded sweetened coconut in the crust. MAKES ONE 9-INCH PIE

FOR THE CRUST

- 6 tablespoons unsalted butter, melted, plus more for pie plate
- ¾ cup sweetened shredded coconut
- 1½ cups chocolate wafer crumbs (from about 25 cookies)
- ¼ cup sugar

FOR THE FILLING

- 1½ cups milk
- 1 cup loosely packed fresh mint leaves
- 1 cup cold heavy cream
- 3 tablespoons crème de menthe
- 2¼ teaspoons unflavored powdered gelatin (1 envelope)
- 5 large egg yolks
- ½ cup sugar

FOR THE TOPPING

Whipped Cream (page 340)

Chocolate shavings (see page 343)

1. Make the crust: Preheat oven to 350°F. Lightly butter a 9-inch pie plate. In a bowl, whisk together coconut, wafer crumbs, and sugar. Add melted butter, and stir until well combined. Press crumb mixture into pie plate. Bake until firm, 10 to 12 minutes. Transfer to a wire rack; let cool completely.

2. Make the filling: Prepare an ice-water bath. Bring milk and mint just to a boil in a saucepan. Remove from heat; cover. Let steep 15 minutes. Pour mixture through a fine sieve into a glass measuring cup. Discard mint, and set milk aside. Beat cream in a chilled medium bowl until stiff peaks form; cover, and refrigerate.

3. Pour crème de menthe into a medium heatproof bowl, and sprinkle with gelatin. Let stand 5 minutes to soften. In another medium bowl, whisk together egg yolks and sugar. Add steeped milk to softened gelatin, whisking until well combined.

4. Set bowl with milk-gelatin mixture over (not in) a pan of simmering water. Cook, whisking constantly, until gelatin is dissolved, about 1 minute. Whisking constantly, pour hot milk mixture in a slow, steady stream into yolk mixture. Return mixture to heatproof bowl; set over simmering water. Cook, whisking constantly, until mixture is slightly thickened and registers 150°F on a candy thermometer, about 8 minutes.

5. Transfer bowl to ice-water bath; whisk until mixture thickens to the consistency of pudding, about 2 minutes. Remove bowl from bath. Whisk in one-third of reserved whipped cream until combined. Gently fold in remaining whipped cream with a flexible spatula. Spoon mixture into piecrust; refrigerate until set, 6 hours or up to 1 day.

6. Top the pie: Slice pie into wedges; spoon dollops of whipped cream onto each, and top with chocolate curls.

Neapolitan Easter Pie

John Barricelli, an excellent baker, television host, and a longtime friend of Martha's, learned to make this Italian grain pie, known as *pastiera*, from his grandfather. The wheat berries are fitting for the Easter holiday, as they symbolize rebirth and renewal. The grains get soaked in water overnight before they are cooked in milk. Afterward, they are mixed with ricotta cheese and pastry cream to make an exceptionally delicious filling. John sells the pies—and many other wonderful baked goods—at SoNo Bakery in South Norwalk, Connecticut. MAKES ONE 10-INCH PIE

FOR THE FILLING

- ½ cup plus 2 tablespoons spring wheat berries (4 ounces)
- 2 cups milk
- 1 cup water
- 2 tablespoons unsalted butter
- Pinch of salt
- 1⅓ cups (12 ounces) fresh ricotta cheese
- ¾ cup sugar
- Vanilla Pastry Cream (page 338)

FOR THE CRUST

- 5 cups all-purpose flour, plus more for dusting
- 2 teaspoons baking powder
- Pinch of salt
- 1 cup (2 sticks) unsalted butter, room temperature
- 1 cup sugar
- Finely grated zest of 1 orange
- 3 large eggs, plus 1 large egg for egg wash

1. Place spring wheat berries in a medium bowl. Add enough water to cover by 2 inches. Refrigerate overnight.

2. Make the crust: In a medium bowl, whisk together flour, baking powder, and salt. With an electric mixer on medium speed, beat butter and sugar until pale and fluffy, about 3 minutes. Beat in orange zest. Add 3 eggs, one at a time, beating until each is fully incorporated. Reduce speed to low, and beat in flour mixture.

3. Divide dough into 2 disks, one larger (approximately two-thirds of dough) and one smaller. Press each piece into a disk; wrap in plastic and refrigerate 1 hour or up to 1 day.

4. Make the filling: Drain wheat berries, and transfer to a medium saucepan with milk, water, butter, and salt. Bring to a boil, then reduce to a simmer, and cook until tender, about 1 hour. Drain, and spread on a baking sheet. Let cool about 30 minutes.

5. Preheat oven to 375°F. In a medium bowl, stir together ricotta and sugar. Add cooled wheat berries and pastry cream. Stir to combine.

6. On a lightly floured surface, roll out larger piece of dough to a 14-inch round, about ⅛ inch thick. Fit into a 10-by-2-inch springform pan. Pour filling into shell. Trim excess dough to ½ inch above filling. Roll out remaining piece of dough, ⅛ inch thick. With a pastry wheel, cut into twelve ¾-inch strips. Weave strips into a lattice (see page 328) over filling; trim lattice flush with edge of dough.

7. Lightly beat remaining egg and brush evenly over top of pie. Bake until crust is golden and filling is bubbling, 60 to 90 minutes. Transfer to a wire rack, and let cool 20 minutes. Run a sharp knife around edge to gently loosen pie. Remove outer ring from springform pan. Let pie cool completely. Serve.

Coconut and Berry Passover Tart

This fresh berry tart defies the notion that Passover desserts are any less indulgent than those that contain flour and dairy. The "missing" ingredients are more than made up for by the chewy coconut crust, soft vanilla-almond filling, and flavorful fruit on top. It's perfect for Passover—or any other time of the year. MAKES ONE 9-INCH TART

FOR THE CRUST

- 2 cups unsweetened shredded coconut
- ½ cup sugar
- 2 large egg whites
- 1 tablespoon pure vanilla extract
- ¼ teaspoon salt

FOR THE FILLING

- ½ vanilla bean, halved lengthwise
- ½ cup vanilla soy milk
- ¼ cup sugar
- 2 large egg yolks
- 2 teaspoons arrowroot or cornstarch
- 2 tablespoons almond paste
- 1 cup almond flour
- ½ cup soy cream cheese, preferably Tofutti
- ¼ cup plus 1 tablespoon apricot jam
- 4 cups mixed fresh berries, such as sliced strawberries, blueberries, and raspberries

1. Make the crust: Preheat oven to 350°F. In a bowl, combine coconut, sugar, egg whites, vanilla, and salt. Press into bottom and up sides of a 9-inch round fluted tart pan.

2. Make the filling: Scrape vanilla seeds into a small saucepan, and add pod. Stir in soy milk and 2 tablespoons sugar, and bring to a boil. In a bowl, whisk egg yolks, arrowroot, and remaining 2 tablespoons sugar. Add hot soy-milk mixture in a slow, steady stream, whisking until combined. Return to pan, and whisk over medium heat until thickened, about 2 minutes. Discard vanilla pod.

3. With an electric mixer on medium, beat soy-milk mixture and almond paste 5 minutes. Beat in almond flour and soy cream cheese. With an offset spatula, spread mixture evenly over crust. Bake 15 minutes. Cover edges with a foil ring (see page 324). Bake until set, 15 to 25 minutes more. Let tart cool completely in pan on a wire rack. Unmold. In a small saucepan, heat jam until loose. With an offset spatula, spread jam evenly over tart. Arrange berries on top, and serve.

Buttermilk Cream Tart

It's as nice a Mother's Day present as a bouquet of fresh flowers, but even sweeter: Delicate poached apple slices, rolled up to resemble blooms, make a pretty arrangement atop a bed of buttermilk cream in a flaky puff-pastry shell. You can bake the pastry and poach the apple slices a day ahead; refrigerate apples submerged in the poaching liquid. Because the filling needs half an hour to set, spread it on the cooled baked pastry and shape the roses (page 342) while you wait. SERVES 6

All-purpose flour, for dusting

1 box store-bought puff pastry, preferably all butter, thawed, or ¼ recipe Puff Pastry (page 334)

1 large egg, lightly beaten

1 tablespoon plus ¼ cup sugar

⅔ cup heavy cream

2¼ teaspoons unflavored powdered gelatin (1 envelope)

1¼ cups low-fat buttermilk (not nonfat)

Pinch of salt

Poached Apple Roses (page 342)

1. On a lightly floured surface, roll out and trim dough to a 9-by-12-inch rectangle. (If necessary, overlap edges of 2 smaller pieces to form a larger rectangle; brush overlap with water to seal, then roll out.) Cut off four 1-inch-wide strips, 2 from one short end and 2 from one long side. Set strips aside. (Rectangle should be 7 by 10 inches.) Transfer rectangle to a parchment-lined baking sheet. Pierce dough all over with a fork; brush with beaten egg. Lay pastry strips on edges to create a border. Trim strips to fit, overlapping at corners. Brush egg over strips and underneath ends to seal. Cover with plastic wrap; refrigerate or freeze until firm, about 30 minutes.

2. Preheat oven to 400°F. Sprinkle dough evenly with 1 tablespoon sugar. Transfer to oven; reduce heat to 350°F. Bake until shell is just golden and puffed all over, about 15 minutes. Using an offset spatula, press down on middle of shell (leave border puffy). Return shell to oven; bake until golden brown, about 15 minutes more. Transfer to a wire rack; press down on middle of shell again. Let cool completely. Tart shell can be stored at room temperature, wrapped in plastic, up to 1 day.

3. With an electric mixer on medium speed, beat ⅓ cup cream until soft peaks form. Sprinkle gelatin over ¼ cup buttermilk in a medium bowl; let stand until softened, 5 minutes.

4. In a small saucepan, over medium heat, bring remaining ⅓ cup cream and remaining ¼ cup sugar to a simmer. Cook, stirring, until sugar has dissolved. Pour hot cream mixture into softened gelatin; stir until gelatin has dissolved. Stir in remaining 1 cup buttermilk and the salt. Pour through a cheesecloth-lined sieve into a medium bowl. Using a flexible spatula, fold in whipped cream. Refrigerate 30 minutes.

5. Pour filling into prepared shell. Spread out to border using an offset spatula. Refrigerate until filling is set, 30 minutes. Arrange roses over filling. Fold leftover peeled-apple slices into ruffles, and fill in gaps. Refrigerate, covered, until ready to serve (up to 6 hours).

Rocky Road Tart

Treat Dad to something special on Father's Day: an over-the-top, unforgettable chocolate dessert. Just like the fudge and the ice-cream variety of the same name, our Rocky Road Tart is jam-packed with mini marshmallows, salted almonds, and chocolate chunks, all in an easy graham-cracker crust. It's sure to become an annual tradition.

MAKES ONE 9-INCH TART

FOR THE CRUST

- 11 graham cracker sheets (about 6 ounces)
- 1 tablespoon sugar
- ⅛ teaspoon salt
- 5 tablespoons unsalted butter, melted

FOR THE GANACHE AND FILLING

- 15 ounces semisweet chocolate (preferably 55 percent cacao)
- 1¾ cups heavy cream
- 2 large egg yolks, lightly beaten
- 2 cups mini marshmallows
- 1 cup whole toasted salted almonds

FOR THE TOPPING

- ¾ cup mini marshmallows
- ¼ cup whole toasted salted almonds, coarsely chopped
- 2 ounces semisweet chocolate (preferably 55 percent cacao), coarsely chopped

1. Make the crust: Preheat oven to 350°F. Pulse graham crackers, sugar, and salt in a food processor until finely ground. Transfer to a bowl, and stir in butter until combined.

2. Press mixture into a 9-inch springform pan or cake ring set on a parchment-lined baking sheet. Press mixture evenly into bottom and up sides of pan. Bake until crust just starts to turn golden brown, about 15 minutes. Let cool completely on sheet on a wire rack.

3. Make ganache: Coarsely chop 10 ounces semisweet chocolate. In a large heatproof bowl set over (not in) a pan of simmering water, melt chocolate. Keep warm. Meanwhile, bring cream just to a simmer in a medium saucepan; remove from heat. Whisk about ¼ cup hot cream into beaten yolks, then whisk yolk mixture into remaining cream in saucepan. Whisk cream mixture into melted chocolate, and remove from heat.

4. Coarsely chop remaining 5 ounces semisweet chocolate, and transfer to a large bowl. Toss in 2 cups mini marshmallows and 1 cup whole toasted almonds. Scatter mixture over bottom of cooled crust. Reserve 1 cup chocolate-egg mixture for topping, and pour the rest evenly into crust (do not overfill). Refrigerate tart, uncovered, until firm, about 1 hour. Meanwhile, cover reserved chocolate-egg mixture with plastic wrap, and set aside at room temperature.

5. Make the topping: Toss together mini marshmallows, chopped almonds, and chocolate; sprinkle over filling. Drizzle reserved 1 cup chocolate-egg mixture over tart, and refrigerate 10 minutes more before unmolding and slicing. Tart can be refrigerated, covered, up to 3 days.

Note: The eggs in this recipe are not fully cooked; it should not be served to pregnant women, babies, young children, the elderly, or anyone whose health is compromised.

Stars and Stripes Mini Pies

Single-serving patriotic pies—each slightly different from the rest—are embellished with a host of cutout and appliquéd shapes. Use cookie cutters to make pastry-dough stars in various sizes, and a pastry wheel to cut strips that stand in for stripes; arrange them in whatever patterns you please. Here, a top crust is spangled with tiny star cutouts; a ring of stars frames a bed of blueberries; and stripes and stars suggest the American flag. Red raspberries, sliced strawberries, blueberries, or blackberries in the fillings carry along the Fourth of July color scheme.

MAKES 6

All-purpose flour, for dusting

2 recipes Pâte Brisée (page 322; do not divide into disks)

7½ cups mixed fresh berries, such as blackberries, blueberries, raspberries, or sliced strawberries

¼ cup fresh lemon juice (from 2 lemons)

¼ cup cornstarch

1 cup plus 2 tablespoons granulated sugar

Pinch of salt

2 large egg yolks, for egg wash

2 tablespoons heavy cream, for egg wash

Fine sanding sugar, for sprinkling

1. On a lightly floured surface, roll out half of dough about ⅛ inch thick. Cut out six 6-inch rounds, and fit into bottoms and up sides of six 5-inch pie plates. Refrigerate or freeze until firm, about 30 minutes.

2. Stir together berries, lemon juice, cornstarch, granulated sugar, and salt. Divide mixture evenly among pie shells.

3. Whisk together egg yolks and cream in a small bowl. Roll out remaining dough ⅛ inch thick. Using mini cookie cutters and a pastry wheel, cut out stars and stripes. Decorate tops of pies as desired (lightly brush bottoms of cutouts with egg wash to help them adhere). Brush pies with egg wash; sprinkle with sanding sugar. Freeze pies until firm, 1 hour.

4. Preheat oven to 375°F. Bake pies on a parchment-lined rimmed baking sheet until crusts are deep golden brown and juices are bubbling, 45 to 50 minutes. Tent with foil if crusts are browning too quickly. Let cool to room temperature on a wire rack. Pies can be kept up to overnight at room temperature, covered tightly with foil.

Flag Berry Tarts

For this edible interpretation of Old Glory, rows of raspberries, some glazed with jam and some dusted with powdered sugar, form the American flag's red and white stripes; blueberries represent the starry field of blue. One tart will have seven rows of berries; the other six. Use smaller berries for the seven-row tart. If you have only one tart pan, you can bake the shells consecutively; let the first shell cool completely in the pan before removing. The interior of each tart shell is brushed with melted chocolate before it is filled; this is an optional step for added flavor. An easy variation (on the following pages) yields three solid-colored tarts in blue, white, and red—also the colors of the French flag—perfect for a Bastille Day celebration. MAKES TWO 14-BY-4-INCH TARTS

All-purpose flour, for dusting

Pâte Sucrée (page 333)

8 ounces cream cheese, room temperature

½ teaspoon pure vanilla extract

½ cup crème fraîche

½ cup confectioners' sugar, plus more for dusting

4 ounces semisweet chocolate (preferably 55 percent cacao; optional), chopped

½ cup raspberry jam

2 tablespoons water

½ cup apricot jam

20 ounces (about 4 cups) fresh red raspberries

12 ounces (about 2 cups) fresh blueberries

1. On a lightly floured surface, roll out 1 disk of dough into an 18-by-8-inch rectangle, ⅛ inch thick. Fit dough into a 14-by-4-inch fluted tart pan; trim excess dough flush with rim. Pierce bottom of shell all over with a fork. Refrigerate or freeze until firm, about 30 minutes. Repeat with second disk of dough.

2. Preheat oven to 375°F. Place pans on a rimmed baking sheet. Line shells with parchment, leaving a 2-inch overhang. Fill shells with pie weights or dried beans. Bake until edges are just starting to color, about 25 minutes. Remove parchment and weights; continue baking until crusts are dry and evenly browned, 10 to 15 minutes more. Transfer to a wire rack; let cool completely before unmolding.

3. With an electric mixer on medium speed, beat cream cheese and vanilla until soft. In a separate bowl, whisk crème fraîche until it holds soft peaks. Whisk a third of crème fraîche into cream-cheese mixture to lighten. Fold in remaining crème fraîche while gradually sifting confectioners' sugar over top; fold just until combined. Cover with plastic wrap; refrigerate until ready to use, up to 2 hours.

4. In a bowl set over (not in) a pan of simmering water, heat chocolate, if using, until just melted, about 1½ minutes; stir until smooth. Using the back of a spoon, spread half of chocolate over each crust; refrigerate until set, at least 5 minutes. Meanwhile, heat raspberry jam in a small saucepan with 1 tablespoon water; strain into a bowl. Heat apricot jam in a small saucepan with remaining 1 tablespoon water; strain into a bowl. (directions continue on page 264) >

Flag Berry Tarts (CONTINUED)

5. Spread crème fraîche filling over chocolate layer in each crust. Make top tart: Starting from right, arrange 3 rows of unglazed raspberries two-thirds the length of tart, leaving space between each row on both long sides (below, left). Dust with confectioners' sugar until raspberries are coated white (below, center). Toss blueberries with apricot jam; fill open third of tart with layers of glazed blueberries arranged snugly in rows. Gently brush more raspberries with strained raspberry jam (enough to fill empty rows), and carefully arrange, rinsing hands as needed (below, right).

6. Make bottom tart: Starting at top left, arrange 3 rows of unglazed raspberries the length of tart, leaving space between each row, and at bottom. Dust with confectioners' sugar until raspberries are coated white. Gently brush remaining raspberries with strained raspberry jam, and carefully arrange to fill empty rows, rinsing hands as needed. Finished tarts will hold at room temperature several hours; don't refrigerate tarts more than 30 minutes, or sugar may begin to liquefy.

French flag variation: Start with 2 recipes of pâte sucrée. Bake 3 tart shells as described on page 262 (reserve 1 disk for another use). If using chocolate, increase to 6 ounces, and heat until melted; coat shells with melted chocolate. Beat 12 ounces cream cheese and ¾ teaspoon vanilla until soft. In a separate bowl, whisk 6 ounces crème fraîche until it holds soft peaks. Incorporate crème fraîche into cream-cheese mixture as described on page 262, and fold in ¾ cup confectioners' sugar. Spread one-third crème fraîche mixture in each chocolate-lined shell. Heat ¾ cup raspberry jam with 1½ tablespoons water until loose; strain. Arrange two layers of red raspberries (12 ounces) in one tart shell, brushing each layer with strained raspberry jam. Fill second shell with 12 ounces golden raspberries, and dust with confectioners' sugar to completely coat. Heat ¾ cup apricot jam with 1½ tablespoons water until loose; strain. Toss 12 ounces blueberries in strained apricot jam; tumble into third shell. Arrange tarts on serving tray to resemble the French flag.

ARRANGING RASPBERRIES IN ROWS

SUGARING RASPBERRIES TO MAKE WHITE STRIPES

ARRANGING GLAZED RASPBERRIES BETWEEN SUGARED ROWS

Pumpkin Chocolate Spiderweb Tart

Serve this tart at a Halloween party, and watch as unsuspecting guests get lured into its chocolate web. The lightly spiced chocolate crust is coated with melted chocolate, then filled with creamy pumpkin purée. More melted semisweet chocolate is piped in a spiderweb pattern to add a frightful finish; the web also serves as an excellent guide for slicing.

MAKES ONE 10-INCH TART

FOR THE CRUST

- 1 cup all-purpose flour, plus more for dusting
- ¼ cup plus 1 tablespoon granulated sugar
- ¼ cup unsweetened cocoa powder
- ½ teaspoon salt
- ½ teaspoon ground cinnamon
- ¼ teaspoon ground cloves
- ½ cup (1 stick) cold unsalted butter, cut into small pieces
- 1 large egg
- 4 ounces semisweet chocolate (preferably 55 percent cacao), finely chopped

FOR THE FILLING

- 1 can (15 ounces) unsweetened pumpkin purée
- ¾ cup packed light brown sugar
- 1 cup crème fraîche or sour cream
- 3 large eggs
- 1 teaspoon ground cinnamon
- 1 teaspoon ground ginger
- ¼ teaspoon freshly grated nutmeg
- ¼ teaspoon salt
- ⅛ teaspoon ground cloves

FOR THE TOPPING

- 2 ounces semisweet chocolate (preferably 55 percent cacao), finely chopped

1. Make the crust: Whisk together flour, granulated sugar, cocoa, salt, cinnamon, and cloves in a bowl. Add butter; with an electric mixer on low speed, beat until butter is the size of small peas, about 5 minutes. Add egg; mix just until ingredients form a dough. Wrap dough in plastic; refrigerate 1 hour or up to 2 days.

2. Preheat oven to 350°F. On a lightly floured surface, roll out dough to just more than ⅛ inch. Press dough into bottom and up sides of a 10-inch tart pan with a removable bottom. Trim excess dough flush with rim. Pierce bottom of shell all over with a fork. Refrigerate or freeze until firm, about 30 minutes or up to 1 day.

3. Bake shell on a parchment-lined rimmed baking sheet until dry, about 15 minutes. Immediately sprinkle the 4 ounces chocolate evenly over crust; let it begin to melt, then smooth with an offset spatula.

4. Make the filling: In a medium bowl, whisk together pumpkin, brown sugar, crème fraîche, eggs, cinnamon, ginger, nutmeg, salt, and cloves until smooth. Pass mixture through a fine sieve into a clean bowl (discard solids). Pour filling into prepared crust, just to top edge.

5. Bake until filling is set, about 40 minutes. Transfer to a wire rack, and let cool at least 30 minutes.

6. Make the topping: Place the 2 ounces chocolate in a heatproof bowl set over (not in) a pan of simmering water; heat until melted, stirring occasionally. Transfer chocolate to a parchment cone or resealable bag with a tiny hole cut in one corner. Pipe about 15 evenly spaced lines radiating out from center of tart. Pipe curved lines around perimeter of tart, connecting each spoke. Continue piping curved lines, spacing them closer together as you near the center. Refrigerate tart until set, 1 hour or up to 1 day.

Mini Jack-o'-Lantern Tarts

Facial features for these grinning jack-o'-lanterns are carved from piecrust instead of pumpkins. Chilling the pastry cutouts helps ensure crisp, clean edges, and baking them separately from the tarts keeps them from shrinking into the spiced pumpkin filling. MAKES 1 DOZEN

All-purpose flour, for dusting

Pâte Sucrée (page 333)

1 can (15 ounces) unsweetened pumpkin purée

3 large whole eggs

½ cup honey

¼ cup packed light brown sugar

1 cup heavy cream, plus 2 tablespoons for egg wash

1 teaspoon ground cinnamon

½ teaspoon ground ginger

¼ teaspoon ground cloves

1 teaspoon coarse salt

1 large egg yolk, for egg wash

1. On a lightly floured surface, roll out 1 disk of dough ⅛ inch thick. Cut out six 6-inch rounds. Fit rounds in bottoms and up sides of six 3¾-inch fluted tart pans. Trim excess dough flush with rims (reserve scraps). Transfer pans to a rimmed baking sheet. Refrigerate or freeze until firm, about 30 minutes.

2. Repeat with second disk of dough, lining 6 more tart pans. Transfer to a parchment-lined baking sheet. Refrigerate or freeze until firm, about 30 minutes.

3. Preheat oven to 375°F. Whisk together pumpkin, whole eggs, honey, brown sugar, 1 cup cream, the cinnamon, ginger, cloves, and salt in a large bowl.

4. Divide filling among tart shells. Bake tarts until golden brown on edges and filling has set, about 30 minutes. Let cool on sheets on wire racks.

5. On a lightly floured surface, roll out scraps to ⅛ inch thick. Using a paring knife or aspic cutters, cut out jack-o'-lantern eyes, noses, and mouths. Place on a parchment-lined baking sheet. Freeze about 15 minutes.

6. Lightly beat egg yolk and remaining 2 tablespoons cream in a small bowl, and brush over features. Bake features until golden brown, about 12 minutes. Transfer to a wire rack and let cool completely. Arrange features on tarts before serving.

Pumpkin Mousse Tart

Elegantly piped ruffles of whipped cream and a fluted crust make for a decidedly more stylish version of the holiday classic. The velvety pumpkin mousse filling is flavored with all the traditional Thanksgiving spices—ginger, cinnamon, nutmeg, and allspice—and a healthy dose of brandy for good measure. Graham-cracker crumbs are combined with cocoa powder in the crust. MAKES ONE 10-INCH TART

FOR THE CRUST

- 18 graham cracker sheets, or 2¼ cups graham cracker crumbs
- ⅓ cup plus 2 tablespoons granulated sugar
- 3 tablespoons unsweetened Dutch-process cocoa powder
- ¼ teaspoon ground cinnamon
- Pinch of grated nutmeg
- ¾ cup (1½ sticks) unsalted butter, melted

FOR THE FILLING

- ¼ cup brandy
- 2 tablespoons plus ¼ cup water
- 2 tablespoons unflavored powdered gelatin (from 3 envelopes)
- 3 large eggs, room temperature
- ¾ cup granulated sugar
- 1½ cups (12 ounces) canned unsweetened pumpkin purée
- ¼ cup sour cream
- ¼ teaspoon ground allspice
- ¼ teaspoon ground ginger
- ½ teaspoon ground cinnamon
- ¼ teaspoon grated nutmeg
- ½ teaspoon salt

FOR THE TOPPING

- 1½ cups heavy cream
- 2 tablespoons confectioners' sugar
- ½ teaspoon pure vanilla extract

1. Make the crust: Preheat oven to 325°F. In a food processor, combine graham cracker sheets, sugar, cocoa, cinnamon, and nutmeg; process until finely ground. Transfer to a medium bowl; mix in butter.

2. Press mixture into bottom and up sides of a 10-inch tart pan with a removable bottom. Place on a parchment-lined rimmed baking sheet; bake until dry, 12 to 15 minutes. Let cool completely on a wire rack.

3. Make the filling: In a small heatproof bowl, combine brandy and 2 tablespoons water. Sprinkle gelatin over liquid; let soften 10 minutes.

4. With an electric mixer on medium-low, beat eggs. While eggs are beating, combine remaining ¼ cup water and the granulated sugar in a small saucepan over medium-high heat. Cook, stirring occasionally, until mixture registers 245°F on a candy thermometer, about 5 minutes.

5. Immediately raise mixer speed to high. Pour sugar mixture down side of mixing bowl in a thin stream; whisk until mixture increases in volume and is pale yellow, about 5 minutes more.

6. Place bowl with softened gelatin over (not in) a pan of simmering water; stir until gelatin has dissolved. Reduce mixer to low speed; whisk in gelatin mixture, the pumpkin, sour cream, allspice, ginger, cinnamon, nutmeg, and salt. Pour into piecrust; refrigerate until set, 4 hours or up to 1 day.

7. Make the topping: Whisk cream, confectioners' sugar, and vanilla in a medium chilled bowl until stiff peaks form. Using a pastry bag fitted with a ⁷⁄₁₆-inch star tip (such as Ateco #825), pipe whipped cream over tart.

Maple Nut Tart

Consider this tart a welcome alternative—or an addition—to pecan pie at Thanksgiving. The recipe is virtually the same, but with walnuts filling in for half the pecans, and maple syrup replacing the corn syrup. You can incorporate other nuts, such as almonds and hazelnuts, as long as the total volume remains the same. MAKES ONE 9-INCH TART

All-purpose flour, for dusting

½ recipe Pâte Brisée (page 322)

2 large eggs

¼ cup packed light brown sugar

¼ teaspoon salt

1 cup pure Grade A maple syrup

1½ cups coarsely chopped pecans

1½ cups coarsely chopped walnuts

1. Preheat oven to 350°F. On a lightly floured surface, roll out dough to an 11-inch round. Fit into bottom and up sides of a 9-inch tart pan with a removable bottom. Trim excess dough flush with rim.

2. In a medium bowl, whisk together eggs, sugar, and salt; whisk in maple syrup. Add nuts, and mix to combine thoroughly. Place tart pan on a parchment-lined rimmed baking sheet, and pour in filling. Bake until filling is set and crust is slightly golden, 55 minutes to 1 hour. Transfer to a wire rack and let cool completely in pan. Unmold before serving.

Cranberry Tart

In a season filled with supersweet treats of all sorts, this aptly named tart stands out for its mouth-puckering flavor. Serve it on Thanksgiving or Christmas—it's equally suited to both holidays. To keep the crust from becoming soggy when the cranberries are added, brush lightly beaten egg white onto the partially baked shell. MAKES ONE 9-INCH TART

½ cup water

16 ounces (about 4 cups) fresh cranberries

1½ cups sugar

1 whole cinnamon stick

All-purpose flour, for dusting

½ recipe Pâte Sucrée (page 333)

1 large egg white, lightly beaten

1 cup heavy cream

½ cup crème fraîche

1. Bring the water, berries, sugar, and cinnamon to a simmer in a medium saucepan. Cook over medium-high, stirring, until the berries start to pop, about 5 minutes. Drain in a sieve set over a bowl. Return strained liquid and cinnamon stick to pan; reserve berries in bowl. Simmer liquid until thickened, about 15 minutes. Pour syrup over berries; let cool. Discard cinnamon stick.

2. On a lightly floured surface, roll out dough ⅛ inch thick. Transfer to a 9-inch square tart pan with a removable bottom. Trim dough, leaving a ½-inch overhang. Tuck overhang under to create a double thickness, and press firmly against sides of pan. Refrigerate or freeze until firm, about 30 minutes.

3. Preheat oven to 400°F. Line shell with parchment, and fill with pie weights or dried beans. Bake until golden brown, about 25 minutes. Transfer to a wire rack. Remove pie weights and parchment. Let cool completely. Reduce heat to 350°F.

4. Brush tart shell with egg white. Fill with cranberry mixture and syrup. Bake until syrup is only slightly runny and berries begin to brown, 45 minutes to 1 hour. If edges brown too quickly, tent with foil.

5. Meanwhile, beat cream in a chilled bowl until soft peaks form. Beat in crème fraîche; refrigerate, covered, until ready to serve.

6. Let tart rest on a wire rack until cool enough to unmold. Serve warm, with crème fraîche whipped cream.

Gingerbread-Raspberry Snowflake Tart

This Yuletide variation on the popular Austrian linzertorte (page 236) features an innovative gingerbread crust surrounding a homemade raspberry-jam filling. Snowflake and dot shapes are cut out from the top; sprinkle the snowflake cutouts—and any others cut from dough scraps—with sugar and bake them to serve as cookies alongside.

MAKES ONE 10-INCH TART

2¼ cups all-purpose flour, plus more for dusting

1½ teaspoons baking powder

1 teaspoon ground ginger

1 teaspoon ground cinnamon

½ teaspoon ground cloves

¼ teaspoon freshly ground pepper

½ teaspoon salt

½ cup packed dark brown sugar

½ cup (1 stick) unsalted butter, room temperature

⅓ cup unsulfured molasses

2 large egg yolks plus 1 large egg white, for egg wash

1¼ cups Raspberry Jam (recipe follows) or best-quality store-bought jam

1. Sift flour, baking powder, ginger, cinnamon, cloves, pepper, and salt into the bowl of an electric mixer. Add sugar; mix on medium-low speed until combined. Add butter; mix until combined, about 2 minutes. Add molasses and egg yolks; mix until dough just comes together, about 30 seconds.

2. On a lightly floured surface, roll out two-thirds of dough to a 12-inch round, ¼ inch thick. Fit into a 10-inch tart pan with a removable bottom. Spread jam over shell; refrigerate about 30 minutes.

3. Roll out remaining dough between lightly floured pieces of parchment to a 10-inch round, ¼ inch thick. Transfer round and parchment to a baking sheet; refrigerate or freeze until firm, about 30 minutes. From round, cut out dot shapes with metal pastry tips, and snowflake shapes with cookie cutters. (If desired, reserve snowflake cutouts and sprinkle tops with sugar. Bake 10 minutes at 350°F.) Refrigerate round on baking sheet until firm, about 30 minutes.

4. Lightly beat egg white; brush rim of tart shell. Carefully slide dough round over shell; press edges to adhere. Refrigerate or freeze until firm, about 30 minutes.

5. Preheat oven to 375°F. Transfer tart to a rimmed baking sheet. Bake until crust is golden brown and filling is bubbling, 50 min-utes to 1 hour. Let cool completely on a wire rack.

....

RASPBERRY JAM
Makes about 2 cups

18 ounces (4 cups) fresh raspberries

2 cups sugar

1. Stir together 3 cups raspberries and the sugar in a medium sauce-pan (off heat). Let stand 15 minutes, stirring occasionally, until berries begin to give off their juices.

2. Bring mixture to a boil over medium-high heat, stirring oc-casionally. Skim off foam. Reduce heat; simmer, skimming foam occasionally, until slightly thick-ened, about 5 minutes.

3. Stir in remaining raspberries; simmer just until berries break up, about 1½ minutes. Let cool completely. Refrigerate until set, at least 4 hours, or up to 1 week.

Chocolate Stencil Tarts

Dark chocolate–on-chocolate tartlets lend themselves well to bold decorative patterns stenciled with white confectioners' sugar. Snowflake-shaped stencils are appropriate for the winter holidays, but any shape will do, depending on the occasion. You could also use this recipe and apply the technique with letter stencils to spell out a holiday message or birthday greeting. MAKES SEVEN 4½-INCH TARTS

All-purpose flour, for dusting

½ recipe Pâte Sucrée, Chocolate Variation (page 333)

1 cup heavy cream

¼ cup milk

2 tablespoons granulated sugar

9 ounces semisweet chocolate (preferably 55 percent cacao), coarsely chopped

2 large eggs, lightly beaten

1½ teaspoons pure vanilla extract

Unsweetened Dutch-process cocoa powder, for dusting

Confectioners' sugar, for dusting

1. Preheat oven to 375°F. On a lightly floured surface, roll out dough ¼ inch thick. Cut out seven 6-inch rounds and fit each into a 4½-inch tart pan with a removable bottom. Trim excess dough flush with rims, and pierce bottoms of shells all over with a fork. Refrigerate or freeze until firm, about 30 minutes.

2. Line shells with parchment and fill with pie weights or dried beans. Bake 15 minutes; remove weights and parchment, and bake 10 minutes more. Transfer pans to a wire rack to cool completely.

3. In a small saucepan over medium-high heat, cook cream, milk, and granulated sugar until cream and milk are scalded, stirring to dissolve sugar. Place chocolate in a medium heatproof bowl. Pour scalded mixture over chocolate; let stand 1 minute and whisk to combine. Add eggs and whisk gently to combine. Whisk in vanilla.

4. Transfer tart shells to a rimmed baking sheet. Divide chocolate filling evenly among tart shells. Bake until filling has set, about 25 minutes. Let cool in pans on a wire rack. Unmold tarts. Tarts can be refrigerated, wrapped in plastic, up to 2 days.

5. Before serving, using a small sieve, sift cocoa over tarts. Stencil one tart at a time: Set snowflake stencil on tart and sift confectioners' sugar over; carefully remove stencil. Serve immediately.

savory

Not all pies and tarts are destined for the dessert course. Some, like the ones that follow, offer wonderful options for main courses at brunch, lunch, or dinner. In a few cases, they make terrific bite-size hors d'oeuvres. They rely on the same techniques and many of the same crusts used to produce their sweet counterparts, but with deliciously savory fillings. Each is versatile in its own way and encourages experimentation. Take the Vegetable Tartlets as but one example: Once you've made the recipe with the vegetables suggested here, you'll surely begin to develop winning flavor combinations of your own, depending on the season.

VEGETABLE TARTLETS, RECIPE PAGE 303

Leek and Olive Tart

Baby leeks, sautéed until meltingly tender and arranged end to end, top this showstopping first course. Other components include Niçoise olives and two types of cheese—one fresh (Pavé d'Affinois, a soft cow's milk cheese similar to Brie); the other aged (Parmigiano-Reggiano). If you can't find baby leeks, you can use regular leeks, or if it's springtime, look for ramps at a farmers' market. MAKES ONE 14-BY-6-INCH TART

15 to 20 baby leeks or 3 large leeks, white and pale green parts only

1 tablespoon unsalted butter

2 tablespoons extra-virgin olive oil

¼ teaspoon coarse salt

1 teaspoon finely chopped fresh thyme leaves

1 box store-bought puff pastry, preferably all butter, thawed, or ¼ recipe Puff Pastry (page 334)

1 large egg beaten with 1 tablespoon water, for egg wash

¼ cup grated Parmigiano-Reggiano

Scant ¼ cup Niçoise olives, pitted

4 ounces Pavé d'Affinois or other soft-ripened cheese (such as Camembert), thinly sliced

1. If using baby leeks, halve lengthwise and trim to about 3 inches long. If using large leeks, cut crosswise into 3-inch pieces; halve each piece lengthwise, then cut into ½-inch-thick strips (about 5 cups). Rinse well to remove any grit, and drain.

2. Melt butter with oil in a medium sauté pan over medium heat. Add leeks and salt; cook, stirring occasionally, 5 minutes. Reduce heat to medium low; cover, and cook, stirring occasionally, until leeks are tender but not browned, about 15 minutes. Stir in thyme. Leeks can be cooled completely and refrigerated in an airtight container up to 1 day; bring to room temperature before assembling tart.

3. Roll out or trim dough to a 14-by-6-inch rectangle. (If necessary, overlap edges of two smaller pieces to form a large rectangle; brush overlap with water to seal, then roll out.) Place on a parchment-lined baking sheet (reserve remaining dough for another use). Score a ¾-inch border on all sides (do not cut all the way through). Brush border with egg wash; sprinkle with grated cheese. Refrigerate 30 minutes.

4. Preheat oven to 375°F. Bake until golden, 10 to 15 minutes. Using an offset spatula, press down on center of shell (leave edges raised). Arrange leeks end to end in rows within border of crust. Scatter olives over leeks. Bake until crust is golden brown, about 10 minutes more. Use a wide spatula to lift to check bottom of crust; if it's still soft, bake 3 to 5 minutes more.

5. Arrange soft cheese over top. Using a large offset spatula, slide tart onto a wire rack; let cool slightly. Cut crosswise into pieces; serve warm or at room temperature. Tart can be kept at room temperature up to 1 hour before serving.

Spinach-Feta Turnovers

Puff pastry replaces phyllo dough to produce handheld individual servings of spanakøpita, a Greek spinach-and-feta pie. As such, the turnovers are quicker to assemble (no buttering and stacking of sheets necessary) yet still bake to a crisp, golden, flaky finish. You can prepare and freeze the turnovers two months in advance, then bake them straight from the freezer. Because feta cheese is on the salty side, taste the filling before seasoning it. MAKES 8

2 tablespoons olive oil

2 onions, finely chopped

2 garlic cloves, minced

4 boxes (10 ounces each) frozen chopped spinach, thawed and squeezed dry

2 cups (8 ounces) crumbled feta

2 to 4 tablespoons fresh lemon juice

⅛ teaspoon cayenne pepper

Coarse salt and freshly ground black pepper

All-purpose flour, for dusting

1 17-ounce box store-bought puff pastry, thawed, or ½ recipe Puff Pastry (page 334)

1 large egg, for egg wash

2 tablespoons water, for egg wash

1. In a skillet, heat oil over medium; add onions and garlic. Cook, stirring occasionally, until tender, 5 to 7 minutes. Transfer to a large bowl; mix in spinach, feta, lemon juice, and cayenne. Season filling with salt and black pepper.

2. Preheat oven to 375°F. On a lightly floured surface, roll out each portion of dough to a 12-inch square; cut each into quarters to form a total of eight 6-inch squares.

3. Dividing evenly, spoon filling onto center of each square. Beat egg and water; lightly brush 2 adjoining edges of each square with egg wash. Fold these edges over filling to form a triangle; press firmly to seal (dough should be tightly pressed around filling). With a floured fork, crimp edges.

4. Transfer turnovers to 2 parchment-lined rimmed baking sheets; brush tops with remaining egg wash. Bake until golden and puffed, 35 to 40 minutes. Serve warm or at room temperature.

To freeze: Freeze unbaked turnovers on a parchment-lined baking sheet. Wrap frozen turnovers individually in plastic wrap; store in a resealable plastic bag in the freezer up to 2 months. Unwrap frozen turnovers, and bake as in step 4, adding 5 to 10 minutes to the baking time.

Cherry Tomato, Mozzarella, and Zucchini Pie

This pie combines the ease of a galette—no need to attach a top crust or crimp any edges—with the convenience of oven-to-table serving. Before the tender dough is fitted in the pie plate, it is cut into flaps around the edge for neat, even folding over the filling. When the pie emerges from the oven, the tomatoes will be near bursting, their juices mingling with the cheeses, zucchini, and basil. It just might remind you of another delicious savory pie: pizza. MAKES ONE 9-INCH PIE

FOR THE CRUST

- 2¼ cups all-purpose flour, plus more for dusting
- ½ cup finely grated Parmesan cheese
- 1 teaspoon coarse salt
- ¾ cup (1½ sticks) cold unsalted butter, cut into pieces
- 1 large egg yolk, plus 1 large egg yolk, for egg wash
- ¼ to ½ cup ice water
- 1 tablespoon heavy cream, for egg wash

FOR THE FILLING

- 2 tablespoons extra-virgin olive oil
- 1 shallot, finely chopped
- 1 small zucchini, halved lengthwise and cut crosswise into ½-inch-thick half-moons
- 1½ pounds cherry tomatoes
- ½ cup grated Parmesan cheese
- 4 ounces bocconcini (fresh mozzarella balls) or fresh mozzarella (1-inch pieces)
- 3 tablespoons fresh basil leaves, chopped
- ¼ cup plus 2 tablespoons all-purpose flour
- Coarse salt and freshly ground pepper

1. Make the crust: Pulse flour, cheese, salt, and butter in a food processor until mixture resembles coarse meal. Add 1 egg yolk; pulse to combine. Drizzle in ¼ cup ice water, and pulse until dough just comes together. (If dough is still crumbly, add up to ¼ cup more water, 1 tablespoon at a time.) Form dough into a disk, and wrap in plastic. Refrigerate or freeze until firm, about 30 minutes.

2. Make the filling: Heat 1 tablespoon oil in a skillet over medium. Add shallot; cook, stirring occasionally, until softened, about 3 minutes. Add zucchini; cook, stirring occasionally, until light golden and liquid has been released, about 5 minutes. Transfer to a large bowl.

3. Halve one-third of the tomatoes. Stir halved and whole tomatoes, both cheeses, basil, and flour into shallot-zucchini mixture. Season with salt and pepper.

4. On a lightly floured surface, roll out dough to a 13-inch round, about ¼ inch thick. Make seven 3-inch-long cuts around edge of dough, evenly spaced. Transfer to a 9-inch pie plate. Drizzle shell with remaining tablespoon oil. Transfer filling to shell. Fold in flaps of dough, slightly overlapping. Refrigerate until dough is firm, about 30 minutes.

5. Preheat oven to 375°F. Whisk cream and remaining egg yolk in a small bowl, and brush over crust. Bake pie on a parchment-lined rimmed baking sheet until crust is golden brown and juices are bubbling, 70 to 80 minutes. Transfer to a wire rack to cool slightly. Serve warm.

Brie and Apple Custard Tart

Just a sliver of this ultra-rich tart will satisfy even the heartiest appetites. It features a quick herb-infused custard, made by blending softened Brie, eggs, and cream in a food processor, then pouring over sautéed Granny Smith apples in a deep *pâte brisée* shell. MAKES ONE 9-INCH TART

All-purpose flour, for dusting

½ recipe Pâte Brisée (page 322)

1 tablespoon olive oil

2 tart, firm apples, such as Granny Smith, peeled and cored, each cut into 6 wedges

6 ounces very ripe Brie cheese, room temperature

1 large whole egg plus 2 large egg yolks

½ cup heavy cream

½ cup milk

2 teaspoons coarsely chopped fresh thyme leaves

Coarse salt and freshly ground pepper

1. Preheat oven to 400°F. On a lightly floured surface, roll out dough to an 11-inch round. Fit into a 9-inch springform pan or tart ring set on a parchment-lined baking sheet, with dough extending up slightly over sides. Pierce the bottom of shell all over with a fork. Refrigerate or freeze until firm, about 30 minutes.

2. Line shell with parchment, extending above sides by about 1 inch. Fill with pie weights or dried beans. Bake 20 minutes. Carefully remove parchment and weights. Bake until crust is golden all over, 10 to 12 minutes more. Transfer to a wire rack to cool slightly before filling. Reduce heat to 325°F.

3. Heat oil in a medium saucepan over medium-high. Add apples; cook until browned on all sides, 2 to 3 minutes total. Remove from heat.

4. In a food processor fitted with plastic blade, process Brie 15 seconds. Add whole egg and the yolks one at a time; process after each until well combined. Add heavy cream, and process until smooth. Transfer mixture to a large mixing bowl; slowly stir in milk until smooth. Stir in thyme, and season with salt and pepper.

5. Arrange sauteéd apples around bottom of crust. Pour custard around apples. Bake until custard is just set when gently touched with your finger, about 35 minutes. Transfer to a wire rack to cool slightly. Serve warm or at room temperature.

Swiss Chard and Goat Cheese Galette

Pies and tarts filled with Swiss chard, pine nuts, and raisins are common in southern France and Italy, where they may be served for dessert, sprinkled with confectioners' sugar or toasted almonds. Goat cheese and anchovies make this galette decidedly savory, while the crust departs from the standard with wholesome oats and whole-wheat flour. SERVES 6

FOR THE CRUST

- ½ cup all-purpose flour, plus more for dusting
- ½ cup whole-wheat flour
- ½ cup old-fashioned rolled oats
- 1 teaspoon salt
- ½ cup (1 stick) cold unsalted butter, cut into small pieces
- 3 ounces cream cheese
- 1 large egg yolk, plus 1 large egg yolk, for egg wash
- 1 tablespoon heavy cream, for egg wash

FOR THE FILLING

- 12 ounces green Swiss chard, washed, stems removed and reserved
- 2 tablespoons extra-virgin olive oil
- 1 large onion, sliced lengthwise ¼ inch thick
- 3 tablespoons balsamic vinegar

  Coarse salt and freshly ground pepper
- 3 anchovy fillets, coarsely chopped (optional)
- 2 tablespoons fresh thyme leaves
- 6 ounces fresh goat cheese, room temperature
- 2 tablespoons heavy cream
- ½ teaspoon grated nutmeg
- 2 tablespoons pine nuts, toasted (see page 343)
- 2 tablespoons golden raisins

1. Make the crust: In a food processor, pulse flours, oats, and salt to combine. Add butter, cream cheese, and 1 egg yolk, and process until dough just comes together, 15 to 20 seconds. Press dough into a disk. Wrap in plastic, and refrigerate 1 hour or up to 1 day.

2. Make the filling: Slice chard stems into ¼-inch pieces. In a large skillet, heat 1 tablespoon oil over medium. Add stems and onion slices, and cook, stirring, until slightly brown, 8 to 10 minutes.

3. Cover skillet, and reduce heat to low. Cook, stirring occasionally, until stems are very soft, about 15 minutes. Add vinegar, and cook, stirring, until liquid is reduced by half, about 2 minutes. Season with salt and pepper. Remove from heat, and transfer onion mixture to a nonreactive bowl.

4. Heat remaining 1 tablespoon oil in same skillet over medium-high. Add anchovies, if using; sauté, stirring frequently, 1 minute. Add chard leaves, and sauté until slightly wilted, about 1 minute. Stir in thyme; season with salt and pepper.

5. With an electric mixer on medium speed, mix goat cheese and cream. Beat until smooth, about 1 minute. Stir in nutmeg; season with salt and pepper.

6. On a lightly floured surface, roll out dough to a 12-inch round, ¼ inch thick. Arrange onion mixture evenly over dough, leaving a 3-inch border around edge. Spread goat-cheese mixture over onion mixture, and top with chard-leaves mixture. Sprinkle with pine nuts and golden raisins. Fold in edges of dough, and press down gently to seal. Transfer tart, on parchment, to a rimmed baking sheet. In a small bowl, beat remaining 1 egg yolk with remaining 1 tablespoon cream; brush exposed dough. Refrigerate until dough is firm, about 30 minutes.

7. Preheat oven to 375°F. Bake until crust is golden, 40 to 45 minutes. Transfer to a wire rack to cool slightly. Serve warm or at room temperature.

Mini Chicken Potpies with Herb Dough

It's hard to improve upon a standard, but this recipe for chicken potpie does just that. Each individual serving is topped with a ruffle-edged round of herb-flecked dough. The filling contains all the usual, well-loved components, but the creamy sauce is brightened with lemon zest. MAKES 8

1 whole chicken (4 pounds), rinsed and patted dry

4 cups homemade or low-sodium store-bought chicken stock

1 large onion, halved

2 bay leaves

½ teaspoon black peppercorns

3 sprigs fresh thyme, plus 2 tablespoons thyme leaves

1 celery stalk, cut into thirds

5 tablespoons unsalted butter

9 ounces red potatoes, cut into ½-inch chunks

12 white, red, or yellow pearl onions, peeled (halved lengthwise if large)

1 leek, white and pale green parts only, cut into ¼-inch-thick rounds and rinsed well

2 carrots, peeled and cut into ¼-inch-thick rounds

6 ounces white mushrooms, trimmed and halved (quartered if large)

¼ cup plus 1 tablespoon all-purpose flour, plus more for dusting

1 cup milk

2 tablespoons chopped fresh flat-leaf parsley

Finely grated zest of 1 lemon

2 teaspoons coarse salt

½ teaspoon freshly ground pepper

Pâte Brisée (page 322; omit sugar)

2 tablespoons mixed fresh herb leaves, such as flat-leaf parsley, sage, chives, thyme, dill, rosemary, and oregano

1 large egg, lightly beaten with 1 tablespoon water, for egg wash

1. Put chicken, stock, onion, bay leaves, peppercorns, thyme sprigs, and celery in an 8-quart pot. Add water to cover. Cover pot; bring to a boil. Uncover; reduce heat. Simmer 1 hour.

2. Transfer chicken to a cutting board. When cool enough to handle, remove skin and discard. Cut meat from bones; discard bones. Using a fork, shred into bite-size pieces.

3. Pour stock through a fine sieve into a large bowl; discard solids. Set aside 2 cups stock. (Reserve remaining stock for another use.)

4. Melt butter in a large skillet over medium-high heat. Add potatoes and pearl onions. Cook, stirring occasionally, until potatoes begin to turn golden, about 5 minutes. Add leek, carrots, and mushrooms; cook, stirring occasionally, until softened, about 5 minutes more. Add flour; cook, stirring, 1 minute.

5. Stir in reserved 2 cups stock and the milk. Bring mixture to a simmer; cook, stirring constantly, until thick and bubbling, 2 to 3 minutes. Stir in shredded chicken, chopped parsley, thyme leaves, zest, salt, and pepper. Divide chicken mixture among eight 4-by-2-inch ramekins, filling almost to top. Let cool slightly.

6. Preheat oven to 375°F. On a lightly floured surface, roll out dough ¼ inch thick. Arrange herbs on top; roll out dough ⅛ inch thick, gently pressing herbs.

7. Using a 4½-inch fluted cutter, cut out 8 rounds of dough. Brush edges of ramekins with egg wash. Place dough rounds over filling. Gently press to seal. Freeze until dough is firm, about 10 minutes.

8. Place ramekins on a rimmed baking sheet. Brush dough with egg wash. With a paring knife, cut 4 steam vents in each round. Bake until golden brown and filling is bubbling, 35 to 40 minutes. Transfer to a wire rack; let cool 10 to 15 minutes, and serve.

Savory Apple Galettes

Chopped fresh rosemary, grated parsnip, and cheese flavor the crust of these sensational little tarts. More cheese is sprinkled over the apple-and-onion filling. The tarts are perfect for an autumn picnic, harvest party, or other outdoor occasion. MAKES 6

FOR THE CRUST

- 1 small parsnip (about 4 ounces), peeled
- 2 cups all-purpose flour, plus more for dusting
- 1 teaspoon salt
- 1 teaspoon sugar
- ¼ teaspoon freshly ground pepper
- ¾ cup (1½ sticks) cold unsalted butter, cut into small pieces
- ½ cup finely grated manchego cheese (about 1½ ounces)
- 2½ teaspoons finely chopped fresh rosemary
- 1 large egg yolk
- ¼ cup ice water

FOR THE FILLING

- 1 tablespoon extra-virgin olive oil
- 1 tablespoon unsalted butter
- 3 Gala apples, peeled, cored, halved, and sliced ¼ inch thick
- 8 medium yellow onions, halved and thinly sliced
- 3 tablespoons cider vinegar
- ½ teaspoon coarse salt
- 1 cup coarsely grated manchego cheese (2 to 3 ounces)

  Freshly ground pepper, to taste

1. Make the crust: Finely grate parsnip (you will need ½ cup). Place on a clean kitchen towel (do not use paper towels), and squeeze to extract as much liquid as possible.

2. Pulse parsnip, flour, salt, sugar, pepper, butter, cheese, and rosemary in a food processor. Add egg yolk, and pulse to combine. Drizzle ice water evenly over mixture; pulse until dough just comes together. Shape into a disk, and wrap in plastic. Refrigerate 1 hour or up to 2 days.

3. Make the filling: Heat oil and butter in a large skillet over medium-high. Add apples and onions, and cook until golden brown, about 15 minutes. Cover, reduce heat to low, and cook until very soft and caramelized, about 35 minutes. Add vinegar and salt, and cook 5 minutes. Remove from heat and let filling cool completely.

4. On a lightly floured surface, roll out dough ⅛ inch thick. Cut out six 7-inch rounds, gathering scraps and rerolling dough, if needed. Place on large parchment-lined baking sheets.

5. Purée half the apple-onion mixture in a food processor until smooth. Using an offset spatula, spread 3 tablespoons apple-onion purée over each round, leaving a 1-inch border around edges. Sprinkle each with 2 tablespoons cheese. Season with pepper. Top each with a generous tablespoon of remaining apple-onion mixture, and sprinkle with 2 teaspoons cheese. Fold in edges of dough, crimping with your fingers. Refrigerate until dough is firm, about 30 minutes. Meanwhile, preheat oven to 350°F.

6. Bake until edges are golden brown, 40 to 45 minutes. Serve warm or at room temperature.

Red and Golden Beet Cheese Tart

Thin slices of roasted red, golden, and striped beets overlap atop a combination of ricotta and goat cheeses to produce a stunning shingled tart. The beets are sprinkled with grated fontina before baking. Use beets in a variety of colors if you can find them. MAKES ONE 13-BY-9-INCH TART

All-purpose flour, for dusting

Pâte Brisée (page 322; do not divide into 2 disks)

1½ pounds (without greens) beets, preferably a combination of red, golden, and Chioggia

2 tablespoons extra-virgin olive oil, plus more for drizzling

Coarse salt and freshly ground pepper

1 pound fresh goat cheese, room temperature

½ scant cup fresh ricotta cheese (4 ounces)

2 teaspoons finely chopped fresh thyme, plus about 1 teaspoon whole leaves

½ cup grated fontina cheese (about 2 ounces)

1. Preheat oven to 375°F. On a lightly floured surface, roll out dough ⅛ inch thick. Press firmly into a 13-by-9-inch rimmed baking sheet, leaving a 1-inch overhang on all sides. Tuck overhang under to create a double thickness; press firmly against pan. Pierce bottom of shell all over with a fork. Refrigerate or freeze until firm, about 30 minutes.

2. Line shell with parchment; fill with pie weights or dried beans. Bake until golden brown, about 30 minutes. Remove weights and parchment. Transfer to a wire rack to cool completely. (Keep oven on.)

3. Trim all but ½ inch of stems from beets; rinse well. Toss with oil and 1 teaspoon salt. Transfer to a rimmed baking sheet; cover with parchment, then tightly with foil. Roast until beets are tender, 45 minutes to 1 hour. When cool enough to handle, peel beets with a paring knife. Cut into thin rounds. Raise heat to 425°F.

4. Stir together goat cheese, ricotta, and chopped thyme until well combined; season with pepper. Spread mixture over tart shell, filling all the way to edges.

5. Arrange beets over cheese mixture, overlapping slices slightly and alternating colors, if possible. Lightly season with salt. Sprinkle fontina and whole thyme leaves on top. Lightly drizzle with oil, and season with pepper. Bake until golden brown, about 25 minutes. Serve warm.

Roasted Cauliflower Hand Pies

A savory short crust flavored with manchego envelops Spanish-inspired hand pies filled with oven-roasted cauliflower, toasted hazelnut paste, chopped rosemary, and more of the grated cheese. Serve them as an appetizer, with slices of membrillo (Spanish quince paste often served alongside cheese, for tapas) and a glass of fine sherry. MAKES 8

FOR THE CRUST

- 2¼ cups all-purpose flour, plus more for dusting
- ½ cup finely grated manchego cheese
- Pinch of sugar
- 1 teaspoon coarse salt
- ¾ cup (1½ sticks) cold unsalted butter, cut into pieces
- 1 large egg yolk, plus 1 large egg yolk, for egg wash
- ¼ to ½ cup ice water
- 1 tablespoon heavy cream, for egg wash

FOR THE FILLING

- 1 small head cauliflower, florets separated and thinly sliced (about 4 cups)
- 3 tablespoons plus ¼ cup extra-virgin olive oil
- Coarse salt and freshly ground pepper
- ⅔ cup hazelnuts, toasted and skinned (see page 343)
- 1 garlic clove
- 1 teaspoon finely grated lemon zest
- 2 teaspoons finely chopped fresh rosemary
- 5 ounces manchego cheese, thinly sliced

1. Make the crust: Pulse flour, cheese, sugar, salt, and butter in a food processor until mixture resembles coarse meal. Add 1 egg yolk; pulse to combine. Drizzle in ¼ cup ice water, and pulse until dough just comes together. (If dough is still crumbly, add up to ¼ cup more water, 1 tablespoon at a time.) Divide dough in half, and shape into disks. Wrap each in plastic. Refrigerate until firm, about 1 hour.

2. Make the filling: Preheat oven to 375°F. Toss cauliflower with 3 tablespoons oil in a medium bowl; season with salt and pepper. Spread on a large rimmed baking sheet. Roast until golden brown, about 7 minutes. Flip cauliflower; roast 5 minutes more. Let cool.

3. Put nuts and garlic in a food processor. With machine running, slowly add remaining ¼ cup oil until mixture is finely chopped. Add zest and 1 teaspoon rosemary; season with salt and pepper. Process until mixture is combined into a paste.

4. On a lightly floured surface, roll out 1 disk of dough ¼ inch thick. Cut out eight 4-inch rounds. Transfer to a parchment-lined rimmed baking sheet. Spread 2 teaspoons hazelnut mixture onto each round, leaving a ¼-inch border. Divide cauliflower among rounds. Top with cheese and remaining teaspoon rosemary, dividing evenly; sprinkle with pepper. Whisk cream and remaining yolk in a small bowl, and brush edges of dough. If dough gets too soft to handle, refrigerate until firm.

5. On a lightly floured surface, roll out remaining disk of dough ¼ inch thick. Cut out eight 4-inch rounds. With a small flower-shaped cookie cutter, cut out 8 flowers from dough scraps. Place a dough round on top of each pie; gently press edges with a fork to seal. Brush crusts with egg wash; place a flower on each pie. Brush flowers with egg wash. Refrigerate until firm, about 30 minutes. Bake until crust is golden brown, 30 to 32 minutes. Serve warm or at room temperature.

Scallion Tartlets

Combined with garlic, fresh chile, walnuts, olives, and Parmesan, the humble scallion is the basis for a delightfully earthy, toss-together topping for puff-pastry squares. As the tartlets bake, the scallions caramelize, turning golden, sweet, and intensely flavorful. Instead of individual tartlets, you can form the dough and filling into two large tarts: Roll out and cut pastry into two eight-inch squares, divide filling evenly between crusts, and bake thirty minutes. MAKES 8

All-purpose flour, for dusting

1 box store-bought puff pastry, preferably all butter, thawed, or ¼ recipe Puff Pastry (page 334)

8 bunches scallions (2¼ pounds), trimmed and cut into matchsticks

1 garlic clove, minced

1 red Thai chile, ribs and seeds removed, minced

½ cup walnuts, finely chopped

½ cup Kalamata olives, pitted and coarsely chopped

2 tablespoons extra-virgin olive oil

Coarse salt and freshly ground pepper

1 large egg yolk, for egg wash

1 teaspoon ice water, for egg wash

½ cup grated Parmesan cheese (2 ounces)

1. Preheat oven to 400°F. On a lightly floured surface, roll out and trim dough into two 9-inch squares. Cut each piece into 4 squares; place on a parchment-lined baking sheet 2 inches apart. Refrigerate or freeze until firm, about 30 minutes.

2. Toss together scallions, garlic, chile, walnuts, olives, and oil in a medium bowl. Season with salt and pepper.

3. In a small bowl, whisk together egg yolk and ice water. Brush ½-inch border around edges of dough squares. Divide scallion mixture among squares, leaving ¼-inch border; sprinkle squares evenly with cheese.

4. Bake until crust is golden brown, about 20 minutes. Transfer to a wire rack to cool. Serve warm or at room temperature.

Vegetable Tartlets

It's not so important which vegetables you use in these colorful, nutritious tarts—rather, that there is a seasonal bounty. Here, eggplant, red onion, zucchini, yellow squash, cherry tomatoes, kale, and red bell peppers fill cornmeal crusts, but you could easily use green beans, corn, or mushrooms. The crust is light and crisp, with less butter than many pastry doughs. To make free-form versions, spoon filling onto center of each dough round, and fold the edges inward. Serve each tartlet with a dollop of fresh ricotta cheese, if desired. Add a green salad to balance out a healthy lunch. MAKES 6

FOR THE CRUST

- 2 cups all-purpose flour, plus more for dusting
- ½ cup yellow cornmeal, preferably stone-ground
- 1 teaspoon sugar
- 1 teaspoon coarse salt
- ½ cup (1 stick) cold unsalted butter, cut into small pieces
- ½ cup ice water

FOR THE FILLING

- 3 tablespoons extra-virgin olive oil
- 2 red bell peppers, stems and seeds removed, cut into ¼-inch strips
- 1 zucchini, thinly sliced
- 1 yellow squash, thinly sliced
- 1 Italian eggplant, thinly sliced
- 1 small red onion, quartered
- 1 cup dry white wine
- ¼ teaspoon coarse salt
  Freshly ground black pepper
- 2 cups coarsely chopped kale (8 ounces)
- 2 cups (about 1 pint) cherry tomatoes
- ⅓ cup fresh basil leaves, coarsely chopped
  Pinch of red pepper flakes

1. Make the crust: Pulse flour, cornmeal, sugar, and salt in a food processor. Add butter; pulse until mixture resembles coarse meal. Drizzle ice water evenly over mixture; pulse just until dough holds together. Divide dough in half, and shape into disks. Wrap in plastic. Refrigerate until firm, about 1 hour.

2. On a lightly floured surface, roll out each disk of dough ⅛ inch thick. Cut out six 8-inch rounds, gathering scraps and rerolling dough. Fit rounds into 4-inch springform pans or tart pans with removable bottoms, pleating dough along edge. Trim excess dough flush with rims. Refrigerate or freeze until firm, about 30 minutes.

3. Preheat oven to 350°F. Make the filling: Heat oil in a large skillet over medium. Add bell peppers, and cook until just tender, 4 to 5 minutes. Add zucchini, squash, eggplant, and onion; cook, stirring, 2 minutes. Add wine and salt; season with black pepper. Cook, stirring, until liquid has evaporated. Add kale, and cook until wilted, 2 to 3 minutes. Remove from heat. Stir in tomatoes, basil, and red pepper flakes.

4. Transfer shells to a rimmed baking sheet. Spoon 1¼ cups vegetable mixture into each tart shell. Bake until crust is golden brown, 40 to 50 minutes. Transfer to a wire rack to cool slightly. Serve warm or at room temperature.

Summer Squash Lattice Tart

The lattice top is taken to a new level with this yellow-and-green basket-weave design made from strips of summer squashes. The tart offers as good a reason as any to head to a farmers' market—or, if you're lucky, your own garden—for zucchini and yellow squash. Use a mandoline or other adjustable-blade slicer to slice the squashes lengthwise. MAKES ONE 14-BY-4-INCH TART

All-purpose flour, for dusting

½ recipe Pâte Brisée (page 322; omit sugar)

2 medium green zucchini (about 10 ounces)

2 medium yellow squash (about 10 ounces)

Coarse salt and freshly ground pepper

2 tablespoons extra-virgin olive oil, plus more for brushing

2 large leeks (about 12 ounces), white part only, washed well and cut into ⅓-inch dice

½ cup grated Gruyère cheese

1 large whole egg plus 1 large egg yolk

¼ cup heavy cream

WEAVING SQUASH LATTICE

1. Preheat oven to 375°F. On a lightly floured surface, roll out dough to a 16-by-6-inch rectangle. Fit dough into a 14-by-4-inch rectangular tart pan with a removable bottom (or a bottomless tart form) set on a parchment-lined rimmed baking sheet, and trim excess dough flush with rim. Pierce bottom of shell all over with a fork. Refrigerate or freeze until firm, about 30 minutes.

2. Line shell with parchment. Fill with pie weights or dried beans. Bake until crust is just beginning to brown, about 15 minutes. Remove weights and parchment. Bake until golden brown, about 10 minutes more. Let cool completely on a wire rack. (Keep oven on.)

3. Using a mandoline or sharp knife, very thinly slice 1 zucchini and 1 squash lengthwise. Place slices in a single layer on a wire rack over a rimmed baking sheet and sprinkle lightly with salt. Let drain 30 minutes.

4. Cut remaining zucchini and squash into ⅓-inch dice. Heat olive oil in a large skillet over medium-high. Add diced zucchini, diced squash, and leeks, and season with salt and pepper. Cook until golden brown but still firm, 8 to 10 minutes. Let vegetables cool slightly. Spread in an even layer in prepared crust; sprinkle cheese evenly on top.

5. In a bowl, whisk together whole egg, egg yolk, and cream, and season with salt and pepper. Carefully pour egg mixture over cheese and vegetables.

6. Place salted squash slices in between double layers of paper towels. Gently press down to remove as much liquid as possible. Alternating squash colors, weave lattice pattern over top of filling, covering the entire surface. Trim or tuck in ends to fit.

7. Using a pastry brush, coat lattice with olive oil. Bake, loosely covered with aluminum foil, until custard is set, 30 to 35 minutes. Uncover, and cool slightly on a wire rack before unmolding and serving.

Alsatian Potato Pie

Inspired by the robust cooking of Alsace, a region in northeastern France bordering Germany, this flaky pie features a rich filling of potatoes, Comté (or Gruyère) cheese, leeks, and garlic-infused cream. Rather than adding the cream to the filling at the beginning, it is poured through the vents on top of the pie only after the pastry has turned golden brown, and then the pie is baked ten minutes more. This allows the crust to crisp properly and keeps the potatoes from soaking up all the cream before the pie has finished baking. SERVES 6

3 Yukon Gold potatoes (about 1½ pounds), peeled and cut into ¼-inch-thick rounds

Coarse salt and freshly ground pepper

1 cup heavy cream

5 garlic cloves, crushed with flat side of a large knife

½ teaspoon freshly grated nutmeg

2 tablespoons unsalted butter

1 leek, white and pale green parts only, halved lengthwise, thinly sliced crosswise, and washed well

¼ cup chopped fresh flat-leaf parsley

1 large egg yolk, for egg wash

All-purpose flour, for dusting

1 box store-bought puff pastry, preferably all butter, thawed, or ¼ recipe Puff Pastry (page 334)

1½ cups grated Comté or Gruyère cheese (about 5 ounces)

1. Cover potatoes with water in a medium saucepan. Bring to a boil. Season water with salt; cook until just tender, 13 to 15 minutes. Drain, and let cool.

2. Bring ¾ cup plus 3 tablespoons cream, the garlic, and nutmeg to a boil in a small saucepan. Cook mixture until reduced by half. Season with salt and pepper.

3. Melt butter in a skillet over medium heat. Add leek; cook, stirring occasionally, until softened, about 5 minutes. Remove from heat. Stir in parsley; season with salt and pepper.

4. Whisk egg yolk and remaining 1 tablespoon cream in a small bowl. On a lightly floured surface, roll out and trim dough into two 13-by-6-inch rectangles. (If necessary, overlap edges of two smaller pieces to form a larger rectangle; brush overlap with water to seal, then roll out.) Set 1 rectangle on a parchment-lined baking sheet. Top with half the potatoes, leaving a ½-inch border all around and overlapping potatoes slightly. Top with half the leek mixture and half the cheese; season with salt and pepper. Repeat layering with remaining potatoes, leeks, and cheese. Brush edges of dough with egg wash. Cover with remaining dough rectangle; gently press edges with a fork to seal. Cut 2-inch slits crosswise in center of crust, 2 inches apart, to let steam escape. Brush with egg wash. Refrigerate pie until firm, about 30 minutes.

5. Preheat oven to 400°F. Bake until golden brown and puffy, about 35 minutes. Remove from oven. Pour cream mixture into pie vents with a metal funnel. Bake 10 minutes more. Transfer pie to a wire rack, and let stand 15 minutes before serving.

Quiche

Essentially a custard of eggs, cream, and savory fillings baked in a pastry crust, quiche is simple to prepare, and takes well to a variety of flavors. For example, you can follow the recipe below to prepare quiches with the suggested fillings—mushroom, bacon and caramelized onion, or leek and corn—or substitute any other ingredients you prefer. You can bake a quiche in a plain pie plate, but the sharper edges of a tart tin better support the crust's sides. In addition, blind-baking the shell will prevent the crust from undercooking and getting soggy. A perfectly cooked quiche will be completely set (it shouldn't jiggle in the center), slightly puffed, and lightly browned across the surface. MAKES ONE 10-INCH TART

All-purpose flour, for dusting

½ recipe Pâte Brisée (page 322)

Mushroom and Shallot Filling (page 310), Bacon and Caramelized Onion Filling (page 310), or Leek and Corn Filling (page 310)

½ cup milk

½ cup heavy cream

2 large eggs plus 1 large egg yolk

Pinch of freshly grated nutmeg

Coarse salt and freshly ground pepper

1½ cups grated Gruyère cheese (about 5 ounces)

1. On a lightly floured surface, roll out dough to a 14-inch round, about ⅛ inch thick. Fit into a 10-inch round fluted tart pan with a removable bottom, gently pressing dough to fit. With a small knife or rolling pin, trim excess dough flush with rim. Pierce bottom of shell all over with a fork. Refrigerate or freeze until firm, about 30 minutes.

2. Preheat oven to 375°F. Line shell with parchment, and fill with pie weights or dried beans. Bake until crust is beginning to brown at edges, about 30 minutes. Remove parchment and weights; bake until bottom of crust is dry but not yet golden brown, 5 to 10 minutes more. Transfer shell to a wire rack to cool slightly.

3. Meanwhile, make the filling of your choice, then prepare the custard: In a medium bowl, whisk together milk, cream, eggs, and yolk until combined, then whisk in nutmeg and season with salt and pepper.

4. Place tart pan on a rimmed baking sheet. Sprinkle half the cheese evenly over bottom of crust. Sprinkle with filling, then top with remaining cheese. Carefully pour custard over cheese. Bake until just set in the center, 30 to 35 minutes. Transfer to a wire rack to cool at least 10 minutes before serving. Serve warm or at room temperature.

Mini quiche variation: To make individual quiches instead of one large one, roll out dough as described in step 1, cutting into five 6-inch rounds and fitting them into 4-inch tart pans. Chill shells. Line shells with parchment, and fill with pie weights; bake until golden, 15 to 20 minutes. Remove parchment and weights, and transfer shells to a wire rack to cool completely. Continue with recipe; once assembled, bake individual quiches 20 to 25 minutes.

Quiche Fillings

MUSHROOM AND SHALLOT FILLING

2 tablespoons extra-virgin olive oil

2 shallots, thinly sliced

1 pound white button mushrooms, quartered

Coarse salt and freshly ground pepper

Heat oil in a large skillet over high. Cook shallots, stirring constantly, until translucent, about 1 minute. Add mushrooms and season with salt and pepper. Cook, stirring frequently, until mushrooms are dark golden brown, 8 to 10 minutes. (Mushrooms will release liquid at first; cook until it has evaporated, adjusting heat as necessary.) Transfer to a bowl, and let cool slightly.

BACON AND CARAMELIZED ONION FILLING

1 tablespoon extra-virgin olive oil or unsalted butter

6 strips bacon, cut into 1-inch pieces

2 onions, cut into small dice

Heat oil in a large skillet over medium. Cook bacon until fat renders and bacon is crisp and brown, about 8 minutes. Use a slotted spoon to transfer to paper towels to drain, leaving rendered fat in skillet. Add onions and cook over medium-low heat, stirring frequently, until dark golden brown and caramelized, 30 to 45 minutes. Combine onions and bacon in a small bowl, and let cool slightly.

LEEK AND CORN FILLING

2 tablespoons extra-virgin olive oil or unsalted butter

1 leek, white and pale green parts only, cut into ½-inch pieces and washed well

2 ears corn, kernels sliced from cobs (about 2 cups)

1 teaspoon fresh thyme leaves (from 2 sprigs)

Coarse salt and freshly ground pepper

Heat oil in a large skillet over high. Cook leek until translucent, about 1 minute, stirring constantly to prevent browning. Add corn and thyme, and season with salt and pepper. Cook, stirring frequently, until corn is fork-tender, about 5 minutes. Transfer to a bowl, and let cool slightly.

the basics

On the pages that follow, you should find everything you need to know in order to produce consistently beautiful, delicious pies and tarts. We've included ingredient and equipment glossaries, as well as illustrated techniques. You'll learn to properly roll out dough, weave a lattice crust, make a meringue topping, and more. You'll also find essential recipes for the most frequently used crusts, fillings, and finishes.

NET WT. 4 OZ. (113g)

NET WT. 4 OZ. (113g)

ingredients

BAKING STAPLES

1. FLOUR When mixed with water, flour forms the gluten proteins that give baked goods their structure. All-purpose flour has just the right amount of protein for most pie dough—producing crusts that are neither too tough nor too crumbly—and is used for nearly all of the crusts in this book. The exception is puff pastry, which requires a small amount of cake flour (not the self-rising variety) along with all-purpose flour to achieve a lofty, lightweight texture. Flour can be used as a thickener in fruit pies as well, and is used in almost every pie recipe for dusting a work surface when rolling out dough. Store flour in an airtight container at room temperature up to one year. See page 343 for tips on how to properly measure flour.

2. BUTTER Fat is what gives pastry crusts their flaky layers and tender texture. Butter is most commonly used in the recipes in this book because of its incomparably pure, rich flavor. When cut into flour to make dough, butter should be very cold; warmer butter will begin to melt as you work with it, resulting in a tough—not flaky—crust. Butter is also melted and tossed with cookie crumbs to make crumb crusts, stirred into creams and curds, and dabbed onto fruit fillings before baking to help them thicken. Choose unsalted butter, and start with fresh sticks: Since butter readily absorbs odors from the foods around it, older butter may impart an off taste to baked goods. Butter freezes nicely for up to six months (thaw overnight in the refrigerator before using).

3. SUGAR White granulated sugar, made from refined sugarcane or sugar beet, is the most widely used variety, especially for baking. Sanding sugar has large crystals and is better for decoration: Sprinkle it over a top crust that's been brushed with an egg wash before baking for a sparkly finish. Turbinado sugar and other "brownulated" sugars can be used in place of sanding sugar in some recipes. Confectioners' sugar dissolves easily into whipped toppings, and can be dusted over the top of a finished dessert. It often forms clumps, so you may want to sift with a fine sieve before using. Brown sugar is a combination of granulated sugar and molasses; dark-brown sugar has a higher molasses content than light-brown sugar, and a deeper color and flavor. See page 343 for how to measure brown sugar. After opening, seal the package securely or transfer brown sugar to an airtight container to keep it

from hardening. (To soften hard brown sugar, place a wedge of apple in the bag and reseal; leave a day or two, until sugar is sufficiently soft, then remove apple.)

4. SALT A little bit of salt in any recipe—sweet or savory—enhances the primary flavors. The recipes in this book call for salt (table salt), coarse salt (kosher salt), or, in a few recipes, sea salt, such as fleur de sel or Maldon. If you don't have coarse salt, you can substitute table salt—just use about a quarter of the amount called for. Do not, however, substitute table salt for sea salts, which are used primarily for flavor; table salt doesn't compare.

5. EGGS Eggs are the basis for custards, curds, and pastry cream; the whites form the structure of airy meringues. Certain pastry doughs—such as pâte sucrée and pasta frolla—contain eggs as well: The fat in the egg yolks makes these crusts more tender, while the additional protein simultaneously strengthens them. Use large room-temperature eggs. If separating yolks from whites, do so while eggs are still cold, then bring them to room temperature.

6. HEAVY CREAM Sweetened or unsweetened whipped cream is a favorite pie topping (see page 340 for a recipe). Use heavy cream (or whipping cream); light cream will not whip. Cream can also be brushed onto a piecrust, on its own or combined with a beaten egg in an egg wash.

7. MILK Combine milk with egg yolks, sugar, and cornstarch to make custard or pastry cream. Whole milk is used for the recipes in this book.

8. CREAM CHEESE Pie dough made with cream cheese is easy to work with; the finished crust has a tender texture. Cream cheese can also be incorporated into baked or unbaked fillings.

9. SOUR CREAM The addition of sour cream (or its French cousin, crème fraîche) gives baked custard fillings a tangy flavor that pairs especially well with fresh fruit toppings.

10. YOGURT An unbaked filling, such as mousse made with yogurt, can be a fresh-tasting alternative to pastry cream. Use plain, full-fat yogurt for the recipes in this book unless otherwise specified.

SPECIALTY INGREDIENTS

1. NUTS Nuts may be used whole as the main component of a pie or tart filling, or finely chopped and mixed into a crust. Almonds and other nuts, such as hazelnuts, are used to make frangipane, a rich batter for fruit tarts and other classic French desserts. Nuts are naturally high in oils, which give them their rich flavor but also cause them to turn rancid quickly. Buy nuts from a source with high turnover, and store them in an airtight bag or container in the freezer for up to six months.

2. COOKIES A press-in cookie-crumb crust is easy to make and is the traditional choice for many cream pies and icebox pies. Graham crackers are common, as are chocolate and vanilla wafers (such as Nabisco Famous Wafers and Nilla Wafers), gingersnaps, and shortbread (such as Walkers). All cookies can be ground in a food processor; or, if you don't have a food processor, place them in a large resealable plastic bag and crush them with a rolling pin. Prepackaged graham-cracker crumbs are also sold in most supermarkets. For measuring purposes, in this book the term "graham cracker sheet" refers to a 5-by-2½-inch rectangle.

3. CORNMEAL Incorporating stone-ground cornmeal—white or yellow—into a crust along with the flour adds a delightful crunch. Store cornmeal in an airtight bag or container, away from sources of heat and light, and be sure to check the sell-by date on the bag; it has a shorter shelf life than flours and other dry ingredients.

4. CHOCOLATE Solid chocolate is used in many applications in pie and tart making, including ganache and cream fillings. It can also be melted and drizzled over desserts or shaved into curls for garnishes. When buying chocolate for baking, look for the best quality bar, block, or chips you can find; Valhrona, Callebaut, El Rey, and Scharffen Berger are all premium brands. The higher the percentage of cacao (often noted on the label), the deeper the flavor. Milk chocolate must contain a minimum of 10 percent cacao, while unsweetened chocolate is 100 percent; dark chocolate (including bittersweet and semisweet) contains at least 35 percent. We like semisweet chocolate with 55 percent cacao, and dark chocolate with at least 70 percent. Use a serrated knife to finely chop chocolate, or a vegetable peeler to make chocolate curls (see page 343).

5. COCOA POWDER You'll find two types of cocoa powder available for baking: natural (sometimes called "nonalkalized cocoa") and Dutch-process, which is treated with an alkaline solution that reduces cocoa's natural acidity and gives the powder a milder flavor and darker color. Use the type of cocoa specified in the recipe. If it is not specified, either type should work fine.

6. VANILLA Always choose extract labeled "pure"— never "imitation." Some recipes call for vanilla beans instead of extract for a more complex flavor and fragrance. To release the seeds, lay the bean flat on a cutting board; holding one end, slice it open lengthwise with a paring knife, then run knife along each cut side. You can generally substitute 1 tablespoon extract for the seeds of one whole bean. Save the pod and use it to make vanilla sugar, which is excellent for baking or sweetening drinks: Place split pod in a jar of sugar, seal the lid, and leave for at least a week (shake daily to distribute flavor); use sugar within several months.

equipment

TOOLS FOR MAKING DOUGHS AND FILLINGS

1. DRY MEASURING CUPS Dry ingredients (such as flour and sugar) and semisolid ingredients (such as jam, sour cream, and peanut butter) should be measured in graduated dry measuring cups. Level ingredients with a straightedge, such as an offset spatula, for the most accurate measurements. See page 343 for more on measuring dry ingredients.

2. LIQUID MEASURING CUPS Use a clear liquid measuring cup (preferably made of heat-resistant glass) with a spout and a handle to measure liquid ingredients. Set the cup on a flat surface, and read measurements at eye level.

3. GRADUATED MEASURING SPOONS Measure both dry and liquid ingredients with a set of graduated metal measuring spoons. Level dry ingredients, such as salt, with a straightedge; pour liquids, such as vanilla extract, to the rim of the spoon. Never measure directly over the bowl.

4. SIEVE A fine-mesh sieve can be used to sift ingredients (such as flour or cocoa powder) into a bowl, or to dust confectioners' sugar or cocoa over the top of a baked pie or tart as a garnish.

5. RASP GRATER The small, sharp blades of a rasp grater are perfect for zesting citrus fruits: they remove the flavorful zest but leave the bitter white pith behind. A rasp grater can also be used to finely grate chocolate, nutmeg, and fresh ginger.

6. WHISK A whisk with a bulbous shape, also called a balloon whisk, quickly and thoroughly incorporates dry and liquid ingredients, and is also used to whip heavy cream by hand. Choose a sturdy stainless-steel whisk that won't bend out of shape.

7. HEATPROOF FLEXIBLE SPATULA A silicone spatula (which is heatproof, unlike a rubber one) is handy for transferring custards, creams, and batters from a bowl or pan, and for evenly spreading fillings and toppings.

8. PASTRY BLENDER Use a pastry blender to cut butter into dry ingredients by hand (some bakers prefer this tool to a food processor). Press down and turn with the pastry blender to work the butter into the flour, taking care not to overwork it.

9. ROLLING PIN The most common rolling pin design features two handles on an axis around which the pin rotates. Many professional bakers, however, prefer a long, slender wooden pin without handles or tapered ends, as this type allows for the most control and lets you "feel" the dough as you roll. Whichever you choose, opt for a longer pin that will accommodate a large piecrust. Wood is the standard, but marble is an excellent choice (and Martha's favorite) because it stays cool as you work and is less likely to stick to the dough.

10. PASTRY WHEEL Use a double-sided pastry wheel to create lattice strips or to cut straight edges for free-form pies; the fluted wheel creates scalloped edges. For straight-edged strips, you can use a pizza cutter in place of a pastry wheel.

11. RULER Using a ruler ensures perfectly even lattice strips. It's also handy for measuring dough as you roll it out on a work surface. A long ruler (such as 18 inches) is most helpful.

12. LARGE OFFSET SPATULA To release dough that is beginning to stick to the work surface, slide an offset spatula at least 10 inches long underneath. Do this periodically as you roll, and lightly flour the spatula if necessary.

13. KITCHEN SHEARS Trim excess dough from the edges of bottom and top crusts with a pair of kitchen shears; they're easier to maneuver than a knife.

14. PASTRY BRUSHES Choose pastry brushes with natural, tightly woven bristles that are securely attached to the handle, and label one brush for dry tasks and one for wet. Use a large brush to remove excess flour from rolled-out dough and to apply glazes and egg washes to piecrusts; use a small brush to apply egg wash to appliquéd or shingled piecrusts. Let brushes dry completely before storing.

TOOLS FOR BAKING PIES AND TARTS

1. OVEN THERMOMETER Because oven temperature is critical to successful baking, an oven thermometer is one of the baker's most important gadgets. Place it in the center of your oven to monitor the temperature, and adjust your oven's dial accordingly.

2. RIMMED BAKING SHEET Juicy fruit pies can bubble and drip during baking, making a mess of your oven. To protect your oven and for easier cleanup, set the pie on a rimmed baking sheet lined with parchment paper or a silicone baking mat. You can also use a rimmed baking sheet to hold a batch of tartlets or miniature pies as they bake, and to bake a rectangular "slab" pie.

3. PARCHMENT PAPER With a multitude of uses, this heat-resistant, nonstick, disposable paper is indispensable in the kitchen. Use it to line your work surface, to contain pie weights when blind-baking pastry shells, and to line baking sheets beneath pie plates. Waxed paper is not an acceptable substitute.

4. SILICONE BAKING MAT A reusable, versatile alternative to parchment paper, a silicone baking mat provides a nonstick surface for baked goods. Use it to line a baking sheet underneath a fruit pie, as described above, or when baking cookie-like tuile tartlet shells, such as those on page 198.

5. COOLING RACK A raised wire rack allows air to circulate around baked goods as they cool. Choose a rack with stainless steel mesh and feet on the bottom, with bars that go in both directions.

6. COOKIE CUTTER Double-crust pies require vents or holes to let steam escape as they bake. These are usually cut with a sharp knife, but for a decorative touch, use a small cookie cutter instead. You can then appliqué the cutout shapes to the top crust with a bit of egg wash (cutouts can also be used to decorate the edges of single-crust pies, as shown on page 25, or to top jam tartlets such as the ones on page 204).

7. PIE WEIGHTS You can buy ceramic or metal pie weights at baking-supply stores, or use dried beans or rice. All prevent a blind-baked crust from shrinking and puffing up as it bakes.

8. GLASS PIE PLATE Tempered glass (such as Pyrex) is the best choice for pie plates, as it disperses heat well, allowing for more even browning. The clear glass also lets you see the color of the bottom crust as it bakes.

9. METAL PIE TIN Although it does not conduct heat as well as a glass plate, a metal pie tin has an old-fashioned appeal. Tins are also available in miniature sizes.

10. CERAMIC BAKING DISH Pie plates and other baking dishes made of earthenware or porcelain conduct heat well and are lovely enough to go from oven to table.

11. FLUTED TART PAN Tarts gain much of their elegant appearance from the pans in which they're baked. The pans have short, fluted sides and removable bottoms, and are sold in a variety of sizes and shapes, the most common of which are round and rectangular.

12. TARTLET PAN Miniature tart pans, available in multiple shapes and sizes, are used to produce an array of tiny treats. Baked tarts are usually small enough to flip right out; no removable bottoms are needed. Small brioche molds can be used in their place.

13. SPRINGFORM PAN Traditionally used to make cheesecake, a springform pan is also excellent for baking modern-looking straight-sided tarts and savory pies such as quiche. Once it has cooled completely, unhinge the clasp on the side to open the pan and release the tart inside.

14. CAKE RING Cake, tart, and flan rings can all be used to bake single-crust pies and tart shells. The bottomless molds—positioned on parchment-lined baking sheets—lift off easily after baking and produce elegant results.

recipes + techniques

Pâte Brisée

The rich flavor, delicate texture, and versatility of *pâte brisée* have made it the standard at *Martha Stewart Living* and in this book, where it is used for pies and tarts both sweet and savory. From three main components—flour, fat, and water—plus a little sugar and salt, you get a crust that is incomparably flaky, yet sturdy enough to contain nearly any filling. An all-butter *pâte brisée* tastes best, but some cooks use shortening or lard for additional tenderness. The name *pâte brisée* means "broken pastry," and refers to cutting the butter into the flour, either by hand or with a food processor. The butter-flour mixture should resemble coarse meal, with some pieces of butter the size of small peas, before cold water is drizzled into it; these bits of unincorporated butter give *pâte brisée* its famously flaky texture by releasing steam as they melt. **MAKES ENOUGH FOR ONE 9-INCH DOUBLE-CRUST PIE OR TWO 9-INCH SINGLE-CRUST PIES**

2½ cups all-purpose flour

1 teaspoon salt

1 teaspoon sugar

1 cup (2 sticks) cold unsalted butter, cut into small pieces

¼ to ½ cup ice water

1. Pulse flour, salt, and sugar in a food processor (or whisk together by hand in a bowl). Add butter, and pulse (or quickly cut in with a pastry blender or your fingertips) until mixture resembles coarse meal, with some larger pieces remaining. Drizzle ¼ cup water over mixture. Pulse (or mix with a fork) until mixture just begins to hold together. If dough is too dry, add ¼ cup more water, 1 tablespoon at a time, and pulse (or mix with a fork).

2. Divide dough in half onto two pieces of plastic wrap. Gather into two balls, wrap loosely in plastic, and press each into a disk using a rolling pin. Refrigerate until firm, well wrapped in plastic, 1 hour or up to 1 day. (Dough can be frozen up to 3 months; thaw in refrigerator before using.)

Shortening Variation: Replace ½ cup (1 stick) butter with ½ cup cold vegetable shortening, cut into small pieces.

Lard Variation: Replace ½ cup (1 stick) butter with ½ cup cold lard. For the best quality, it's worth seeking out leaf lard. You can buy rendered leaf lard from online vendors, or from artisanal butcher shops.

Cornmeal Variation: Replace ½ cup flour with ½ cup coarse cornmeal.

Cheddar Variation: Reduce butter to ¾ cup (1½ sticks) and add 1½ cups shredded sharp cheddar to the flour mixture along with the butter. Increase sugar to 1 tablespoon.

PÂTE BRISÉE HOW-TO

1. COMBINING INGREDIENTS Be sure all ingredients—even the dry ones—are cold before you begin (refrigerate them for 30 minutes). Pulse flour, salt, and sugar in a food processor. Cut butter into small pieces and add to processor.

2. CUTTING IN BUTTER Pulse just until mixture resembles coarse meal, with some larger pieces remaining (up to 1/2 inch), about 10 seconds.

3. ADDING THE WATER Drizzle 1/4 cup ice water evenly over mixture, and pulse until the dough just begins to hold together. Pinch off a piece of dough with your fingers: It should just hold together when squeezed without being wet, sticky, or crumbly. Add up to 1/4 cup more water, by the tablespoon, if necessary.

4. CHILLING THE DOUGH Turn out dough onto plastic wrap. Use your hands to quickly gather wrap to shape the dough into balls; flatten slightly. Unwrap; rewrap loosely, leaving half an inch of air space around the dough. Roll to 1/2 inch thick, filling space. Refrigerate until dough is firm, 1 hour or up to 1 day.

5. ROLLING OUT THE DOUGH If necessary, let dough sit at room temperature 10 minutes to soften. On a lightly floured surface, roll dough, working from center out to edges. Turn dough one-eighth of a turn with every roll, loosening it with a large offset spatula. Remove excess flour with a dry pastry brush.

6. FITTING THE DOUGH INTO DISH Once the dough is rolled out to its proper dimension, roll it back up over the pin. Next, carefully unroll to drape the dough over the pie plate, and gently press to fit it into the dish.

SINGLE-CRUST PIE HOW-TO

TRIMMING THE DOUGH
Trim excess dough to a 1-inch overhang. Crimp edges (as shown, right) with your thumb and forefinger, or create another decorative edge (see opposite page).

DOCKING THE CRUST
Piercing the unbaked crust with a fork (called "docking") allows steam to escape from inside, preventing the crust from puffing as it bakes. Chill shell after docking.

BLIND-BAKING THE CRUST
Line chilled pie shell with parchment and fill with pie weights or dried beans. For a partially baked shell, bake just until the edges begin to brown. Remove weights and parchment. For a completely pre-baked shell, continue baking until bottom of crust is lightly browned.

MAKING A FOIL RING
A foil ring protects a crust's edges from browning too quickly. Press a piece of foil onto an empty pie plate to shape; trim the outer edge and cut out the center to make a ring that's about 2 inches wide.

PIECRUST EDGES

To make a checkerboard border (1), snip the dough at even intervals and bend every other section toward the center. Cutouts can be adhered with an egg wash or water: Overlapping tiny triangles form an arrowhead pattern (2), while strips of dough are woven into a braid (3). Traditional crimping with a thumb and forefinger can be varied to make a diagonally pinched (4) or fork-crimped edge (5).

1. CHECKERBOARD

2. ARROWHEAD

4. PINCHED

5. FORK-CRIMPED

3. BRAIDED

DOUBLE-CRUST FRUIT PIE HOW-TO

1. FILLING Pile the filling evenly into the pastry shell, mounding it in the center. Dotting a tablespoon or two of butter, cut into small pieces, on top of the filling will help emulsify the juices and add richness.

2. ADDING THE TOP CRUST Brush the edge of the bottom crust with some egg wash. Center and drape the top crust over the filling.

3. SEALING EDGES Trim excess dough to leave a 1-inch overhang. Fold edge of top crust under bottom edge and press to seal. To crimp edges: With thumb and index finger of one hand, press dough against thumb or knuckle of other hand; continue around edge of pie.

4. FINISHING TOUCHES Use a paring knife to cut several slits (for steam vents) in the top crust, each about 3 inches long (or cut vent into a shape using a small cookie cutter). Brush top crust with egg wash (see opposite page) and sprinkle evenly all over with fine or coarse sanding sugar.

1. EGG YOLK AND CREAM

2. HEAVY CREAM

3. EGG YOLK AND WATER

EGG WASHES

Washes made with different ingredients or proportions of ingredients can alter the look and texture of a baked top crust. A wash made of one egg yolk and one tablespoon heavy cream whisked together (1) is Martha's favorite. It creates a lovely golden color. Heavy cream (2) imparts a paler finish than egg but adds a nice shine. Egg yolk and water (3) is the standard; use one tablespoon cold water to one egg yolk. An egg simply whisked and then brushed onto unbaked pastry results in a rich, golden color and a shiny surface (4). Brushing on water by itself (5) creates a crisp, crackly, pale-colored surface. It works well to adhere sugar, and is good in a pinch.

4. WHOLE EGG

5. WATER

LATTICE CRUST HOW-TO

1. Cut an even number of strips (we cut 10) of rolled-out pie dough using the plain or fluted edge of a double-sided pastry wheel. (If you don't have a pastry wheel, you can use a pizza cutter or sharp knife in its place.) The strips pictured are about 1 inch wide; make them as wide or as narrow as you like. Wide strips are easier to work with, especially for beginners.

2. Lay half the strips vertically and evenly spaced across the pie, starting in the center and working out toward the edge.

3. Fold back the odd-numbered strips, as shown, and lay a horizontal strip across the center of the pie.

4. Unfold the odd-numbered dough strips, then fold back the even-numbered pieces; lay another perpendicular strip as shown. Repeat, unfolding and folding alternating strips of dough.

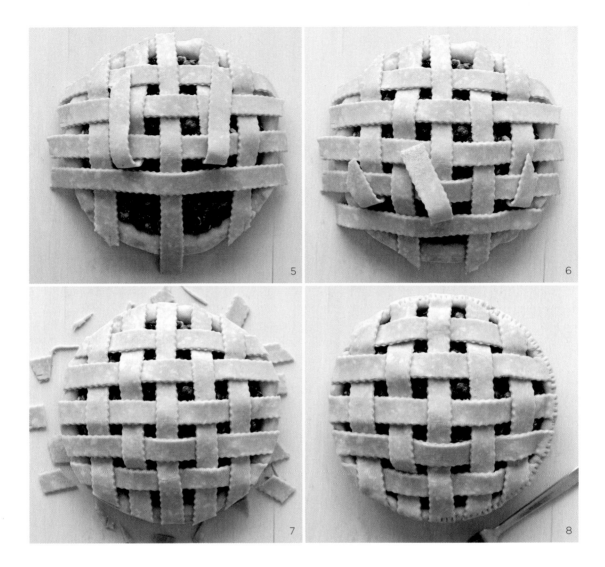

5. Continue on the other side of the pie, folding back the even-numbered strips and placing another horizontal piece.

6. Unfold the even-numbered dough strips, and fold back the odd-numbered pieces; place the last horizontal strip. Unfold strips.

7. Trim excess on ends of dough strips flush with the overhang of the bottom crust (but not flush with rim of pan).

8. Fold lattice ends and edge of bottom crust under. Crimp edge with a fork or your thumbs. Finish by brushing the entire surface with the egg wash of your choice and sprinkling with fine or coarse sanding sugar (not shown).

Cream Cheese Pie Dough

Those new to working with pastry would do well to start with a cream cheese dough. The combination of butter and cream cheese produces a supple, forgiving dough that rolls out quickly and smoothly, thanks to the high moisture content of the cream cheese. It also has a tender crumb and a pleasingly tangy flavor that pairs well with sweet or savory fillings. MAKES ENOUGH FOR ONE 9-INCH SINGLE-CRUST PIE

2 teaspoons cold water

1 teaspoon cold cider vinegar

1½ cups all-purpose flour, plus more for dusting

½ teaspoon salt

½ cup (1 stick) cold unsalted butter, cut into small pieces

4 ounces cold cream cheese, cut into small pieces

1. Combine water and vinegar in a small bowl. Combine flour and salt in another bowl. Using a pastry blender or your fingers, cut butter and cream cheese into flour mixture until mixture resembles coarse meal, with some larger pieces remaining. (Alternatively, pulse ingredients in a food processor.)

2. Add water mixture to dough in a slow, steady stream, stirring (or pulsing), until mixture just begins to hold together. Turn out onto plastic, and wrap. Press dough into a disk using a rolling pin. Refrigerate until firm, 1 hour or up to 1 day. (Dough can be frozen up to 3 months; thaw in the refrigerator before using.)

1. SETTING UP As with all pie doughs, cold ingredients are essential to producing a flaky texture. Measure all ingredients, cutting the butter and cream cheese into small cubes, and then refrigerate everything (including the flour and salt in the bowl) for 30 minutes before you start.

2. MAKING THE DOUGH Avoid overmixing as you cut the butter and cream cheese into the flour mixture. The dough is meant to be a bit crumbly, with pieces ranging in size from coarse meal to about ½ inch, all evenly coated in the flour mixture.

3. WRAPPING THE DOUGH Covering the dough with plastic compresses the ingredients while protecting them from warming under your hands. Turn out dough onto plastic wrap, then use the plastic to gather dough into a ball. Flatten into a disk; refrigerate at least 1 hour or up to 1 day.

Graham Cracker Crust

The crumbly texture of a graham cracker crust pairs best with creamy fillings; it is extremely easy to make—just combine cookie crumbs with melted butter and a small amount of sugar, press the mixture into a pie plate, and bake. MAKES ONE 9-INCH CRUST

12 graham cracker sheets (6 ounces), broken into pieces, or 1½ cups graham cracker crumbs

6 tablespoons butter, melted and cooled, plus more for pie plate

3 tablespoons sugar

Pinch of salt

Preheat oven to 375°F. Lightly butter a 9-inch pie plate. In a food processor, pulse graham crackers until finely ground. In a bowl, combine crumbs, butter, sugar, and salt. Press mixture firmly and evenly into bottom and up sides of pie plate. Bake until lightly browned, about 12 minutes. Let cool completely on a wire rack. (Crust can be stored up to 1 day, loosely covered with foil, at room temperature.)

Chocolate Wafer Crust

Chocolate wafers (or nearly any wafer cookie) make a delicious crumb crust, especially for cream pies. MAKES ONE 9-INCH CRUST

25 chocolate wafers (6 ounces), broken into pieces, or 1½ cups wafer-cookie crumbs

5 tablespoons unsalted butter, melted

3 tablespoons sugar

Pinch of salt

Preheat oven to 350°F. In a food processor, pulse wafers until finely ground. Add butter, sugar, and salt, and process until well combined. Press mixture firmly into bottom and up sides of a 9-inch pie plate. Bake until crust is firm, about 10 minutes. Let cool completely on a wire rack. (Crust can be stored up to 1 day.)

FORMING A CRUMB CRUST For a firm, evenly packed crust, use the flat bottom of a dry measuring cup to press the crumbs into the bottom and up the sides of the pan.

Rich Chocolate Pie Dough

This crumbly cocoa-enriched shell is used to make the Chocolate-Caramel Cream Pie on page 116; it pairs nicely with other cream fillings as well. **MAKES ENOUGH FOR ONE 9-INCH SINGLE-CRUST PIE**

1¼ cups all-purpose flour, plus more for dusting

⅓ cup sugar

2 tablespoons unsweetened Dutch-process cocoa powder

½ teaspoon salt

6 tablespoons cold unsalted butter, cut into small pieces

3 large egg yolks

½ teaspoon pure vanilla extract

In a food processor, pulse flour, sugar, cocoa, and salt until combined. Add butter, and pulse just until mixture resembles coarse meal. Add yolks and vanilla, and pulse until mixture just begins to hold together. Shape dough into a disk. Wrap in plastic, and refrigerate until firm, 1 hour or up to 2 days.

Pâte Sablée

Pâte sablée is essentially a sugar-cookie dough used to produce a crumbly, sandy pastry crust. In fact, "sablée" comes from the French word for "sand." Because the dough is very soft, it can be difficult to roll out; instead, press it gently into the pan. Any scraps of dough can be cut out and baked into cookies. **MAKES ENOUGH FOR ONE 9-INCH TART**

¾ cup (1½ sticks) unsalted butter, room temperature

½ cup confectioners' sugar

1½ cups all-purpose flour

¾ teaspoon salt

With an electric mixer on medium, beat butter and sugar until pale and fluffy, 3 minutes. Reduce speed to medium-low. Add flour and salt; beat until just combined and crumbly (do not overmix). Shape dough into a disk, and wrap in plastic. Refrigerate 1 hour or up to 2 days, or freeze up to 3 months (thaw in refrigerator before using).

Pâte Sucrée

Pâte sucrée, or "sweet pastry," is a sturdy dough, thanks to its proportion of sugar and the addition of egg yolks. It's a good choice for tarts, which are most often unmolded before serving. It is also more tender than pâte brisée, breaking cleanly under a fork instead of shattering into flakes.

MAKES ENOUGH FOR TWO 8- OR 9-INCH TARTS, OR TWO DOZEN 3-INCH TARTS

2½ cups all-purpose flour

¼ cup sugar

¼ teaspoon salt

1 cup (2 sticks) cold unsalted butter, cut into small pieces

2 large egg yolks, lightly beaten

2 to 4 tablespoons cold heavy cream or ice water

Pulse flour, sugar, and salt in a food processor until combined. Add butter, and pulse just until mixture resembles coarse meal. Add yolks and drizzle 2 tablespoons cream evenly over mixture; pulse just until dough begins to come together, no more than 30 seconds. If dough is too dry, add remaining cream, 1 tablespoon at a time, and pulse. Divide dough in half, pat each half into a disk, and wrap in plastic. Refrigerate 1 hour or up to 2 days, or freeze up to 3 months (thaw in refrigerator before using).

Citrus Variation: Add 2 teaspoons finely grated orange zest and 1 teaspoon finely grated lemon zest to the dry ingredients.

Poppy Seed Variation: Add 2 tablespoons poppy seeds to the dry ingredients.

Chocolate Variation: Replace ¼ cup flour with ¼ cup unsweetened Dutch-process cocoa powder.

Cornmeal-Lemon Variation: Replace ¾ cup flour with ¾ cup coarse cornmeal; reduce sugar to 2 tablespoons. Add 1 teaspoon lemon zest to the dry ingredients.

Puff Pastry

The texture of puff pastry comes from the way its essential ingredients—flour, butter, water, and salt—are combined. You begin by making two separate components. The first, the dough package, or *détrempe* in French, is mostly flour with just a bit of butter worked in (a combination of all-purpose and cake flour results in just enough protein to support the dough as it puffs). The second, the butter package, or *bourrage* ("filling"), is mostly butter, with a little flour worked in. The two packages are combined by repeatedly rolling and folding the dough, creating a total of 1,458 distinct layers. In the heat of the oven, the steam that is produced by the butter in the dough creates pockets of air and expands the many layers. Tarts made with a puff pastry base are among the simplest to assemble. The following recipe makes enough pastry for four large tarts (freeze unused pastry up to 3 months). **MAKES ABOUT 2½ POUNDS**

FOR THE DOUGH PACKAGE

- 3 cups all-purpose flour, plus more for dusting
- ¾ cup cake flour (not self-rising)
- 1½ teaspoons salt
- 4 tablespoons cold unsalted butter (cut stick lengthwise; use other half to make the butter package), cut into ½-inch pieces
- 1¼ cups cold water

FOR THE BUTTER PACKAGE

- 1 tablespoon all-purpose flour
- 1¾ cups (3½ sticks, halve last stick lengthwise and use other half for the dough package) cold unsalted butter

1. Make the dough package: In a large bowl, whisk to combine both flours with the salt. Scatter butter pieces over flour mixture; using a pastry blender or your fingers, cut in butter just until mixture resembles coarse meal. Form a well in center of mixture, and pour the water into well. Using your hands, gradually draw flour mixture over water, covering and gathering until mixture is well blended and begins to come together. Gently knead mixture in bowl just until it comes together to form a dough, about 15 seconds. Pat dough into a rough ball, and turn out onto plastic wrap. Wrap tightly, and refrigerate 1 hour.

2. Make the butter package: Sprinkle 1½ teaspoons flour on a sheet of parchment. Place sticks of butter on top, side by side, and sprinkle with remaining 1½ teaspoons flour. Top with another sheet of parchment; using a rolling pin, pound butter to soften and flatten to about ½ inch. Remove top sheet of parchment, and fold butter package in half onto itself. Replace top sheet of paper, and pound again until butter is about ½ inch thick. Repeat process 2 or 3 times, or until butter becomes quite pliable. With a large offset spatula and parchment paper, shape butter package into a 6-inch square. Wrap well and refrigerate until chilled but not hardened, no more than 10 minutes. (*directions continue on page 336*) >

PUFF PASTRY HOW-TO

1. Make the dough package. Form dough into a ball, wrap in plastic, and refrigerate 1 hour.

2. Make the butter package: Place 3½ sticks butter on a sheet of floured parchment paper, sprinkle with more flour, and top with a second sheet of parchment. Pound the butter with a rolling pin until it is flattened to about ½ inch thick. Remove top piece of parchment, and fold butter in half onto itself. Replace paper, and pound again until butter is about ½ inch thick.

3. Repeat process two or three times, until butter becomes pliable. With a large offset spatula and parchment paper, shape butter into a 6-inch square; wrap in plastic and refrigerate for no more than 10 minutes.

4. Remove dough package from refrigerator and lightly dust with flour.

5. Roll dough package into a 9-inch circle.

6. Place butter package in the center of the dough round. Lightly score dough with a paring knife or offset spatula to outline the butter square; remove butter. *(directions continue on page 337)* >

Puff Pastry (CONTINUED)

USING STORE-BOUGHT PASTRY
Homemade puff pastry is incomparably buttery and flaky. While not difficult to make, it does require multiple steps over the course of several hours. This recipe yields four 11-ounce pieces—enough for four large tarts; freeze the unused portion up to 3 months. If you choose to use store-bought frozen puff pastry, look for an all-butter brand, such as Dufour, which is sold in a 14-ounce rectangular sheet. Pepperidge Farm frozen puff pastry, which is made with vegetable oil, is sold in a 17-ounce box, with two square sheets per box. The recipes in this book allow for some flexibility when it comes to puff pastry: You may use one 11-ounce sheet of homemade pastry, one 14-ounce box of store-bought all-butter pastry, or one 17-ounce box (two sheets) interchangeably. Simply roll or cut the pastry to the desired size. To combine 2 smaller pieces into 1 larger rectangle, overlap the 2 pieces slightly, brushing the overlap with water to seal. Then roll or cut the pastry as directed.

3. Remove dough package from refrigerator and lightly dust with flour. On a lightly floured surface, gently roll dough package into a 9-inch round. Place butter package in center of dough round. Using a paring knife or bench scraper, lightly score dough to outline butter square; remove butter. Starting from each side of center square, gently roll out dough with rolling pin, forming four flaps, each 4 to 5 inches long; do not roll the raised square in center of dough. Replace butter package on center square (remove parchment). Fold flaps of dough over butter package so that it is completely enclosed. Gently press with your hands to seal. (If at any point in rolling process, dough becomes too soft or elastic, return it to refrigerator to rest at least 30 minutes.)

4. Using rolling pin, press down on dough at regular intervals, repeating and covering entire surface area, until it is about 1 inch thick. Gently roll out dough into a large rectangle, about 9 by 20 inches, with a short side closest to you. Be careful not to press too hard around edges, and keep corners even as you roll out dough by squaring them with the side of the rolling pin or a large offset spatula. Brush off excess flour. Starting at near end, fold rectangle in thirds as you would a letter; this completes first single turn. Wrap well in plastic; refrigerate 45 to 60 minutes.

5. Repeat process in step 4, giving dough five more single turns. Always start with flap opening on right as if it were a book. Mark dough with your knuckle each time you complete a turn to help you keep track. Refrigerate 1 hour between each turn. Dough can be made in advance through fourth turn and then kept overnight in refrigerator or up to 1 month in freezer before continuing. After sixth and final turn, wrap dough in plastic; refrigerate at least 4 hours or overnight before using. Divide into 4 pieces. Freeze unused portions for up to 3 months (thaw in refrigerator overnight before using.)

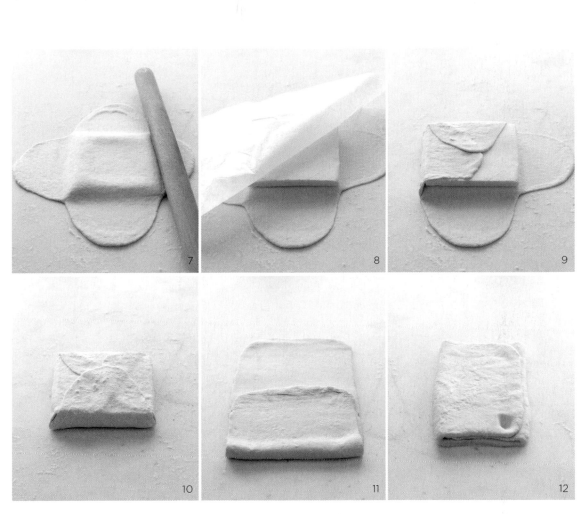

PUFF PASTRY HOW-TO (continued)

7. Starting from each side of the center square, gently roll out dough to form four flaps, each 4 to 5 inches long. (Do not roll over raised square.)

8. Place butter package in the center of the dough package.

9. Fold flaps over butter package.

10. Once butter package is completely enclosed, seal with your hands.

11. With a rolling pin, press down on the dough at regular intervals until it is about 1 inch thick. Roll out dough into a large rectangle with the short side closest to you. Starting at near end, fold rectangle into thirds as you would a letter. This completes the first turn. Wrap dough in plastic and refrigerate 45 to 60 minutes.

12. Repeat steps 10 and 11, giving dough 5 more single turns. Always start with flap opening on the right as if it were a book. Mark dough with your knuckle each time you complete a turn to help you keep track. Refrigerate dough 1 hour between each turn.

Vanilla Pastry Cream

Pastry cream is the classic filling for French fruit tarts; it can also be folded into other fillings, such as whipped cream or the rich ricotta custard in the Neapolitan Easter Pie on page 253. Like many other custards, it is thickened with eggs and cornstarch; the mixture must be brought to a full boil to activate the starch and set properly. We use a whole vanilla bean, but you can substitute vanilla extract in its place.

MAKES 1½ CUPS

2 cups milk

1 vanilla bean, halved lengthwise and seeds scraped (or 1 tablespoon pure vanilla extract; omit step 1 if using)

4 large egg yolks

½ cup sugar

¼ cup cornstarch

1. Bring milk and vanilla-bean seeds and pod to a simmer in a medium saucepan. Remove from heat. Cover; let stand 20 minutes.

2. In a large bowl, whisk egg yolks until smooth. In a medium saucepan, combine sugar and cornstarch. Gradually add milk mixture (or milk and vanilla extract, if not using vanilla bean) in a slow, steady stream and cook over medium heat, stirring constantly, until mixture thickens and begins to bubble, about 5 minutes.

3. Whisking constantly, slowly pour one-third of milk mixture into egg yolks. Pour mixture into remaining milk in saucepan. Cook over medium heat, whisking constantly, until mixture comes to a full boil and is thick enough to coat the back of a spoon, 2 to 4 minutes. Remove from heat.

4. Strain mixture through a fine sieve into a heatproof bowl; discard solids. Cover with parchment or plastic wrap, pressing directly on surface to prevent a skin from forming. Refrigerate until well chilled and firm, at least 2 hours or up to 2 days. Whisk to soften slightly just before using.

Lemon Curd

MAKES 1¾ CUPS

6 large egg yolks

1 tablespoon finely grated lemon zest plus ½ cup fresh lemon juice (from 3 lemons)

¾ cup sugar

Pinch of salt

½ cup (1 stick) cold unsalted butter, cut into pieces

Whisk together yolks, zest, juice, sugar, and salt in a heavy saucepan. Bring to a simmer over medium heat, whisking constantly. Cook until thickened, 8 to 10 minutes. Strain through a fine sieve into a bowl. Whisk in butter, one piece at a time, until smooth. Press plastic wrap directly onto surface, and refrigerate until cold, 1 hour or up to 1 day.

Candied Lemon Slices

Use this technique to make other candied citrus slices, such as lime, orange, or kumquat. MAKES 3 DOZEN

3 lemons, washed well and dried

4 cups water

4 cups sugar

1. Using a very sharp knife or an adjustable-blade slicer, cut lemons into very thin slices (remove and discard seeds). In a heavy saucepan, bring the water and the sugar to a boil, stirring to dissolve sugar.

2. Add lemon slices to pan, and cover with a round of parchment to keep lemons submerged; return to a boil. Remove from heat, and let cool to room temperature. Candied citrus slices can be refrigerated (in syrup) in an airtight container up to 1 week. Place on a wire rack to dry before using.

SLICING LEMONS   COOKING LEMON SLICES   DRYING LEMON SLICES

Mile-High Meringue Topping

This recipe yields an extraordinarily lofty topping. You may halve the recipe for a meringue with less volume. Either way, be sure to spread meringue until it completely covers the filling to prevent shrinking or "weeping." MAKES ENOUGH FOR ONE 9-INCH PIE

8 large egg whites

¼ teaspoon cream of tartar

¾ cup sugar

½ teaspoon pure vanilla extract

1. With an electric mixer on medium speed, whisk egg whites and cream of tartar until foamy. Gradually add sugar. Increase speed and whisk until meringue is glossy and forms stiff peaks. Whisk in vanilla.

2. Spoon meringue onto surface of the pie until it reaches the crust, then use an offset spatula to create a swirling pattern.

3. If desired, use a kitchen torch to toast the meringue, moving flame back and forth until evenly browned. Or brown the meringue under the broiler, but keep an eye on it—a minute or two is all you need.

FORMING STIFF PEAKS   SPREADING MERINGUE OVER FILLING   BROWNING MERINGUE

Whipped Cream

You can adjust the amount of sugar in this recipe to suit your preference; for unsweetened whipped cream, simply omit the sugar. MAKES ABOUT 2 CUPS

1 cup heavy cream, chilled

2 tablespoons confectioners' sugar

With an electric mixer on medium-high speed (or by hand), whisk cream in a well-chilled bowl until soft peaks form. Add confectioners' sugar, and whisk until medium-stiff peaks form.

Crushed Hazelnut Praline

You can make praline from any variety of toasted nuts (preferably blanched or skinless). The Butterscotch Praline Cream Pie on page 95 features this variation, crushed and folded into the whipped cream and sprinkled over the top. MAKES ENOUGH FOR 1 CUP

Vegetable-oil cooking spray
½ cup sugar
1 teaspoon light corn syrup
1 tablespoon water
Pinch of salt
⅓ cup toasted and skinned hazelnuts (see page 343)

Coat a rimmed baking sheet with cooking spray. Combine sugar, corn syrup, water, and salt in a small saucepan over medium-high heat, stirring constantly until sugar dissolves. Continue to cook, without stirring, until deep amber. Remove from heat and stir in nuts. Immediately pour mixture onto prepared baking sheet, and spread into an even layer. Let cool completely on sheet on a wire rack. Break praline into medium-size pieces, and transfer to a resealable plastic bag. Using a rolling pin, crush into pea-size portions.

Cranberry Compote

MAKES 2 CUPS

8 ounces (about 2 cups) fresh cranberries
1 teaspoon finely grated orange zest plus 3 tablespoons fresh orange juice
1 cup sugar
¼ teaspoon ground cinnamon
½ teaspoon pure vanilla extract

In a saucepan, over medium-high heat, combine all ingredients and cook 7 to 10 minutes, stirring occasionally, until berries start to pop but are still whole. Transfer to a bowl to cool. Compote can be refrigerated in an airtight container up to 3 days.

Vanilla Poached Pears

MAKES 10 PEAR HALVES

1 cup dry white wine

3 cups water

¼ cup honey

1 vanilla bean, halved lengthwise and seeds scraped

5 ripe, firm Bartlett or Comice pears

1. Bring wine, water, honey, and vanilla-bean seeds and pod to a simmer in a large saucepan. Cook over medium-low heat 5 minutes.

2. Meanwhile, cut a round of parchment the same diameter as the saucepan. Peel pears and halve lengthwise. Use a small spoon or melon baller to scoop out cores, seeds, and stems. Trim fibrous strip from center with a paring knife. Gently lower pears into pot. Place parchment round directly on pears to keep them submerged (this will help keep them from turning brown).

3. Cook until a paring knife slides easily into pears, meeting slight resistance, 15 to 20 minutes. Remove from heat; let cool in liquid 30 minutes. Use a slotted spoon to transfer pears to a large bowl; cover with cooking liquid and let cool completely. Pears can be refrigerated in an airtight container up to 3 days.

Poached Apple Roses

MAKES 9

4 cups water

¼ cup fresh lemon juice (from 1 to 2 lemons), plus 1 lemon, halved

2 cups sugar

3 golden apples, such as Golden Delicious

2 red apples, such as Gala, McIntosh, or Red Delicious

1. Bring the water, lemon juice, and sugar to a boil in a medium saucepan. Remove syrup from heat; cover. Cut a round of parchment the same diameter as the saucepan.

2. Core apples. Peel golden apples; using 1 lemon half, rub flesh. Squeeze juice from remaining half into hollows of (unpeeled) red apples. Using a mandoline or a sharp knife, cut all apples crosswise into paper-thin (less than ⅛ inch) slices. Transfer to syrup; shake pan to coat slices. Place parchment directly onto surface of apple mixture. Let syrup cool completely, about 40 minutes.

3. Remove slices from syrup. Cut slices into semicircles. Stack 1 red apple slice on top of 1 golden slice, with cut edges nearest you. Wrap slices together into a cone shape to form a "bud." Stack 2 more slices. Placing them slightly above base (to create a staggered appearance), wrap them around bud. Repeat, wrapping until rose is about 2½ inches in diameter. Reserve leftover peeled slices for garnish.

FORMING APPLE ROSES

recipe tips and techniques

MEASURING DRY INGREDIENTS Measure dry ingredients (such as flour and sugar) and semisolid ingredients (such as peanut butter and sour cream) in graduated dry measuring cups. For flour, dip the cup into the flour and fill to overflowing, then level with a straightedge such as an offset spatula. (Never shake the cup or tap it on the counter to level; both will lead to inaccurate measurements.) If a recipe calls for "sifted flour," sift the flour first, and then measure it; if it calls for "flour, sifted," measure first and then sift. When measuring brown sugar, pack firmly into a dry cup.

MEASURING LIQUID INGREDIENTS Measure liquid ingredients such as milk in a liquid measuring cup; to read, set the cup on a flat surface and view the measurement at eye level.

TOASTING AND GRINDING NUTS To toast nuts such as pecans, walnuts, and almonds, spread them on a baking sheet and cook in a 350°F oven until fragrant, about 10 minutes. (Start checking after 6 minutes if toasting sliced or chopped nuts.) Toast pine nuts at 350°F for 5 to 7 minutes. Toast hazelnuts in a 375°F oven until skins split, about 10 to 12 minutes; when cool enough to handle, rub warm nuts in a clean kitchen towel to remove skins. Chop cooled nuts coarsely or finely with a chef's knife, or pulse them in a food processor to grind. Do not over-process, or nuts will turn into a paste.

STORING GROUND SPICES Keep ground spices in a cool, dark place for up to a year; labeling the jars when you buy them will remind you when it's time to replace them.

GRATING NUTMEG Nutmeg has a nutty, spicy flavor that beautifully complements aromatic spices such as cinnamon and ginger. Grating fresh nutmeg results in a more complex, nuanced flavor (whole nutmeg also has a longer shelf life). Use a specialty nutmeg grater or a rasp grater. If you would like to substitute ground nutmeg for freshly grated, use half the amount.

MELTING CHOCOLATE Melt chocolate in a metal bowl set over (not in) a pan of simmering water, or in a double-boiler. Alternatively, you can melt chocolate in the microwave: In a microwave-safe bowl, heat chocolate in 30-second intervals, stirring after each, until almost melted. Remove from microwave and stir to melt completely.

MAKING CHOCOLATE CURLS AND SHAVINGS Use a vegetable peeler to shave tight chocolate curls from a large block of slightly warm chocolate (heat in microwave for 5-second intervals, checking after each, until just warm to the touch). To make uneven shavings, finely slice a block of chocolate lengthwise with a large chef's knife.

ZESTING CITRUS Use a rasp grater such as a Microplane to remove citrus fruits' flavorful zest while leaving the bitter white pith behind. A citrus zester (a small tool with a row of small, sharp holes at one end) makes decorative curls for garnishes.

PITTING CHERRIES Use a cherry pitter to remove the pits from cherries. Or gently press down on each cherry with the flat side of a chef's knife until it splits open, then remove the pit. As an alternative, you can use a paper clip: Unbend the clip at the center; insert the tip of one bent end slightly into the stem end of cherry. Twist the clip to loosen the pit, and pull to remove.

PEELING PEACHES AND APRICOTS With a paring knife, lightly score the bottom of each peach with an X before blanching. Working in batches of 3 or 4, add peaches or apricots to boiling water for about 1 minute. Use a slotted spoon to transfer them to an ice-water bath to stop the cooking. Remove skin with a paring knife.

MAKING PUMPKIN PURÉE One small sugar pumpkin (about 4 pounds) will yield about 3 cups pumpkin purée. Heat oven to 425°F. Halve pumpkin and roast, cut sides down, on a rimmed baking sheet until soft, 50 minutes to 1 hour. Let cool completely; roasted pumpkin can be refrigerated in an airtight container overnight. Discard seeds and scoop out flesh using a large spoon; transfer to a food processor. Process until smooth, about 1 minute.

sources

BAKING TOOLS AND EQUIPMENT

BRIDGE KITCHENWARE 800-274-3435 or bridge kitchenware.com. Metal pie tins, tart and mini tartlet pans, springform pans, flan rings, brioche molds, rolling pins, pastry bags and tips.

BROADWAY PANHANDLER 866-266-5925 or broadway panhandler.com. Metal and ceramic pie plates, tart pans, springform pans, rolling pins, pastry bags and tips.

COPPER GIFTS 620-421-0654 or coppergifts.com. Cookie cutters.

MACY'S 800-289-6229 or macys.com. Martha Stewart Collection pans (baking sheets, springform pans, standard and mini muffin tins), rolling pins, pastry blenders, cookie cutters, cake stands.

WILLIAMS-SONOMA 877-812-6235 or williams-sonoma.com. Metal and ceramic pie plates, tart pans, rolling pins, pie weights, kitchen torches, pastry blenders, pastry wheels, pastry bags and tips.

RECIPES

Page 34: **TARTE TATIN** Mauviel copper tarte Tatin pan, Williams-Sonoma, see previous.

Page 69: **CRÈME BRÛLÉE TARTS** Kitchen torch, Williams-Sonoma, see previous.

Page 85: **CARAMELIZED LEMON TART** Kitchen torch, Williams-Sonoma, see previous.

Page 89: **PUMPKIN FLANS IN PASTRY SHELLS** 5½-inch flan rings (ABFR-P-140), Bridge Kitchenware, see previous.

Page 133: **HONEY AND PINE NUT TART** Golden Nectar leatherwood honey, My Brands, 888-281-6400 or mybrands.com.

Page 165: **CHOCOLATE-ESPRESSO TART** 14-by-4½-inch rectangular flan mold, Bridge Kitchenware, see previous.

Page 190: **PORT CARAMEL CHOCOLATE TARTLETS** Matfer 2⅜-inch tartlet mold (TTL-DS-60), Bridge Kitchenware, see previous.

Page 202: **COCONUT MACAROON TARTLETS** 2¼-inch brioche mold (ABBM-N-60), Bridge Kitchenware, see previous.

Page 211: **BLACKBERRY AND CREAM TARTLETS** St. Germain elderflower liqueur, K&L Wine Merchants, 877-559-4637 or klwines.com; 3½-inch brioche mold (ABBM-N-90), Bridge Kitchenware, see previous.

Page 219: **CONCORD GRAPE JAM TART** Taylor Classic Candy & Deep Fry Thermometer, Cheftools.com, 206-933-0700.

Page 220: **PEAR-CRANBERRY PIE WITH FAUX LATTICE** Similar ¾-inch mini square cookie cutter, Copper Gifts, see previous.

Page 223: **SHINGLED-LEAF BRANDY APPLE PIE** Similar 2½-inch mini aspen leaf cookie cutter, Sugarcraft, 513-896-7089 or sugarcraft.com.

Page 232: **LINZER TART WITH LINGONBERRY JAM** 14-ounce lingonberry preserves, igourmet .com, 877-446-8763.

Page 235: **STRAWBERRY BANDANNA TART** Ateco aspic cutter set, Broadway Panhandler, see previous.

Page 245: **MINI BLACK AND WHITE CHOCOLATE TARTLETS** Similar 2-inch round (ATTL-PL-3) and 3½-by-1½-inch rectangular tartlet pan (ATTL-TS-1R), and similar 2¼-inch brioche mold (BBM-N-60), Bridge Kitchenware, see previous.

Page 246: **PEAR-RASPBERRY HEART PIE** Similar 2-inch heart cookie cutter (#264), Copper Gifts, see previous.

Page 249: **CHOCOLATE GANACHE HEART TARTLETS** 5-inch heart tart pan (#21411) or 10½-inch heart tart pan (#21426), Fante's, 800-443-2683 or fantes.com.

Page 253: **NEAPOLITAN EASTER PIE** Spring wheat berries, Nuts Online, 800-558-6887 or nutsonline.com.

Page 261: **STARS AND STRIPES MINI PIES** 5-inch pie pan (#1541), Fante's, see previous.

page 268: **MINI JACK-O'-LANTERN TARTS** Ateco ½-inch aspic cutter set, Broadway Panhandler, see previous.

Page 276: **GINGERBREAD-RASPBERRY SNOWFLAKE TART** Similar mini snowflake cookie cutter (#4830), Copper Gifts, see previous.

Page 279: **CHOCOLATE STENCIL TARTS** Similar holiday stencils, Copper Gifts, see previous.

photo credits

All photographs by **JOHNNY MILLER,** except:

CAREN ALPERT: pages 256, 342

SANG AN: pages 91, 184, 223

JAMES BAIGRIE: page 83

CHRIS BAKER: pages 199, 330

ROLAND BELLO: pages 71, 100, 101, 242, 248

EARL CARTER: page 54

LISA COHEN: pages 154, 155

SUSIE CUSHNER: page 214

KATYA DE GRUNWALD: page 247

DANA GALLAGHER: pages 58, 140, 148, 152, 156, 197, 202, 203, 234, 298, 306

GENTL & HYERS: pages 36, 42, 46, 48, 49, 64, 65, 72, 144, 188, 222, 263, 264, 265, 289, 304

HANS GISSINGER: pages 75, 143

RAYMOND HOM: page 260

MATTHEW HRANEK: page 220

JOHN KERNICK: pages 22, 23, 132, 135, 139, 294

YUNHEE KIM: pages 45, 280, 302

DAVID LOFTUS: pages 146, 147

JONATHAN LOVEKIN: pages 167, 176, 177, 282

ELLIE MILLER: page 293

MARCUS NILSSON: pages 106, 160, 183, 309, 311

VICKI PEARSON: pages 213, 238

CON POULOS: pages 50, 172, 179, 218, 219, 277, 285

MARIA ROBLEDO: pages 127, 206, 237, 290, 297

MIKKEL VANG: pages 229, 241

SIMON WATSON: page 53

ANNA WILLIAMS: pages 136, 162, 301

index